I0814486

DOCTOR

WHO

DOCTOR WHO

AN ENCYCLOPAEDIA OF COMPANION ACTORS

DANA FOX

WHITE OWL
AN IMPRINT OF PEN & SWORD BOOKS LTD
YORKSHIRE – PHILADELPHIA

First published in Great Britain in 2025 by
PEN AND SWORD WHITE OWL
An imprint of
Pen & Sword Books Ltd
Yorkshire – Philadelphia

ISBN 978 1 39905 082 1

A CIP catalogue record for this book is available from the British Library.

Typeset in Times New Roman 10.5/13.5 by
SJmagic DESIGN SERVICES, India.
Printed and bound in the UK by CPI Group (UK) Ltd, Croydon, CR0 4YY.

The Publisher's authorised representative in the EU for product safety is Authorised Rep Compliance Ltd., Ground Floor, 71 Lower Baggot Street, Dublin D02 P593, Ireland.
www.arccompliance.com

For a complete list of Pen & Sword titles please contact

PEN & SWORD BOOKS LIMITED
George House, Units 12 & 13, Beevor Street, Off Pontefract Road,
Barnsley, South Yorkshire, S71 1HN, England
E-mail: enquiries@pen-and-sword.co.uk
Website: www.pen-and-sword.co.uk

or

PEN AND SWORD BOOKS
1950 Lawrence Rd, Havertown, PA 19083, USA
E-mail: uspen-and-sword@casematepublishers.com
Website: www.penandswordbooks.com

Contents

Contents

Acknowledgements and Thanks

IN THE course of this book I have been greatly aided by so many people.

Thank you to all the actors who have played companions in the show. Thank you for existing.

I extend my warmest thanks to Peter Purves, Mark Strickson, Isabella Courtney, Sophie Aldred and Katy Manning for their kindness and generosity in allowing me to interview them. Your words have lent something very special to this book and to myself.

My heartfelt thanks also go to Aaron Lowe, John Ainsworth and Keith Barnfather for sharing with me their perspectives and experiences. Special thanks to Steve at Big Finish and to Fantom Events and Publishing. Thank you to Alex, Kevan, Owen and Toby at The Who Shop for your encouragement and the tour. My special thanks again to Keith Barnfather for permission to use the fantastic photographs from his collection, as well as to Paul Phipps-Williams of Fantom Events for his photographs too.

Further gratitude goes to Maria Kinsella and Lizzi VonDooLittle for giving me their perspectives and sharing their lived experiences.

Thank you to Lennie and Nat for introducing me to Isabella Courtney. Mine's a Chianti.

To *my* companions, those who have gone, those who remain and those yet to arrive: thank you.

Thank you to Lucius for indulging my love of 'spacey things'. Obsessive as it may be, I still love you more.

It feels inadequate to thank my parents for everything they have done, still do and will continue to do for me. Words cannot express my love for you both.

Foreword

I AWAKEN from the dream again, with a sharp shriek of undefinable panic, one half of my face squished into a crumpled, velvet cushion and the other half twitching in the bright April, midday sun.

It is midday because I was awake until around four in the morning writing this book and the pillow is velvet because I am a Taurus. Whenever I engross myself in a project, I tend to work at night. I am easily distracted, especially at this time of the year when, after what feels like an eternity of bleak, damp and entirely normal British weather, something finally appears which resembles sunshine.

I love the feeling of picking up a project in the afternoon. Just as the rest of the country is thinking about dinner and winding down for the evening, I am sitting at my desk doing the only thing I know how to do: create. I retreat into the dimly lit cavern of my study, lined with books, trailing plants and vinyl records, an empty wine glass nestling shyly on the windowsill and I make things. In my usual life, I make animations and digital art, but for some months I have put that on hold while I make on this book.

At night, I can work for hours without a break, only stopping to think how lucky I am to be able to do it this way.

The trade-off with this nocturnal activity is that whatever vestige remains of my internal clock is less of a circadian rhythm and more like the tail end of an illegal rave on Dartmoor. Trust me, I speak with experience. I have convinced myself that what seems like such a wonderful idea first thing in the afternoon is in keeping with my natural, vampiric state. But in reality it often leaves me waking up feeling like I have been rugby tackled by a small elephant.

Such are my thoughts this morning as I convulse there in bed like a dishevelled newborn. And then I remember the dream. It is the fourth night in a row that I have had the exact same dream.

It is hardly surprising. Nearing the end of writing the *Doctor Who Companion Encyclopaedia,* I have thought of little else but the science fiction series which has been a constant source of safety and comfort since I was 10 years old. Thirty years later, as I race to finish the manuscript before my publisher sends out a search party, it has dominated every waking moment of my life for two months. Carpets have gone un-vacuumed, dinner has shrivelled to a cold, pasta-based husk and I am sure at some point I had a social life.

The dream is always the same. I am in a series of corridors made from angular, shining metal. There is a sharp, bitter taste in the air and fingers of cobalt blue lightning arc through the air.

I look to my left and then to my right, then behind me and ahead of me. It all looks the same, I think, a metallic crossroads. As I am standing there, considering which way to go, I feel an urge to run forward. There is, I sense, danger.

Suddenly I am legging it at full speed because I know that there is someone, or some*thing* chasing me. Anonymous chrome walls pass me, my feet clang on the grilled surface of the floor and I feel a frantic sense of desperation. Whatever was in pursuit is now beside me, effortlessly matching my pace. I refuse to turn and look, unable to acknowledge whatever revenant might have finally caught up with me.

Eventually, I can run no more. As I buckle forwards and stop in my tracks, panting, I lift my head up and turn towards it, my eyes clenched shut, but not for long, for I must face whatever nameless terror has finally closed in. I open my eyes and standing there is … Janet Fielding. And she is asking me, rather angrily, if I have finished the book yet.

No, seriously. It's Janet Fielding. Or maybe it is her character Tegan Jovanka, I am not sure. But there she is, in some dream-like cross between the famous purple air stewardess uniform from 'Logopolis' and the grey military jacket from 'The Power of the Doctor'.

Now, I'm not a Freudian. If anything, my years of studying gestalt psychotherapy have taught me that what appears in one's dreams is an aspect of oneself, often one which has been repressed or unacknowledged. If that is so, then this recurring dream-Janet-Fielding-Tegan-Jovanka must represent something I need to know or to face.

But face *what*? Did I not face her last year when I completely screwed up the *Doctor Who* quiz at her event in Margate? Give me a break, dream-Janet-Tegan.

I could tell you what I think her appearance in my dream means.

The thing is, every one of the actors and their characters will signify something different to each of you. It might depend on your age. If you have watched the show since 'An Unearthly Child' in 1963, then your perspective will likely be different to someone whose first memory is Rose in 2005. If you are from the Black community it may be that you have waited an unimaginably long time to see Martha Jones. If you are queer, it is possible that the arrival of Captain Jack Harkness spoke to you in a way that other companions could not.

Whoever you are, I hope that within this book you will find a celebration, however small, of the companions who you relate to the most. It is also my hope that you will enjoy learning a little about the actors who played them. If you already know it all – you big know-it-all – then there are always the interviews, which are entirely new and conducted by this author.

The only *Doctor Who* serial I remember watching during its original run was 'The Curse of Fenric' (1989). Like many fans of the show, I grew to adore Ace, but I was only about 6 years old then. I remember nothing about the Seventh Doctor and very little about Ace. It would be many years before I began buying VHS tapes and *really* getting into the show, by which time it had been cancelled.

So I did not come to the show in chronological order. During what has come to be known as The Wilderness Years, I bought my first videos of *Doctor Who*: 'Genesis of the Daleks', 'Logopolis', 'The Curse of Fenric' and 'Mawdryn Undead'.

As a result, my Doctors were Tom Baker, Peter Davison and Sylvester McCoy. My first companions were Sarah Jane Smith, Harry Sullivan, Adric, Tegan, Nyssa, Turlough and Ace.

I suppose I could tell you which of these companions I became most attached to and why. I could tell you about my experiences as I discovered more of the show and I could revel in the utter delights of the early twenty-first century, a time when all serials which are not lost, deleted or sitting in someone's attic, are now readily available to watch at the click of a button. I could tell you which of the actors I have met or what I thought of Ben Jackson in a sailor outfit.

I could even tell you why I think dream-Janet-Fielding-Tegan-Jovanka has been appearing in my dreams lately.

All of this might make for a satisfactory, if somewhat confessional, introduction, but I cannot convince myself that it would be of much use to you as a reader. It might fit with the theme of this book, which despite being called the *Companion Encyclopaedia*, is actually more about the actors who played them.

When I am talking about *Doctor Who*, I can justify pretty much any thematic diversion. You can ask my husband for confirmation. But instead, I think I should tell you about the structure of this book, what you will find here and why. The tangential diversions will happen along the way.

I have presented this book as a series of biographical entries. Each actor has their own section in accordance with their chronological appearance on the show. On occasion, companions appeared at pretty much the same time, in which case I have gone with what I feel makes most sense.

Each section begins with the actor's name, date of birth and sadly, in some cases, the date they died. It is fairly common for actors to go by a name other than the one they were given at birth. This is for a variety of reasons, often to do with the union Equity insisting that each actor on their books has a unique name, but sometimes it is simply done out of convenience or vanity. Both are valid as far as I am concerned. Their birth name, where appropriate, appears next to their 'stage name'.

The name of the companion they played then follows, as does the title of their inaugural story and their final regular story, along with the original dates of transmission. I have chosen not to include story numbers or any alphanumerical codes used in production, because, seriously, who has time for that? Where an actor has reprised their role in the television series, I have mentioned it in their entry.

Unlike the Doctor, I *am* limited by space and time and, as such, these entries are by no means exhaustive or comprehensive. I do not think it would be very interesting for you if I simply listed their resumes, nor do I have the word count for such larks.

I have tried to capture the actor's essence in a way that I personally think is relevant and important. Sometimes that is focused on *Doctor Who*, but often there are other aspects of their lives which I have chosen to include in lieu of production anecdotes and information which can be found elsewhere.

I have included an appendix in this volume which contains information regarding personal websites and published works, podcasts and interviews which provide more information than I could ever squeeze in here, but which have been invaluable in my research. I also encourage you to make use of the references and bibliography.

The interviews are a rather special part of this book. During the course of writing, I was privileged to speak with Peter Purves, who played Steven Taylor; Katy Manning who played Jo Grant; Mark Strickson, who played Vislor Turlough; and Isabella Courtney, daughter of Nicholas Courtney who played the Brigadier. These people generously gave me their time and I am sincerely grateful.

I was equally fortunate to be granted interviews with Keith Barnfather of Reeltime Pictures and John Ainsworth from Big Finish Productions, two people who have been involved in the *Doctor Who* universe in a production capacity and have shared with me their thoughts and experiences. I also spoke with Aaron Lowe, Lizzi Von Doolittle and Maria Kinsella, fans of the show who have entrusted me with their perspectives on *Doctor Who* and the people who make it happen.

These interviews are presented as separate chapters, which I have called 'interludes' and they are scattered throughout the book in an order which makes sense – at least to me.

I now invite you to pull up a cushion, velvet or otherwise, and come with me. I am going to take you back to a time when there was no internet, no Wi-Fi and no *Doctor Who*.

Introduction

A Brief History of Television

It may seem to many of us that television has always been around. We can't imagine what it would have been like not to have the sheer volume of choice that we have today, or the simple immediacy of its convenience. On-demand, on your screen, on your phone, always on.

But back in what has come to be known as the Analogue Era, there were, at most, only five channels. If you have trouble imagining that, then hold onto your umbrella, because the first public demonstration of television in Britain was way back in 1926. Although there were numerous transmissions and experimental broadcasts, it wasn't until ten years later that the newly formed British Broadcasting Company began regular transmissions.

Now when I say regular transmissions, I feel I need to point out a few things before you get carried away. Today, high-definition television resolution is around 1080 lines. Hundreds of channels broadcast thousands of movies, TV show and rolling new channels 24 hours a day, ceaselessly, indefatigably. Most people in Britain today have a screen upon which they can watch any of this.

In 1936, the Marconi-EMI 405-line high-definition service broadcast for four hours a day from Alexander Palace, only to people within range of the transmitter in London. There were only around 500 television sets, but they were the first TV consumer audience.

This regular service was, however, to be short-lived. On 1 September 1939, Britain declared war on Germany and television was shut down, ostensibly because it was believed that the signals might be used by the Germans to guide them to potential targets. The last programme shown was a Mickey Mouse cartoon.

On 7 June 1946, the BBC came back on the air, holding dominion over the airwaves until 22 September 1955 when Independent Television (ITV) began broadcasting in the London area. This inaugurated the era of commercial, competitive television. The first advert on ITV was for SR toothpaste, by the way.

Over the next couple of years, several developments took place. Videotape recording became possible in 1958. The BBC and ITV began trying to outdo each other in terms of ratings and programming. By 1960, 95 per cent of people in the UK could now watch BBC, while ITV focused on regional television programming.

Running parallel to what was in and of itself an entertaining stand-off between ITV and BBC, plenty was going down. The demographic which was soon to come of age is now known as the 'Baby Boomers'. More births were registered in this period than ever before and it wasn't long before they were all teenagers – the memories of depression and war were far away.

From the late 1950s onwards, as I understand it, British culture pivoted away from functional modesty of the immediate post-war years into an era of optimism and stability. With television now widespread, there was also the dissemination of transatlantic attitudes into Britain, giving rise to what would be the first youth subcultures.

I don't have the space here to give an extensive chronicle of just how significant – and shocking – the change in attitudes were, but I think that the rebellious counterculture of the late 1950s spawned an era which was conducive, even integral, to the time in which *Doctor Who* came about.

Alongside the excitement of the late 1950s dark storm clouds had already been brewing.

The Cold War, which began in 1947, split the world in half. On one side, the Eastern Bloc comprised of the Soviet Union and its allies. On the other, the Western Bloc, made up of the United States, Britain and the rest of NATO.

Capitalists vs Communists, 'developing' vs 'developed' – whichever way history chooses to typify this period of unease, the resulting atmosphere was the same: the spectre of atomic destruction hung over the human race. There was a pervasive, unfamiliar sensation that perhaps technological advancement had a darker side to it and perhaps those in charge of running the political world were not entirely as wise as the previous generation had believed.

Somewhere in the depths of the BBC in 1963, a conversation was happening. A gap needs to be filled on Saturday evenings, between 5.15 and 5.45.

Enter Sydney Newman, who got wind of of a memo sent by BBC planning assistant John Mair, in which he suggested a science fiction show should occupy the slot.

The precise story of how *Doctor Who* came to be made is the subject of speculation and competing claims. It is generally accepted that Sydney Newman, who was Head of Drama at the time, guided the conception of the show, and Head of Serials, Donald Wilson, and writer CE 'Bunny' Webber, had an enormous amount of input. If you want to make your own mind up,

I suggest you read *Head of Drama: The Memoir of Sydney Newman* (Newman, Burke 2017) for a full account of the communique between all involved.

What is certain is that on 23 November 1963, directed by Waris Hussein and produced by Verity Lambert, the very first episode of *Doctor Who* was aired.

Why Does the Doctor Need Companions?

Doctor Who belongs to a very old and very effective brand of storytelling: science fiction. These days, it can be difficult to pin down exactly what science fiction is. As a postmodernist, multiple definitions of something are what makes my world go round. But I think it will be helpful if I guide you towards something approaching a prerequisite, at least where this book is concerned.

Sci-fi celebrates and imagines. It can also be a warning. It is an example of a storytelling ritual which people use to express and entertain their fears of the world, humanity and its future. To the uninitiated, the tropes of sci-fi usually involve aliens, spaceships, the future and advanced technology, but these are not imperatives. In fact, imperfectly combined, they could be regarded as clichés.

Some successful science fiction has deliberately avoided these tropes. Frank Herbert's *Dune* universe contains no advanced technology. In the series of books, it has been outlawed, although there is interstellar travel and extraterrestrial life.

Films such as *Interstellar* (dir. Christopher Nolan, 2014), *Gattaca* (dir. Andrew Niccol, 1997) have not a single alien civilisation in sight, but the technology depicted, however feasible, is certainly advanced. Many of the works of Ursula K. Guin focus on societal and cultural aspects in lieu of technological or scientific speculation. But they are often set on distant planets in the far future.

What about when contemporary developments in the real world catch up with science fiction or even disprove some of the events contained? Does HG Wells' *The War of the Worlds* (1898) stop being science fiction simply because we now know that Mars is uninhabitable (at least for humans)?

Instead of trying to define what science fiction is, perhaps let us look at what it does.

I hereby invoke Isaac Asimov (1920–1992), who defined science fiction as 'the branch of literature which deals with the response of human beings to changes in the level science and technology'.[1]

Phillip K. Dick went to great lengths to define what science fiction is not. He proposed that a piece of fiction being set in the far future, or involving space travel, does not necessarily meet the criteria for science fiction if the central theme is one of, say, romance. It just happens to occur in a particular setting. He proposed that the central theme of sci-fi is that of a new idea which occurs in a fictitious world, a world generated by what he terms a 'conceptual dyslocation'.[2]

Like Asimov, Dick surmises that the reaction to this change in science or technology is integral to the criteria. Sci-fi is about the human experience and subsequent response to a change in the understanding of science and/or technology. Without a human being experiencing this transformation, we have something which lacks a vital ingredient for effective science fiction.

More specifically, if *Doctor Who* merely contained the Doctor, the show might have been a tool for presenting possible futures, technology or non-human life forms. Without someone to experience these wondrous things for the first time, it might have been visually appealing, at first, but it would essentially be a documentary.

The Doctor's companions experience a sudden change in their understanding of the universe. That's what science fiction is.

When Ian and Barbara first burst into the TARDIS, we are not looking through the eyes of a pair of scientists who immediately begin theorising or interrogating the science involved. No, they are disturbed. It was just a box. We are as in awe of this impossibility as they are.

When the Ninth Doctor confirms to Rose Tyler that he is indeed an alien, her reaction is not to ask what planet he comes from or how he came to be on Earth, but to break down in tears from the ontological shock. The improbable is confirmed, a change has occurred in her scientific understanding and in that moment her perspective on the universe expands.

Outside of this philosophical answer to why we need a companion, a more obvious reason exists and that is one of a narrative proxy for the viewer. The Doctor's companions are overwhelmingly human, often contemporary and therefore relatable. Notable exceptions exist, of course. Adric, Turlough, Nyssa and Romana are all example of non-human companions. Leela, though human, was a member of an isolated and 'regressed' tribe of humans. But human or not, contemporary or distant, they share in our wonder at the Doctor and the complex, surprising journeys they take us on. The companions experience it for us and we can relate to them somehow. We each have our favourites, the ones we understand more than others and who, we imagine, might understand us.

Defining a Companion

Eventually, I knew I would have to write this part. That I had to decide who appears in this book in the first place was challenging enough, but the idea that

I might have to explain myself to the fanbase in some way was a thought that tied me up in knots.

Debate about *Doctor Who* canon and continuity is an ever-present, sometimes contentious discussion. There exist numerous television spin-offs, fan-made movies and other media adjacent to the main *Doctor Who* series. This output has featured companions often played by the same actor. I refer to these frequently, because they form part of the actor's body of work. There exists a debate as to what extent these spin-offs should be considered canonical, the exceptions being *Torchwood* and *The Sarah Jane Adventures*.

Some say that the defining quality which marks a spin-off as official canon is the appearance of the Doctor at some point. However, that argument falls apart when one considers the audio dramas, particularly the Big Finish Productions which do feature the Doctor and have also introduced an entire range of companions who have not appeared on the show. Canon can be entirely subjective and I think that's extraordinary fun.

Fortunately for me, this is not an in-universe study of the show and I can, for the most part, conveniently side-step any debate about continuity. I have chosen to confine this volume to the companion actors who have appeared in the BBC television series, but this decision should not infer a limited perspective of the show's canonical universe.

Many aspects of the show's continuity have been retconned in the main television series too, gifting us with surprises and contradictions. For me, this is not a bug, but a feature, and is entirely emblematic of *Doctor Who*.

In most cases, it was obvious who should be in this book. It was only when I considered the less obvious characters that I had a idea to define what constitutes a companion, in the foolish thought that it might help me make a few cut-throat decisions about which actors to include. As it turns out, this definition was elusive and slippery.

Part of the definition had to be that the person had travelled with the Doctor. That much is obvious. But what about Dr Elizabeth Shaw? She did not travel with the Doctor at all. She never even left Earth and yet she is universally considered to be a companion.

Okay, so perhaps (I thought) I could venture that they had been of assistance to the Doctor. That cannot be too much to ask, surely? But what about Turlough? Although his character arc led to his decision to support the Doctor, he was originally sent by the Black Guardian to kill him, spending quite a few episodes privately wrestling with that fact. There was Adam Mitchell too. Generally considered to be a companion, he was hardly of much use and eventually was ejected from the TARDIS after a silly, selfish betrayal.

Perhaps the answer was in the production aspects. They should have appeared in more than one or two stories, otherwise I would have to include every recurring character in the series. But there are notable exceptions to this: Dr Grace Holloway, Sara Kingdom and Katarina. No help for me there.

Eventually, I concluded that in trying to define this criteria, I was missing the point. The show is different for everybody and I am not going to be able to satisfy everybody in terms of who I include. What defines and constitutes a companion sometimes lies in a grey area, the subject of debate and negotiation.

I have not included the actors Neve McIntosh, Catrin Stewart, or Dan Starkey who played the members of The Paternoster Gang. Nor is there a biography for Penelope Wilton who played Harriet Jones, former Prime Minister (you know who she is), nor have I written about Tony Selby (Sabalom Glitz) or Samuel Anderson (Danny Pink). These characters might come close to being considered companions, but if I had included them, I would find it difficult to reason why I should not include so many others. The book would become much longer, I would not be able to go into as much detail and chaos would reign in the universe.

I had to draw the line somewhere and it is understandable that some readers may disagree with my decisions.

Conversely there may also be some names in this book who, for one reason or another, you might think do not belong here. But I have a responsibility to tell the history of the show and you will not find unhealthy rumour, speculation or salacious controversy within these pages.

You *will* find a celebration of the lives and careers of the remarkable people who played companions *Doctor Who*. It is told in precious fragments, of history, original interviews and all bound together with the threads of what makes the show such a unique phenomenon: magic, love, inclusion and excitement.

1

Carole Ann Ford (Carole Ann Lillian Higgins)

Born	16 June 1940
Companion	Susan Foreman
First Appearance	'An Unearthly Child' (23 November – 14 December 1963)
Final Appearance	'The Five Doctors' (23 November 1983)

CAROLE ANN FORD was born in Ilford, Essex, during an air raid, which I imagine must have been a rather dramatic entrance. She had her first acting job at the age of 8, in *The Last Load* (1948). She began appearing in advertisements and modelling. A versatile actor, she was in a number of films and television shows and a wide variety of genres. Of particular note was the 1963 film adaptation of John Wyndham's *The Day of the Triffids*.

Carole Ann Ford's character in the show is now regarded as the original 'Doctor Who Girl', indeed the title of the first ever episode *An Unearthly Child* refers directly to her. That Ford portrayed the very first companion to the Doctor on screen grants her a unique position in the show's history. She and her co-stars William Hartnell, William Russell and Jacqueline Hill set the precedent for the audience for what was to come.

Sidney Newman, while reviewing the initial ideas for *Doctor Who*, decided that a child character would be needed to move the story along and appeal to a young audience.[1] It was Waris Hussein who recommended her for the role, after he saw her in the BBC studios while she was filming *Suspense* (1962). He was impressed with her presence both on camera and between shots; he and Verity Lambert agreed that she had an 'unconventional beauty' and would be perfect for the role.

At the time, Ford regarded the job – at least initially – as unremarkable. This did not stop her from wanting to bring elements to Susan which were uncommon for female actors at the time. In an interview with *The Telegraph*,[2] Ford said that she would have enjoyed being able to bring a more physical aspect to the role, having had experience in acrobatics and dance. However, to her sadness, Susan became more of a misfit-teenager trope – though of course an extraterrestrial one.

After *Doctor Who*, Ford went back to her first love of theatre. She had, of course, become extremely well-known for her role as Susan, which became something of a double-edged sword. At the Doctor Who Appreciation Society's event at Riverside Studios, Hammersmith,[3] she said that although her roles in theatre productions sold tickets, she felt she had been typecast in terms of television casting.

In later life, from 1977 onwards, Ford became a dialogue coach to public speakers, politicians, businesspersons and actors.

It would seem that, with time, Ford has reconnected in a positive way with her time on *Doctor Who*, despite saying earlier that it actually harmed her acting career.

Although the rights to the character of Susan could not be obtained, Ford appeared as Zorelle in *Shakedown: Return of the Sontarans* (1994), a spin off by Dreamwatch Media. She has been in several Big Finish Productions audio dramas too, including *Doctor Who*: *The Companion Chronicles: The First Doctor* Volume 01 (2015), *Susan's War* (2020) and as Sura in *Gallifrey: Forever* (2011) Big Finish. She has voiced her praise for the revived series of *Doctor Who*.

2

Jacqueline Hill (born Grace Jacqueline Hill)

Born	17 December 1929
Died	18 February 1993
Companion	Barbara Wright
First Appearance	'An Unearthly Child' (23 November – 14 December 1963)
Final Appearance	'The Chase' (22 May – 26 June 1965)

GRACE JACQUELINE HILL was born to Grace and Arthur Hill, at home in Birmingham; she had a brother Arthur who was one year younger than her. In her biography of Jacqueline, Louise Bremner describes Hill's early family life.[1] Jacqueline's grandfather, Morris Roberts, died by suicide and her mother, Grace, gradually became estranged.

In 1937, Hill's father was tragically killed in a bicycle accident, leaving her and her brother effectively orphaned. They were loosely adopted by their grandmother, step-grandfather and great aunt. Due to Birmingham being a vast military and industrial centre during the Second World War, the city was heavily bombed. The children were subsequently evacuated to Wales.

Hill got a job at the prestigious Bourneville factory, which was well-regarded at the time in the community. The factory was set up by the Quakers and Cadbury. The moral principles of the factory was focused on the workers' health and wellbeing.

Hill first became interested in acting while studying at the Bourneville Factory's Day Continuation School,[2] taking roles in *Twelfth Night*, *Mr Bolfrie* and *Pygmalion*. Jacqueline graduated from RADA, supported by a grant and a part-time job waitressing.

She worked in local repertory theatre, with her first West End Show being *The Shrike* in 1953, written by Joseph Kramm.

By 1958, she had made a name for herself starring in various BBC and ITV television plays. She was cast by director Alvin Rakoff, who she would marry that year and who would cast her in many leading roles. In 1959, Hill and Rakoff moved to New York City, where she first met Verity Lambert, before the couple moved back to London.

Jacqueline Hill was cast as Barbara Wright, one of the first ever companions on *Doctor Who*. Hill and Lambert knew each other socially and Lambert thought that, as a person, Hill was right for the part.

Story editor David Whitaker wrote the Writers' Guide to *Doctor Who* during its conception, which would be given to potential script writers.[3] In this six-page document, Hill's character Barbara is described as attractive and courageous, but also mentions that the relationship between her and Ian would remain strictly platonic. Hill confirmed[4] that although there was affection and perhaps an undercurrent of romance between the two characters, it was their shared experience with the Doctor which brought them close.

It is without a doubt that Hill's contribution to the first two season of the show assured its success. Over the course of the stories, strong and varied dynamics played out between the characters. Barbara Wright was anything but the stereotypical female companion. She was something of a mother figure to Susan and Vicki, had a meaningful friendship with Ian and, at times, something of a diplomat between the Doctor and the others. Hill's talent and versatility as an actor is strong, yet subtle, and although it is sure that *Doctor Who* was not solely responsible for Jacqueline's career, Bremner argues that it 'secured her a lasting place in television history'.[5]

Hill has not voiced any regret leaving the show, sharing the sentiment with her co-star William Russell, that the time had come to move on.

In the 1960s, if one had a strong association to a particular show, it was hard to get work afterwards. When Hill left *Doctor Who*, she was 36 years old and had two children, which perhaps meant further leading roles were even less forthcoming. She mainly retired from acting to raise her family. But in 1980, she returned to *Doctor Who* playing the character Lexa, opposite Tom Baker's Doctor in the story 'Meglos'.

Jacqueline Hill appeared at only one *Doctor Who* convention, in 1985, where she spoke fondly and vividly of her time on the show, from its inception and her casting, to her and William Russell's departure.

Jacqueline Hill died in 1993 of cancer.

3

William Russell (born William Russell Enoch)

Born	19 November 1924
Died	3 June 2024
Companion	Ian Chesterton
First Appearance	'An Unearthly Child' (23 November – 14 December 1963)
Final Appearance	'The Chase' (22 May – 26 June 1965)

WILLIAM RUSSELL was born in Sunderland to Eva and Alfred James Enoch. He organised entertainment during his national services in the RAF, then went into repertory theatre.

Russell's character Ian Chesterton was the first male companion, one of the originals, you might say. He was the epitome of the 1960s handsome, self-assured hero. *Doctor Who*'s inception and its formative days were to be the bedrock upon which the next sixty years (and counting) would be built. Nobody knew this at the time, of course.

Russell's character, along with his co-star Jacqueline Hill, were the surrogates for the audience, exemplifying that important quality of science fiction which we discussed in the opening chapter: the human reaction to the shocking changes and experiences they encountered.

Ian Chesterton was a science teacher – a logical and practical man, so his reaction when he and Barbara first entered the TARDIS was not simply that of a layman encountering something he didn't understand. In fact, his character understood a great deal and therefore *knew* what he was seeing was impossible. This lent extra gravity to those famous scenes.

Verity Lambert had admired him for a long time.[1] He was a well known actor, having starred as Sir Lancelot in *The Adventures of Sir Lancelot*. Russell was used to playing the handsome, heroic male character and he played Ian with a similar flair for chivalry and valour. Already an established actor, he played Ian with a degree of confidence and even-tempered righteousness which can only come from a mature actor.

The original TARDIS team became a blueprint for when the show got the casting right, when the blend of actors ends up well-balanced both on-screen and off. In an interview with *Radio Times*,[2] Russell described how well he and his co-stars got on and that Hartnell was an exemplary and professional actor.

After a long run, with the series still going strong (a welcome surprise to everybody involved), Russell decided, along with his co-star Jacqueline Hill, that since they arrived together, they should leave together. The show had become hard work and, like so many others would, Russell knew when the time had come to leave on a high note.

Russell, often going under variations of his birth name, appeared in numerous stage productions. He was MacDuff in *Macbeth* at English Stage Company (1966) and later would appear in *Countryman* at the National Theatre in 1987. He also appeared in *Hamlet* as the ghost, and King James I of Aragon in *The Disputation* in 2001. He held a position as a senior executive in the acting union Equity and was a member of the Royal Shakespeare Company.

It was originally planned that Russell would return in the 1983 *Doctor Who* story Mawdryn Undead, however his conflicting theatre schedule meant that this become sadly impossible.

Russell's television roles were just as abundant. He played Tom Preston in *Harriet's Back in Town* between 1972–1973, for over forty episodes. He would make guest appearances on several other television shows, before eventually joining the cast of *Coronation Street* in 1992, playing Ted Sullivan.

William Russell has reprised his role of Ian Chesterton in many Big Finish Productions, but he has also played the First Doctor on a few occasions, notably *Doctor Who*: *The Early Adventures* starting in 2014. William Hartnell died in 1975, so the fact that Russell, a fellow actor who worked with and greatly respected him, should now be able to play his role is a fitting and poignant tribute.

On 23 October 2022, Russell had a brief and beautiful cameo in *The Power of the Doctor*, appearing in a support group composed of former companions of the Doctor, including Jo Grant, Mel Bush, Kate Stewart, Tegan, Ace and Graham, Dan and Yaz.

William Enoch Russell died at home on 3 June 2024. He was 99 years old.

4

Maureen O'Brien

Born	29 June 1943
Companion	Vicki
First Appearance	'The Rescue' (2–9 January 1965)
Final Appearance	'The Myth Makers' (16 October – 6 November 1965)

MAUREEN O'BRIEN was born in Liverpool, during the Second World War. O'Brien did well academically and was put into the eleven-plus class at just 8 years old. O'Brien described her first experience with maths, which was advanced for her age, and it scared her. She went to Notre Dame School, a grammar school in central Liverpool, close to the Everyman Theatre.

The grammar school was run by the Notre Dame nuns, who she describes as being democratic, intelligent and excellent teachers. One of the sisters, Sister Therese of the Passion, at the school started a drama society.

O'Brien credits Sister Therese as her inspiration for applying at the Central School of Speech and Drama. She did a teaching diploma and learned the Alexander Technique, developed by Frederick Matthias Alexander (20 January 1869 – 10 October 1955) as a way to improve posture and relive musculoskeletal problems by improved awareness of the body.

O'Brien has appeared in many theatre productions, including *An Enemy of the People* (Everyman Liverpool 1964), *Lancelot and Guinevere* (The Old Vic, London 1980) and *Othello* (Bristol Old Vic Company, 1990). She has had some roles on television, namely *Z-Cars* (1969), *Casualty* (1987) and *Jonathan Creek* (1997)

Theatre being her first love and, as we've already seen, television being thought of as comparatively low-brow, O'Brien was reluctant when she was told there was a possibility of a television role. This news came from Harry Moore, one of her instructors at the Central School.

O'Brien was perfectly happy at the Everyman theatre, but her then-boyfriend (who would later become her husband) convinced her to audition.[1]

The character of Vicki was the first 'new' companion to join. O'Brien describes the experience as like joining a family, albeit a changeable one with guest stars. The gruelling schedules differed from her time in theatre where she was used to a lot more rehearsal time and could keep her script close by. O'Brien easily adapted and was able to get into the rhythm after a few weeks.

An unplanned leak alerted the media to O'Brien's role in *Doctor Who* much earlier than the BBC had planned. Journalists apparently laid siege to her home and began harassing her neighbours, which meant she and her boyfriend had to make several furtive exits from their flat when they needed to go somewhere. The additional pressure of being recognised in public caused problems for O'Brien, who was very shy.

Maureen O'Brien's decision to leave *Doctor Who* was a combination of her being constantly recognised, and what she perceived to be a limiting role. O'Brien attempted to encourage the producers to make Vicki more of a complex character, with more humour, intelligence and fight.

It was during the scheduled break in filming for six weeks that O'Brien discovered she had been written out. Although she had received no warning about this, she was relieved.[2]

Maureen O'Brien worked on several Big Finish Productions audio dramas. She's been prolific, in fact, and continues her roles to this day, reprising her role as Vicki in *The Ravelli Conspiracy* (2016) and *Fugitive of the Daleks* (2024), to name but two. O'Brien became enamoured with radio plays and audio dramas because of the freedom it allowed her as an actor – physical qualities and limitations didn't matter.

Popular, lively and, in the opinion of many fans, underrated during her original tenure, O'Brien thrilled the fanbase by returning in the 2023 trailer for the *Doctor Who* Season 2 Blu-Ray boxset, reminiscing with her granddaughter about her travels with the Doctor, but now apparently still content in Ancient Troy where her character stayed.

5

Peter Purves

Born	10 February 1939
Companion	Steven Taylor
First Appearance	'The Chase' (22 May – 26 June 1965)
Final Appearance	'The Savages' (28 May – 18 June 1966)

PETER PURVES was born in New Longton, Lancashire. His father's family was from Preston and his mother's from Newcastle-Upon-Tyne. He describes his childhood as 'unfashionably happy'[1] and rather fun.

In 1942, his father went into business with his friend Arthur Sharples and bought a hotel in Blackpool. The seaside town exposed a young Purves to so much showbusiness that he knew he wanted to become an actor from a very young age. Both his parents were admirers of cinema and stage, so there was already a love of the arts around him. It was in 1948 when Purves, at 9½ years old, had his first role, in *The Pied Piper of Hamelin* – as the Piper.

Purves went to boarding school, very willingly, describing that his peers who were at boarding school were 'always the most interesting'.[2] Much later, he wrote to the local repertory company at Her Majesty's Theatre, Barrow, and successfully completed an audition. He was then cast in his first professional role as the sheriff in a stage version of *The Rainmaker*.

Purves then joined Alsager College, Stoke-on-Trent, as a back-up in case acting didn't work out. It seems he was always destined for acting, however, as he became involved with the Dramatic Society. Shortly after, he got a post teaching maths at a school in Hackney, London, but all he could think about was acting.

After realising that he didn't want to be a teacher, Purves quit and attempted to find an acting agent. He received an invitation back to Her Majesty's Theatre, Barrow, to join as a regular actor. No matter which town, repertory theatre is renowned for being intense, with a different stage show every week and very little time to learn lines. However, this was the most enjoyable work Purves had ever done and he felt fulfilled and contented.

It was in Barrow that Purves met Gillian Emmett, who he married in 1962. In 1963, she became pregnant and the couple moved to London, where they both acted in theatre. Soon, Purves got his first television role on *Z-Cars* and, later, while taking a lunch break from another role in *The World of Wooster*, Purves would meet William Hartnell, taking his own lunch break from filming *Doctor Who*.

In 1965, Purves' agent arranged a meeting with *Doctor Who* director Richard Martin. The audition was for one of the 'menoptera' creatures, but Martin insisted that Purves should have a speaking role and when one was available, he would get in touch. It wasn't long before Martin cast Purves as Morton Dill in episode three of 'The Chase'.

Almost immediately after he finished filming, Purves was asked to join as the new companion. He didn't need to audition for the part of Steven, as Verity Lambert and story editor Dennis Spooner had already enjoyed his performances as Morton Dill.

Sadly, many of the *Doctor* episodes featuring Peter Purves have now been lost entirely, and some stories ('Galaxy 4', 'The Daleks' Masterplan' and 'The Celestial Toymaker') only partially survive. Some of the stories have been reconstructed with animation and, as the audio of episodes survived, Purves has narrated many of the soundtracks to their release.

'The Gunfighters' was Purves' last appearance on *Doctor Who*. Between 1978 and 1981, Peter Purves was the lead presenter for five seasons of the BBC children's sport programme *Stopwatch*. He has also been a presenter for the Darts World Championship, Driver of the Year, *Kickstart* and has had numerous roles in television programmes such as *Z-Cars* and *Girl in a Black Bikini*, though Purves himself states that these roles were small[3] and came at a time when, after *Who*, his acting career had taken 'a bit of a nosedive'.

However, in 1968, he auditioned for the job as presenter of Blue Peter, alongside John Noakes and Valerie Singleton. Though this was initially going be for short time, he ended up presenting the show for ten years. A long-time lover of dogs, Purves has been a commentator for dog show Crufts for over forty years.

Peter Purves is a British household name, no question, and he has continued his association with *Doctor Who*, attending many conventions over the years, as well as reprising his role as Steven in numerous Big Finish Productions audio dramas. Interestingly, Purves has done almost as many audio stories playing William Hartnell's First Doctor.

Interlude 1: Peter Purves Interview

IN 2023, Peter Purves agreed to speak to me about his time on *Doctor Who*. Having already read *Peter Purves The Autobiography: Here's One I Wrote Earlier* (Green Umbrella Publishing, 2009, London), I had lots of questions to ask him.

I must admit being quite nervous on the day we spoke, but Peter was incredibly kind and forthcoming, with a wealth of experience and knowledge of the world of show business and, of course, *Doctor Who*.

I was on Twitter and saw you at Fantom Films Pandorica. It looked really fun.

I have done very few this year. Three. One I couldn't do because I got Covid.

Pandorica is a brilliant one. The staff, you know them all, because you've been to the events before. All the helpers are great. They have very good interviewers on stage who know more about *Doctor Who* than we do. If I'm honest, I'm not really a huge fan of the show. I worked on it, I did it. That was then, this is now. So I have a good time there and it was great because I was busy the entire time. I didn't have any downtime. That was good. I had breakfast, relaxed, went down to the convention and then I was busy from then on! That's how I like them to be.

I thought your autobiography was really sensitively written.

Really? I'm not proud of my writing. I thought it was a bit prosaic, a bit dull. But I do write like I speak. I think I come off the page if that means anything to you.

I enjoyed the nonlinear presentation. From 1979, then to the present day. You said fairly early on in the book that this was the first time you'd addressed the past. Writing an autobiography is a brave thing to do.

Why I don't like it is because it should have been called a memoir. I didn't check anything, I wrote it as if I was telling you. The memories are exactly as I remembered them. Some of them are borrowed memories because I could not remember anything until Mark Ayres asked me to do the commentaries on my episodes. They are the audios from all my missing episodes. So my whole career in *Doctor Who* is on audio. So when I did that, it started to bring it all back.

It unlocked something.

Yes, of course. I remembered some of the script. But there's a sequence in the 'Dalek Master Plan', called the Feast of Steven! It was about slapstick comedy in Hollywood … and I don't remember doing it. Now I know I did, because I'm there on the audio tape, but I don't remember any of it. None of it! It's got custard pie fights. I love silent movies, these are the things I really love. And I don't remember any of it. So I'm not sure if some of the memories aren't recreated. But certainly in my book, the attitudes I express are right.

I was asked a question yesterday at Pandorica. I was asked what was it like as a *Doctor Who* companion. And my answer was that it was a very perilous time. Because companions were being dropped like nobody's business. Maureen O'Brien went after we did two series. She came back from summer break and discovered she'd been written out. Then we started 'Dalek Master Plan' with a new companion who lasted four episodes before they killed her off. There was Jean Marsh who could only do eight weeks before her next job. And then we got Jackie Lane and she only lasted six episodes after I left. And I left with four weeks' notice.

It was a period of great peril. Nobody felt secure. It was a very unusual thing. And we had a changed of producer. I was cast by Verity Lambert, worked through John Wiles and then Ines Lloyd came on.

When you go the job you were cast as Morton Dill, and then by the end of it you were cast as Steven and asked if you wanted to stay on? I imagine the producers running out after you and asking you to please stay.

It was virtually like that. As soon as it was finished, the producers came onto the floor, asked me for a drink and offered me the job. It was largely due to Maureen O'Brien's instigation. She went to Bill Hartnell and she was worried that the replacement hadn't been found for Jackie and Russ. I'd got on very well doing Morton Dill. It was a funny scene, they thought it was funny and they liked it. Maureen went to Bill and said 'You're getting on well with this guy – what do you think?', and so he spoke to Verity Lambert and she and Donald Tosh the editor and writer for the next serial. 'The Time Meddler'. Well he and she watched me in the producers' run through and then watched me carefully on the recording and offered me that job. Morton Dill was my audition and I didn't know it.

Sometimes it's best if you don't know.

Yes, I would have been nervous enough. Terribly nervous. I knew the part inside out. I'd grown up with weekly rep and you learn different parts all the time. You learn it on the Monday and the Tuesday and then you're on stage live. It was easy learning for me. It was a good action piece, but had nothing to do with Steven Taylor!

It's funny you mention weekly rep too. Repertory theatre was so important to actors' early years. This was like boot camp for actors.
It was great fun, high pressure. My description of rep was that it is the most fun, the hardest work and the worst paid job I've ever done. But the most satisfying! It was a great experience. The majority were very talented people, the artistic director working his socks off to make something worthwhile with very little money. It was on a shoestring, but somehow we survived.

The shoestring budgets forces, I think, people to work hard. You can't rely on huge money or CGI.
On *Doctor Who* we didn't have the editing time. The budget allowed for three edits. That means if you have a special effect, that includes the arrival of the TARDIS and its departure. So in any one episode, you have only one edit left. That's all we had. Everything else was recorded with only three times the length of the programme to finish.

Yes, Deborah Watling in her book describes how they would be running around changing and preparing for their next scene, just as the previous scene was being recorded.
It's essentially live television. In the studio, you might have six different sets. Between those, you maybe had five or six cameras. Each of them is cabled to the power, which are on different sides of the studio. On top of that, we didn't have mics. We had a boom, operated by a boom swinger and this huge boom swivelled and turned. That's how it was done. All those things have to move from whichever set they're on to where they're needed. So if you need four cameras and the next scene is at the other end of the studio, you have to know exactly what the shots are so you can free up a camera for the next one. Plus you have personnel, prop men, actors. All sorts. It was incredibly busy and complicated. The directors on any semi-live TV were absolutely brilliant! They worked it all out, shot for shot, on paper – who, where, what and why.

When we get into the studio, the vision mixer cuts where it's written, the shots being called out by a PA. That's going on on the gallery, while we're acting. It's stunning stuff. It would make a thrilling drama! I might write one!

It sounds like it was choreographed like a ballet.
Absolutely. Everything was. This is why the rep connection works. The things you did in theatre, you did in TV. Obviously once things changed you got into single camera shooting, it became easy. But it was very hard back then.

The time that you worked on *Doctor Who* set it up for what it was going to be. You worked with William Hartnell who took the role of The Doctor extremely seriously.
He created it. None of the excitement would exist now if it weren't for his wonderful performance. The BFI release last week for the Blu–ray restoration of 'The Time Meddler' is stunning. Bear in mind how it was shot – it's amazing what we can do with a bit of shrubbery.

I actually watched *The Time Meddler* Last night before talking to you today. It's on Britbox.
Was it a good restoration?

It was a good copy, but I'm interested in the Blu-ray now.
Well it's tremendous. And yes, I loved working with Bill Hartnell. He cast me, he was responsible for me getting the job and was protective of me. He'd give me little tips. I'd do a gesture or something and he would say [does excellent impersonation of William Hartnell] 'Oh Peter you need to do gestures near your face, because TV is very small and it won't be seen!' So things like that he gave to me. He gave me a lot of companionship. Took me for lunch once a week and always a smashing lunch. My wife and I used to take him out too once a month for a good Indian or a good Chinese meal. I got on very well with him. He was an absolute gent and he had a good sense of humour.

He had no understanding of irony, though. Once he was sitting at mine before we went went out, we were watching TV. Kenneth Tynan was on a late night television show where he said 'fuck' for the first time on British television. And William Hartnell said 'That was disgusting. You wouldn't go into someone's living room and use fucking language like that!'

[I'm pretty much inconsolable with laughter at this.]
He didn't understand irony at all. His acting, his general geniality and his humour. Maureen O'Brien and I are as one in that.

I really liked the relationship between you and William Hartnell. There was a warmth to him and I'm aware he had a reputation for being somewhat irascible.
The reason for that is because towards the end of his tenure *Doctor Who* he was having difficulty remembering his lines and it took some time to get him back on script and of course we didn't have the time to edit it, so it went out. And occasionally it was difficult. But he was such a professional that he was furious with himself when he got it wrong, so if someone encountered him

when he was angry about that, they're were likely to get some flack. He was never awkward or discourteous to me once.

I was thinking about something you said in an interview, you said you were surprised people didn't ask more about yet technical aspects of the show.
Well, the technology was crap. Television pictures were made of lines not pixels. So the restoration that's been done on 'The Time Meddler' – watching it on the big screen, it's been restored so well that you can see the 405 lines which made up the picture back then. Anybody seeing anything that's been restored from those 1960s performances, the director never saw the picture as well as we see them now. There were things on the set which you can see now which you weren't meant to, like parts of the set and stage.

I'm fully believing the story that you took the Trilogic Game prop from The Celestial Toymaker home with you. Am I right?
Yep.

And I'm also fully believing that it was bad luck and when you got rid of it, that was when you got the call from *Blue Peter*!
It's a slightly cynical view about it, honestly, but the coincidence … My work has been forged by coincidences. It was coincidence that I played the lead in a play for Alvin Rakoff – who was married to Jacqueline Hill – called *The Girl in the Picture* in 1964. I went to see Richard Martin to play one of the giant insects in *The Web Planet.* The previous night, the play had been transmitted and he'd seen it and said there was nothing for me to play. He said 'when I'm casting decent roles, I'll think of you'.

I took it with a pinch of salt because it's one of those things a director would say to let you down gently. But he was as good as his word. That's why he cast me as Morton Dill and I didn't have to audition.

When I chucked out the Trilogic Game, I got the call the following day. They contacted my agent and said they were looking for a replacement for Christopher Trace on *Blue Peter* and they contacted my agent because they'd been given my name. I didn't know how it happened at the time, but I do now. I got the job.

When I finished on *Blue Peter*, I was given three series by the BBC and so I went to Manchester to do those series. I used to play darts a lot and there was a dartboard in the BBC club and the BBC had just started covering the world championships. I was a good player! So I'm playing regularly and one of the guys who played was Tony Green who was one of the commentators on television. He mentioned to the boss of sport and I ended up presenting presenting darts for seven years.

I did a film about the white helmets on *Blue Peter*. I learned to ride a motorbike, off road, rough ground – and as a result I was given *KickStart* because the director of it was the producer of the *Blue Peter* film. So my career has been a chunk of coincidental hops. My career was extended quite a lot. I had a mainstream series on TV until 1992 and I started in 1965. That's not a bad span!

I'm wary of what I read on the internet, but it says somewhere that you play the organ as an amateur. Is that right?
No. I played the piano until I was about 11. I had singing lessons, music lessons. I dropped the lessons eventually though.

Well there's a very succinct lie floating around on the internet that you played the organ!
I've never been asked that before, so maybe nobody else has seen it!

I was really interested in your experiences in Ethiopia which led to what I might say a bringing into focus of your spiritual perspective or lack thereof. I found that so interesting.
It was a very unfortunate thing. We ran the appeal before Live Aid for famine in Ethiopia. See these people had been turning up at the local capitals and they came from Dintsa, and the plan was to restock them with cattle, because cattle are very important there, to give them ploughs and give them seed to plant. The first thing was that the cattle were near one of the small cities and we were going to take the cattle to them. When we got there the herd was quarantined because they had foot and mouth and we lost them all. And I just said that there isn't a God. I don't believe in God. I am an atheist, a firm one.

And that's what I found so interesting. I think I've spoken to a lot of agnostics, but I don't remember the last time I met someone who was staunchly atheist.
Thank you for sharing that.

What do you think from your formative years most informed the way you live your life?
Well, I had a very loving mother. My father was working a lot, he had a tailoring business in Preston. If they hadn't failed in their business venture with the hotel and had to move, my life would have been very different. Because I was at a very good school and they decided I should stay there because they weren't sure where they would end up. I stayed there at boarding school until I was 18. That

had the biggest effect on my life. The town I grew up in, which was Blackpool, was somewhere I saw and did so much to do with showbiz and I knew I wanted to be an actor from the age of 9. But being at the school tempered me. I'm very much a sole person, on my own. I'm not on my own of course. I'm married, and my wife says I can be very distant at times. I do feel very self-sufficient. I can cope quite well on my own, although I've very often been in a relationship and have been married for forty years – second time – and seventeen years the first time. But I can cope with most things and I'm not particularly neurotic.

If there's one thing you'd like the readers of this book to know about you, what would it be?
Nothing really. I'm a very open book. I don't hide anything. I was a very average sportsman at school. I could have been academic, but I was only academically good in certain ways. I got all the subjects I studied for in exams, but I went off the academic side and in the end I did get maths and qualified as a Maths and English teacher and got a job teaching Maths and English. But I got fed up and then went into rep! That's me in a nutshell.

If there's one thing you'd like the readers of this book to know about life, what would it be?
Experience counts for nothing. It's not regarded. If you're old, you're old. Will that do?

It certainly will! Thank you.

6

Adrienne Hill

Born	22 July 1937
Died	6 October 1997
Companion	Katarina
First Appearance	'The Myth Makers' (16 October – 6 November 1965)
Final Appearance	'The Daleks' Master Plan' (13 November 1965 – 29 January 1966)

ADRIENNE HILL was born in Plymouth, Devon. She trained in acting at the Bristol Old Vic and, with the Old Vic Company, did repertory theatre for a number of years. After an unsuccessful audition for Princess Joanna in 'The Crusade' (a role which went to Jean Marsh), Douglas Camfield who was the *Doctor Who* director at the time, cast her as Katarina.

This came about when she was an understudy for Dame Maggie Smith in *Mary, Mary*. Smith had become ill, so Hill was required to perform. *Doctor Who* Production assistant Viktors Ritelis put her forward, but Camfield rejected her, only to cast her later along with Jean Marsh as Sara Kingdom.

The character of Katarina was extremely short lived and Hill's episodes were filmed back to front. Hill filmed her death scene in 'The Daleks' Master Plan' before her introduction in the *Myth Makers*.

Initially conceived as a replacement for Vicki, the producers of the show quickly realised that her being from Ancient Troy meant she would have an extremely steep learning curve when it came to understanding the crew elements of the show – time travel, technology, extraterrestrials.

It was decided that the show would have become very quickly all about her journey, which, interesting as this may have been, would have taken far too much attention away from the stories. So Katarina was written out in the next story.

Hill had only a brief career in television, with her part in *Doctor Who* being her final screen role. She had success in radio dramas, particularly the BBC drama *Waggoner's Walk* and in the 1980s she appeared in theatre productions, including James O'Brien's *Necropolis* (1988).

She married Dennis Wrattan, with whom she had two children, and whose work she took to Holland, then the USA.[1] After her marriage ended, she return to Britain and became a drama teacher.

On 22 November 1985, Hill was reunited with Peter Purves and Maureen O'Brien on the Children in Need appeal. She also attended some *Doctor Who* conventions.

Adrienne Hill died in 1997.

7

Jean Marsh (Jean Lyndsey Torren Marsh)

Born	1 July 1934
Companion	Sara Kingdom
First Appearance and final appearance	'The Daleks' Master Plan' (13 November 1965 – 29 January 1966)

JEAN MARSH was born in Stoke Newington, London, to a working-class family; her mother worked in a bar and her father was a labourer. She became a dancer by way of recovery and therapy from a childhood illness which left her temporarily paralysed. She attended the Aida Foster Theatre School, ostensibly a stage school, but one which Marsh describes as a 'charm school'[1]

Barbara Windsor also attended the school at the same time and corroborated the emphasis on received pronunciation and 'to be pretty'. (*Desert Island Discs: 70 Years of Castaways*, Sean Magee). Despite the Aida Foster School's curriculum of conformity, Marsh's unconventional appearance landed her some unusual roles, particularly as a cat when she was 15 in the stage play *Pardon My Claws* by Robert Monro (a pseudonym of Sonnie Hale) in 1952.

Marsh went to the Central School of Speech and Drama, worked in repertory theatre and supplemented her income by dancing in film. She went on to have roles in television throughout the 1950s and '60s, both in Britain and America, including *Danger Man*, *The Twilight Zone* and *The Edgar Wallace Mystery Theatre*.

Jean Marsh has quite a history with *Doctor Who*. In 1950, she married Jon Pertwee who would go on to play the Third Doctor, though they divorced in 1960 well before either of them had been in the show. In 1965, she was cast as Lady Joanna in the *Doctor Who* story 'The Crusade', of which only two episodes are currently known to exist.

She returned as Sara Kingdom in 'The Daleks' Master Plan', also in 1965, cast by Douglas Camfield. This story was an epic twelve-part story, which was the only serial to feature Marsh's character; she died at the end. However, Marsh seems to have had a pleasant time filming, and has on more than one occasion told the story about how the smokers on set would often use any vacant Dalek props in which to secret themselves and have a cigarette, given away only by the smoke wafting out through the top of the casings.[2]

Jean Marsh plays an exquisite villain. She played Nurse Wilson/Mombi in *Return to Oz* (1985), Queen Bavmorda in *Willow* (1988) In 1989, Marsh returned to *Doctor Who*, but this time as Morgaine in the story Battlefield (1989).

She has an illustrious film career, appearing in Alfred Hitchcock's *Frenzy* (1972), *Fatherland* (1994) and *Monarch* (2000). Her television career has been equally full and varied, including the character Roz Keith in *9 to 5* (1982–83), Dr Culex in *The Tomorrow People* (1994), Mrs Choker in children's television series *The Ghost Hunter*.

Marsh reprised her role as Sara Kingdom in many of the Big Finish audio dramas, including 'The Five Companions', 'The Destroyers' and 'The Drowned World'.

With actress and screenwriter Eileen Atkins, Marsh created the very popular British drama *Upstairs, Downstairs* and she appeared as Rose Buck for the entirety of its run from 1971 until 1975, later appearing in the 2010 revival, which ran to another season in 2012.

Her role was smaller this time, as in 2011, Marsh had a stroke and a heart attack. With her characteristic spirit, Marsh chose to view this experience as a period of learning and re-learning, a time of self-discovery which she said she found exciting.[3]

In 2021, Jean Marsh was made an Officer of the Order of the British Empire for her services to drama.

8

Jackie Lane (born Jacqueline Joyce Lane)

Born	10 July 1941
Died	23 June 2021
Companion	Dodo Chaplet
First Appearance	'The Massacre' (5 February – 26 February 1966)
Final Appearance	'The War Machines' (25 June – 16 July 1966)

JACKIE LANE was born in Manchester, England. Her father, Jack Lane, was theatrical wig-maker and make-up artist, which of course led to early exposure to the world of theatre and acting.

Determined to be become an actress, she began doing repertory at the Manchester Library Theatre. After that, she moved from Manchester to London where she began taking her first small acting roles.

Her early career involved radio and television production, of particular note Anna Neagle's production of *Wonderful Things* in 1958. She then went on to play roles in *Z-Cars* in 1961, Rosemary Gray in the soap opera *Compact* in 1963, as well as its ITV rival *Coronation Street*.

Remember, this was still a time when the two channels were trying to out-do each other. It's interesting to speculate what actors like Jackie Lane may have thought constantly 'crossing the floor' and what comparison they may have privately made.

Lane very nearly became involved with *Doctor Who* at the show's inception in 1963, when she auditioned for the part of Susan.[1] She was reluctant to be bound by a year-long contract and Lane herself clarified that the initial contract was for a lengthy period to which she was unwilling to commit.

John Wiles, who had succeeded Verity Lambert as the show's producer, had worked with Lane before and she was offered the part of Dodo in 1966. Shortly after, Innes Lloyd took over.

Although her tenure as Dodo was short, Lane has remained a popular character with fans. Her iconic Sixties mini skirt and Dylan cap made her a memorable and recognisable character. Lane brought a feisty determination to the role with a rebellious self-assured demeanour. There are moments in 'The Gunfighters' where Lane's ability to play a daring and demanding character are tense and amusing, for instance holding the character of Doc Holliday at gunpoint and demanding to be taken back to Tombstone. When this request is duly satisfied, Dodo lowers the gun and grins, relieved.

The nuance and energy with which Lane played Dodo is exceptional and the dynamic relationships between her and William Hartnell, Peter Purves and her other co-stars is engaging and fun to watch.

It's difficult to understand why Lane was dropped from the show so suddenly, with what has been described as an anticlimactic ending, something which has not gone noticed among fans of the show, who often remark that she was underrated and deserved a more fitting departure.

After her time on the show she became a diplomatic secretary to the Australian Embassy in Paris. Later, she became theatrical agent, with one of her clients being Tom Baker, who would later play the Fourth Doctor.

Although Jackie Lane chose not to appear on any of the new *Doctor Who* DVD commentaries, she was a guest at Manopticon in 1991, when she give extensive comments about her time on the show. She described feeling welcome[2] and mentioned that her claim to fame is being one of the first women to wear a miniskirt on British television.

Jackie Lane died in 2021 and left behind a brief, but clearly memorable and exciting mark on *Doctor Who*. The fan tributes and obituaries speak in glowing terms and she certainly made an impact.

9

Anneke Wills (Anna Katarina Willys)

Born	20 October 1941
Companion	Polly
First Appearance	'The War Machines' (25 June – 16 July 1966)
Final Appearance	'The Faceless Ones' (8 April – 13 May 1967)

ANNEKE WILLS was born in Fulmer, Buckinghamshire. Her father, Alaric Willys, was in the army and her mother, Anna, was Dutch, having multiple jobs to support her family, including as a gardener and a teacher. As a result, they moved around to various parts of the country.

After training at the Arts Educational School, Wills quickly began a successful and prolific television career, playing roles in *The Blakes* (1955), *The Railway Children* (1957) and *Gamble For a Throne* (1961). In an interview with Mark Ayres for the audio of 'The War Machines', Wills describes her busy career, saying that 1966 was an exciting time. In her personal life, Wills was also a well-connected and popular woman in London's social scene. A frequent patron of the famous Troubadour coffee house on Old Brompton Street and The Establishment on Greek Street, Wills had a colourful and legendary time, embodying the 1960s London scene.

With her reputation, it's no surprise that Wills' character Polly was the archetypal 'Swinging Sixties' girl. She was written to be classy and gregarious, in contrast to her co-star Michael Craze's character Ben, a cockney seaman who first appeared rather sullen and in need of a drink. The initial differences between their on-screen characters could not be more apparent, right from their first scene together in 'The War Machines' (1966), though Ben jumps to Polly's defence after being harassed by a loutish barfly.

Wills recalls playing practical jokes on Patrick Troughton, along with Craze, including once when they both appeared in T-shirts emblazoned with

'Bring Back Bill Hartnell'. Apparently, despite enjoying playing practical jokes, Troughton remained unamused.[1]

When Wills was told about the idea to regenerate the Doctor, she thought it was 'brilliant', though describes the speed from which they went from conception, to audition and to casting, as being very quick. With this innovative way of continuing the series, the show entered a new and exciting phase, Wills continuing with the Second Doctor.[2]

There seems to be some confusion as to why she left the role. Anneke Wills recalls that both she and Craze were asked to stay on, but decided against it. Craze himself did not recall this.

Anneke Wills played a few more roles, notable Judy in *The Avengers* for two episodes In 1966–67, then starring as Evelyn McLean in the inventive crime drama television series *Syringe Report* (1969).

By this time, Wills had two children, a daughter named Polly from her previous relationship with performer Anthony Newley (24 September 1931 – 14 April 1999) and a son, Jasper, with her husband Michael Gough, who sold be well-known to *Doctor Who* fans for his role as 'The Celestial Toymaker' in 1966. She left acting to raise her children and, after she and Gough divorced, she went on a period of reflective travelling, living in America, Canada, India and Vietnam.[3]

Anneke Wills revised her role as Polly in the Big Finish Productions audio dramas many times, as well as narrating some of the Target novelisation audio books and has appeared in multiple documentaries relating to the show.

In 2007, Wills released her autobiography which is a deeply moving, honest and often hilarious account of her life, peppered with precious photographs and sketches done by Wills herself.

10

Michael Craze (Michael Francis Craze)

Companion	Ben Jackson
Born	29 November 1942
Died	7 December 1998
First Appearance	'The War Machines' (25 June – 16 July 1966)
Final Appearance	'The Faceless Ones' (8 April – 13 May 1967)

MICHAEL CRAZE was born in Newquay, Cornwall. He moved around many different parts of Britain, before he and his family settled in London. It was when he was doing Scout shows at the age of 12 that he learned he had a good singing voice, specifically that of a soprano. This led to some early roles, such as *Plain and Fancy* in 1956 and *Damn Yankees* in 1957, though after he went back to school to finish his education he had lost his singing voice.

After graduating he studied the Stanislavsky method for two years, while working some unrelated jobs to support himself and joining repertory theatre companies.[1]

By 1960 he had his first role not only in television, but specifically science fiction, in the programme *Target Luna*, paying the role of Geoffrey Wedgewood. The show was produced by none other than Sidney Newman who, of course, three years later, would go on to co-create *Doctor Who*. Originally believed wiped and lost, the series is now available on DVD.

Just before getting the role of Ben Jackson on *Doctor Who*, Craze was appearing in an episode of *No Hiding Place*, but before that he had suffer a fall and badly injured his nose. At the time of filming, he was still recovering.

The character of Ben Jackson was initially devised to be a replacement for Peter Purves' Steven Tyler, seeing that audiences had become used to a male companion on the show. As William Hartnell's age precluded the possibility of intense action scenes, much like Ian Chester, they developed the character of Ben to be a sailor, a confident and energetic young cockney.

Craze was unaware that the audition would be as a companion, initially believing that the role would be only for a single story, however it soon became apparent through subsequent auditions with Ines Lloyd and director Michael Ferguson that they had further plans for Ben.

The episode which introduced Craze's character, 'The War Machines', featured some of the most extensive location filming in *Doctor Who* at the time, lending a very palpable sense of time and place to the show. Opposite Anneke Wills, Michael Craze embodied the so-called 'Swinging Sixties'. The class divide between the characters, with Wills' Polly being more well-to-do than cockney seaman Ben, led to an exciting, but always platonic, chemistry between them, the script often including friendly wisecracks about each other's accents and presumed background.

Craze had the honour of playing one of the first companions to witness the Doctor regenerate. Although Craze gave glowing comments regarding Hartnell, saying that the show would not have acquired its reputation quite so much had anybody else been in the role, he did find him difficult to work with.[2] Craze was somewhat more full of praise for the Second Doctor, Patrick Troughton, noting his serious professionalism was balanced by his humble, fun-loving nature.

After Craze left *Doctor Who*, it appears he was touched by rather selective early curse of *Doctor Who*, in that he felt typecast by the role. Subsequently, he described his immediate career afterwards as 'precarious'.[3] He did appear in some television programmes, particularly *Journey to the Unknown* (1969), *Ivanhoe* in 1970, *Crown Court* in 1974 and *Z-Cars*. He was no longer a full-time actor however, because at the same time he managed several pubs, particularly one in Shepperton.

In November 1973 *Doctor Who* celebrated its 10th anniversary, and to celebrate *Radio Times* held photoshoots with a number of previous companions, including Michael Craze and his co-star Anneke Wills. Michael, Anneke and two Cybermen were photographed at Stiffkey Marshes and Cley Beach in Norfolk, and afterwards went for lunch at the Jolly Farmer's pub in North Creake. It was the first time Michael and Anneke had been reunited since they left *Doctor Who* in 1967.

In 1992, Craze recorded an introduction for a BBC video release of 'The Tenth Planet', however it turned out that the long-lost episode had not actually been discovered at all and subsequently the introduction has never been released.

On 7 December 1998, Michael Craze sadly passed away after a fall. His co-star Anneke Wills wrote, in an obituary,[4] a moving testament to his life and work, celebrating his humour, generosity and his friendship.

11

Frazer Hines (Frazer Simpson Frederick Hines)

Born	22 September 1944
Companion	Jamie McCrimmon
First Appearance	'The Highlanders' (17 December 1966 – 7 January 1967)
Final Appearance	'The War Games' (19 April – 21 June 1969)

FRAZER HINES was born in Horsforth, just outside Leeds, to Molly and Bill Hines. He is of Scottish descent on his mother's side and has two elder brothers, Ray and Ian.

Soon after he was born, the family moved to Harrogate and Hines describes his upbringing as great fun, recalling in his autobiography how he would regularly play on The Stray, a 200-acre area of public parkland.[1]

From an early age, Hines became well known for his humour, something which he would later share with his co-stars in *Doctor Who* and would occasionally led to him being admonished for his pranks. He was brought up in an extrovert household, his parents both being members of the Harrogate Operatic Society. Hines himself started attending the Margaret Newbury School of Dancing, which was every Saturday. It was during one of their annual shows that he performed a Maurice Chevalier song *Louise*, which made the local newspapers and led to his auditioning for entrance to the Corona Academy of Stage Training.

Hines describes his time at Corona as being fertile ground for himself and other actors of his time. He counted Dennis Waterman and Richard O'Sullivan as classmates.

From 1955 onwards, he was in several roles as a child actor, notably a science fiction film *X the Unknown* (1956) written by Jimmy Sangster. He then became a member of the Shaun Sutton TV rep company, frequently being cast and very rarely being out of work. Although frequently in television, Hines describes theatre work as being the happiest of his professional life.[2]

It seems that Hines never stopped working right from the beginning. He appeared in a string of regular television roles: Napoleon in *Huntingtower* (1957), Jan in *The Silver Sword* (1957–1958), *Emergency Ward 10* (1963–1964).

Shaun Sutton (14 October 1919 – 14 May 2004) was Head of Drama at the BBC when *Doctor Who* producers were casting for the new story 'The Highlanders', one of the final purely historical stories the show did. Sutton knew that Innes Lloyd was looking for a Scotsman; Sutton also knew that Hines could do a very good Scottish accent, so he was cast in the role of Jamie McCrimmon.

Initially, Hines was only due to play Jamie McCrimmon for one story, however the successful dynamic between Hines and Patrick Troughton was obvious, so much so that upon wrapping up filming for 'The Highlanders', Hines was asked to re-shoot his final scene waving goodbye to the TARDIS, but this re-shoot saw him bidding farewell and then walking into it with the Doctor.

A good working relationship between actors undoubtedly reflects on screen – and Hines, Troughton and co-stars Deborah Watling and, later, Wendy Padbury, all had excellent behind-the-scenes bonds. Hines and Troughton were relentless in their practical jokes, once rolling poor Deborah Watling around in special-effects' foam during location filming on 'Fury from the Deep' (1968). Sadly, this episode is one of the many ones still missing, so we will likely not get to see the results.

After *Doctor Who*, Hines went to Ibiza and was called by his agent for a role in *The Last Valley* (1971). His most famous post-*Who* role would be as Joe Sugden in the long-running British soap opera *Emmerdale*. He was part of the original cast in 1972, back when the show was known as *Emmerdale Farm* and he was a series regular for over twenty years. He has appeared in children's television show *Out of Sight* (1997–98), which coincidentally featured and early performance from Sacha Dhawan who would later play an incarnation of the Master.

Hines reprised his role as Jamie McCrimmon in 'The Five Doctors' (1983) and 'The Two Doctors' (1985), and he returned in the Big Finish Productions audio dramas, also recreating Patrick Troughton's Second Doctor in some of the stories. In 2023 Hines released a novelisation of 'Evil of the Daleks'.

Frazer Hines has written two autobiographies: *Films, Farms and Fillies* (1996) and *Hines Sight* (2009), both of which contain a wealth of stories, anecdotes and information regarding what is an impressive career and a mischievous outlook on life.

12

Deborah Watling (Deborah Patricia Watling)

Born	2 January 1948
Died	21 July 2017
Companion	Victoria Waterfield
First Appearance	'The Evil of the Daleks' (20 May – 1 July 1967)
Final Appearance	'Fury From the Deep' (16 March – 20 April 1968)

DEBORAH WATLING was born into a family of actors, in London and was raised in Epping and later Loughton, Essex. Her mother, Patricia Hicks, had appeared on stage in the 1940s, but later quit in order to raise her family.

Watling described her father, Jack Watling (13 January 1923 – 22 May 2001), as being a 'great star of stage and screen'.[1] Among his best known roles are *A Night to Remember* (1958), *The Winslow Boy* (1948) and *Under Capricorn* (1949). It was no surprise that Deborah Watling would become an actor too. Her half-sister Dilys, her sister Nicky and her brother Giles, would all became actors, though Giles would later become a prominent politician, serving as MP for Clacton since 2017.

Her first acting job was when she was about 3 years old, playing a child eating ice cream in a doorway, alongside her sister Dilys. When she was 10, Watling had her first breakthrough in television series of HG Wells' *The Invisible Man*, where she playing regular character called Sally Wilson.

After appearing as Carol Fellows as Carol Fellows in television series *A Life of Bliss* (1960), she went on to have roles in *The Wednesday Play* (1965), in an episode written by the legendary Dennis Potter, and then an episode of anthology science fiction series *Out of the Unknown* in 1966.

In her autobiography, Deborah Watling describes how she met with *Doctor Who* producer Innes Lloyd for a talk about joining the show. However, knowing that the filming schedule was fierce, Lloyd advised Watling to go and get some more experience.[2] A year later, after Watling had indeed gained more experience, she went back and was cast straight away as Victoria Waterfield.

Innes Lloyd was, of course, not lying when he said the filming would be intense. It's interesting hearing about Deborah Watling's experiences while filming *Doctor Who*, in particular the tight costume changes while other scenes were still being filmed and the necessary silence she was required to hold.

The character of Victoria, in partnership with Frazer Hines' Jamie, was extremely popular, the behind the scenes bond as strong as the on-screen portrayals, with many infamous pranks being played, where very few members of the TARDIS team escaped unscathed. In one memorable story, Watling describes how her co-stars Patrick Troughton, Frazer Hines *and* her father, conceived a prank involving the planting of a pair of frilly knickers on set during a take, amusing the then director Douglas Camfield so much that any chance of a reprimand seemed to be out of the question.[3]

Deborah Watling would appear in two *Doctor Who* stories with her father Jack, 'The Abominable Snowmen' (1967) and 'The Web of Fear' (1968). Initially, Jack was sceptical of the role, believing *Doctor Who* to be a children's series, but eventually he was convinced.

The character of Victoria was hard for the producers to let go, but Watling was adamant that she wanted to leave after one year, despite enjoying the role so much. She was invited to take part in 'The Five Doctors' (1983), however Watling had already committed to another job.

After leaving the show, Deborah Watling appeared as a regular in *The Newcomers* in 1969, a television series in which she would again play opposite her father. She had other roles on television, but had also taken to the stage again, appearing in *A Little Bit of Fluff* at the Churchill Theatre in 1978, as Belinda Blair in *Noises Off* for two of its runs in 1987 and 1988.

Watling would revise her role as Victoria Waterfield in the 1995 Reeltime Pictures production *Downtime*, appearing once again alongside Jack Watling who in turn had reprised his role as Professor Travers. A continuation of sorts of the threat posed by 'The Yeti' and the 'Great Intelligence', the direct-to-video release also starred Elisabeth Sladen and Nicholas Courtney, both of whom reprised their roles from *Doctor Who*.

Deborah Watling moved to in Thorpe-le-Soken, Essex, with her husband Steve Turner. She all but retired from acting, appearing in Big Finish Productions audio dramas, but mainly enjoyed the peaceful, supportive community around her, taking part in a gardening business set up by her friend, and being involved in the local community theatre.

Deborah Watling had been diagnosed with lung cancer and, after a short battle with the illness, died on 21 July 2017.

13

Nicholas Courtney (William Nicholas Stone Courtney)

Born	16 December 1929
Died	22 February 2011
Companion	Brigadier Alistair Gordon Lethbridge-Stewart
First Appearance	'The Web of Fear' (3 February – 9 March 1968)
Final Appearance	'Battlefield' (6 – 27 September 1989)

NICHOLAS COURTNEY was born on 16 December 1929, in Cairo, Egypt. His father was a diplomat and his mother was half American. Courtney's stepmother Anne was a central figure in his life, instilling in him a sense of reason and rationality.

Well-travelled from a young age, Nicholas Courtney left Egypt when he was 4 and went to Paris, then England, back to Egypt and eventually Kenya. His first stage role was in *The Pied Piper of Hamelin* and then in 1943 in *Ali the Cobbler*. He acted in several theatre plays.

On 9 December 1948, Courtney did National Service for eighteen months, as did all young men at the time. After being demobbed, he worked in a shop in Holborn. This was when he decided to rejoin the acting world. So in 1950, with a grant from Surrey Council, Courtney joined the Webber Douglas School of Singing and Dramatic art.

Webber D, as it was known, was also attended by John Prescott, Bernard Horsfall (who would later appear in several different *Doctor Who* stories).

Nicholas Courtney did repertory theatre. He describes rep as being 'for my generation where we mastered our craft'.[1] He was on the move a great deal with Birmingham Rep Theatre, appearing in plays in Folkestone, Watford and Richmond.

His first television appearance was on ITV *Playhouse* in 1957. In many of his early television appearances, Courtney often played the adversary.

In fact, his first appearance on *Doctor Who* was as Bret Vyon in 'The Daleks' Master Plan' (1965), where he got to know Peter Purves who was then playing Steven Tyler.

It was three years later that Nicholas Courtney became the character for which he is arguably best known: Brigadier (Sir) Alastair Gordon Lethbridge-Stewart. Initially a Colonel, the character first appeared in 'The Web of Fear' (1968). In fact, we only got to see his boots at first – although these didn't actually belong to Courteney.

In 1968, as the *Doctor Who* stories became Earthbound due to the Doctor's exile, the decision was taken to make the Brigadier a regular character, featuring UNIT HQ, a newly formed group created by writer Derrick Sherwin. The concept of UNIT, a contemporary organisation created to protect the Earth from extraterrestrial incursions, is something which can be seen much later in Torchwood.

The Invasion (1969) was considered a test to see if this idea would work, but Courtney would have to wait several months before filming, so he taught over summer at Corona School, London.

The inauguration of the Pertwee Era began with 'Spearhead From Space'. Initially, filming was tense, owing to strike disruption at the BBC, a new Doctor finding his feet and a disconnection with director Derek Martinus. However, Courtney got along well with Caroline John (Elizabeth Shaw), finding common ground in their Christianity and church attendance together.

In his autobiography, Nicholas Courtney speaks very candid about his sudden depression,[2] while filming 'Terror or the Autons'. Barry Letts was particularly supportive at this time – again a connection was made through spirituality, Letts having a been a practicing Buddhist for some time. Courtney's faith in God and the church helped him during this difficult period.

Nicholas Courtney played the Brigadier regular until 1975, appearing again in 1983 in 'Mawdryn Undead'. Six years later, he would return one final time in 'Battlefield' (1989), having turned down a part in a West End run of *Madame Butterfly*. This was no easy decision, but in the end, his love for the show, friendship with John Nathan-Turner, and understanding that the Brigadier was going to meet his end in 'Battlefield', won out.

Courtney had a great deal of input into the character of the Brigadier and played him for such a long time, portraying a rich and detailed backstory from Colonel, to Brigadier, to retired Sir, finally married to Doris. Thankfully for fans, the character did not die in 'Battlefield', but would return to be played by Courtney in Downtime (1996) and eventually in 'Enemy of the Bane' (2008), a two-part story of *The Sarah Jane Adventures*.

Since his time on *Doctor Who*, Courtney had continued to act, both in theatre and on television, with roles such as Marquis in television series *French*

Fields (1989 – 1991) and *Then Churchill Said to Me* (1993). In 1979, he had the role of the Narrator in *The Rocky Horror Show*.

When *Doctor Who* returned in 2005, Russell T Davies did not ask Courtney to return as the Brigadier, feeling that the show had to start fresh. Although Courtney would have been happy to appear as the Brigadier, it seems that he was at peace with how the show progressed into new territory, for new fans.

He did, however, reprise his roles for numerous Big Finish audio dramas, as well as providing audio commentaries for many of his stories when they were released on DVD.

Nicholas Courtney was married twice. He married Madeleine Seignol in 1962, on lake Geneva. They had two children, Phillip and Isabella. Courtney and Seignol separated in 1976 and subsequently divorced. In 1994, he married Karen Harding.

Nicholas Courtney died on 22 February 2011, aged 81. Fans, friends and former co-stars paid tribute to him, with Sylvester McCoy calling him a true gentleman[3] and Tom Baker making a statement describing his final visit to Courtney while he was ill, praising his strength and humour.[4]

Interlude 2: Isabella Courtney Interview

AS IS often the case, it was by a curious coincidence that I discovered I shared mutual friend with Nicholas Courtney's daughter, Isabella. Life has a funny way of throwing unexpected connections at us.

Isabella Courtney was gracious enough to join me for an interview about her father. During the interview, we spoke about the nature of this book. We discussed how, of course, it contains biographical and factual information about everybody, but that this is also a rough sketch of the actors' lives as human beings and professionals.

Isabella was not only abundant with her time, but also with her memories of Nicholas Courtney, her father, whom she remembers as humble, good-humoured and possessing a warm, popular nature. I found Isabella to be very much the same and it is with immense joy and gratitude that I am able to share our conversation.

So, Isabella, I'm curious. Have you given any interviews about your father before?

Well, as I said, just a few months ago in September, for this Blu-ray DVD that's been commissioned by the BBC, on Nicholas Courtney, the man behind the Brigadier, and some of his ancestral history and his origins. So that will be a really well documented DVD there

And then I was interviewed along with my brother and my cousin. They also interviewed some different people that knew him, obviously family and actors. I have no idea what it's looking like, or anything at all. There should be a showing within the next two or three months.

I look forward to seeing that. Could you tell me about your father? Could you encapsulate the man that you knew?

What can I say about him? He was a very kind, loving person. He had a very, very difficult childhood, extremely difficult. He was abandoned. I mean, he's from a very wealthy background, but his mother basically left him and his sister when he was two years old. So he was motherless from the age of two to eight. Very essential years there. He had those gaps. He had those things that he hadn't been able to develop in his personality and emotionally.

But there was absolutely not a nasty inch within his body at all. He was almost too trusting and almost naive, which sometimes can be seen as endearing. Sometimes you feel just like an idiot. It depends, but ultimately having that openness and vulnerability is something that can be a strength. It can be more on the loving side, as opposed getting hardened and resentful. And so my dad was a very sweet person, very, very popular. He spent a lot of time in the pub.

We didn't have a normal family life. I wouldn't say we were brought up more by my mum, really, but he was very dutiful, and he did his best. And I think that's that really important, and that's what I realised, that he did absolutely the best that he could with what he had.

We would philosophise. I used to love talking with him. We would talk philosophy for hours and hours. I used to love it as a teenager, because he'd listen and I really felt like he addressed me as an adult. I appreciated that. He listened to me and he was also interested in my point of view.

I really appreciated him very much as a younger teenager and then as a child, I just looked up to him. He was this person, this presence, this *voice.* I used to always love to the way he used to hold my hand when we were crossing the road. He would hold on tight.

I understand that when you were growing up, he was away filming a lot of Doctor Who at the time, so it must have been really interesting and unusual.

Yeah, I think that as an adult, when I look back, I sort of thought 'Oh, my dad was pretty absent'. But as a child, you don't judge. It just is what it is. And so it's just normal. I remember us watching Doctor Who and me being very scared, running behind the sofa and going in and out, and him getting pissed off – just either in or out! [Laughs]. It was a bit scary that before the age of 10.

He used to take us to church on Sundays. He was religious. He had that habit of going to church, and we would go to church, and my mum would cook a beautiful meal afterwards. She was French, and so she used to cook delicious food. I remember coming home and that was a great family moment. That ritual – we would go off and it was fun. It was a Protestant church, and we had games, and the kids would do other stuff, so it was fun.

And then my next door neighbour, who was Jewish, we would go to the synagogue with her, and then she would come with us to church on Sunday. I used to enjoy it until I got to about 12 years old and it was really uncool! He was fine about it. He didn't insist in any way.

On Saturday, he would often go to the races. I remember my mum packing him some sandwiches, putting them in aluminium foil and I don't know what the drink was, but off he would go to the races. He loved horse racing and liked to go and bet on on the horses. He'd be there often with his binoculars and his sandwich bag. I remember that was one of his rituals. And if not, he'd watch it on TV.

I don't remember him being around for evening meals. I just remember the Sunday lunch. But then, yes, I would see him on TV, and then I remember sometimes going to some fetes with him, and feeling very privileged and proud, you know – the 'he's my dad' sort of thing.

He had a great sense of humour. He liked to send himself up, you know, self irony, that sort of thing. In family situations, he was more of a back seat man. He would sit back and observe everything and everyone. But apparently, at the pub, he was the life and soul, the one telling his stories and everything. I didn't see that so much.

But he liked it, especially my mom's family, who were a French family. Very, very warm, rowdy, noisy – eating, drinking, crazy. He used to really like that a lot. He spoke perfect French. He was really good. I think he spent some of his school years in Paris. So his French was great. In fact, we spoke French at home before I went to school. It was my first language.

It seems like your father was pretty well travelled, right from an early age, and I get the impression that he must have witnessed a lot of different types of politics and ways of living.

Yeah, he was very interested in politics, absolutely. He wouldn't really have political conversations with me apart from telling me how much he hated Margaret Thatcher. I remember that period, and we were all against Margaret Thatcher. She was cutting the arts funding and all that. That was some time back. But he was always very interested in politics.

In fact, he also went to Equity. He always used to go once a week. He also liked to be involved in charity too. He donated to charities and did his goodwill sort of thing.

You spoke earlier about his approach to religion and spirituality. He took church seriously, but seemed also like a very chilled out man about most things, religion included.

He was very much like that. He just appreciated the differences, the different interpretations, the different perspectives. He had this acceptance of all different creeds, beliefs and respect for others. He was genuinely, through and through, a respectful, kind person, I never heard him slagging anyone off. He just wouldn't. He didn't have that judgment thing.

He didn't seem to be short of acting work in his in his life at all.

You know, there were some times I remember – I don't know which point this was, before or after Doctor Who – sometimes he would say, 'Well, I'm resting', or this sort of thing. He did work once in a shop at a certain point, selling those little battle soldiers. Some people have those set-ups, a whole battle. I had a cousin like that. Do you know what I mean?

Ah, like the little historical reenactment boards?

That's it. So he wasn't always working. He was out of work too. And even with Doctor Who, it wasn't constant. They'd do a series, then break. He did a lot of theatre and radio as well. He liked theatre a lot. He was very much a stage actor. He was kind of that way, you know – it's an old-fashioned way of acting. I used to love going backstage, all the makeup and the lights and the costumes and that smell! All these actors with their perfumes. I enjoyed that, I have to say. You got to experience quite a lot of that.

I remember numerous times, going backstage in London. I remember in Bournemouth once as well, when he was on a tour or something. It would go on for months and then I would go along and I would be able to go backstage after. I just got this taste of a world which I was enchanted with, absolutely. I wanted to be an actress, but, but my mum was absolutely against it. I didn't go in that direction in the end.

How did your father take to Doctor Who fandom, conventions and things? Doctor Who fun fans are ... highly exuberant.

I think he very much took it in his stride. This is my opinion. I remember him going to fetes or signing sessions, and being around him a few times. I remember his piles of photos and him signing, signing, signing.

So I think it was pretty run of the mill. It kind of went with the package, and as long as he had his box of Californian rosé – which is probably the worst wine I've ever tasted – and people would come and ask him questions, he was happy. Happy to speak to people too. I think ultimately, he loved the attention. He needed that attention particularly and I think somehow, through the acting, he got his recognition, his sense of worth.

And then there were the huge cruises, which started in the 1990s. Three or four days – or maybe more – of a convention on a cruise ship. They were intense events. I don't know how much he enjoyed that, because it must have been very demanding. But he adapted and one his friends started to get him to be paid for it, because initially he was doing it for free. So it was an income too.

The way he lived was very simple. My dad was not an extravagant man. He was very contained, had a normal car for ten or fifteen years and he had a very simple way of living. And he was always so comfortable.

I admired him very much, because whatever question anyone would ask him, he would answer with such nonchalance. He was just happy to share it all. He never put on a face. He was just himself.

14

Wendy Padbury

Born	7 December 1947
Companion	Zoe Heriot
First Appearance	'The Wheel in Space' (27 April – 1 June 1968)
Final Appearance	'The War Games' (19 April – 21 June 1969)

WENDY PADBURY was born in Stratford-upon-Avon. Initially, she trained in ballet, but due to fallen arches (commonly known as 'flat feet'), she took drama instead and trained at the Aida Foster Stage School, of which notable alumni include Barbara Windsor and Kate O'Mara. Padbury left grammar school at 15 after her application to stage school was successful.

From early on, Padbury began getting roles, the first of which was in 1966 on the BBC's arts programme *Monitor*, where she played a bit-part Dickensian child as part of promotion for John Dankworth and Cleo Lane's jazz LP.

Padbury's big break in television was undoubtedly when she joined the regulars of *Crossroads* in 1966, playing Stephanie Harris.

Padbury was put forward by her agent to replace the outgoing Deborah Watling. Having been a fan of the show, Padbury was familiar with the stories and with the current Doctor at the time. Patrick Troughton. The audition process involved several stages, but eventually she was welcomed by her new co-stars Frazer Hines and Patrick Troughton.

Padbury's character Zoe Heriot was remarkably different to former female companions, at least initially. She was an astrophysicist, from the twenty-first century and extremely intelligent. At this point in the show's history, having a companion who had such a self-assured intellectual nature was usually reserved for the male companions, if at all.

By all accounts, Padbury and Hines shared a similar sense of humour and continued the 'messing around'[1] and giggling at unintentional innuendos. Quite a few intentional ones as well, we imagine.

In a very enlightening interview, Padbury acknowledged that she did not experience any sort of typecasting after leaving the show.[2] Padbury had a recurring role in television series *Freewheelers* between 1971 and 1973, and appeared in cult horror classic T*he Blood on Satan's Claw* in 1971, which also guest starred Anthony Ainley, who would later go on to play the Master.

Wendy Padbury continued to have a connection to *Doctor Who* in many subsequent ways. Growing dissatisfied with acting, she became a theatrical agent and throughout her sixteen-year tenure, ended up representing Nicholas Courtney, Mark Strickson and Colin Baker. She describes the responsibility of being an actors' agent as 'enormous' (*Sirens of Audio*), but also frustrating as the contemporary acting world was substantially tougher than what she had experienced herself.

During her time in *Doctor Who*, 'fandom' as it has come to be known was not a thing. It's worth noting that the show had been going for five years and by this point, we had seen one regeneration. However, Padbury regarded her time playing Zoe Heriot as just a job, one of many.

It wasn't until John Nathan-Turner invited her to her first convention that she began to make frequent appearances at *Doctor Who* conventions and events, and has given many interviews, although is now retired.

15

Caroline John (born Caroline Frances John)

Born	19 September 1940
Died	5 June 2012
Companion	Elizabeth Shaw
First Regular Appearance	'Spearhead From Space' (3 – 24 January 1970)
Final Regular Appearance	'Inferno' (9 May – 20 June 1970)

CAROLINE JOHN was born in York to Vera and Alexander John. She was one of eight children. Her father was a theatre director, got the Belgrade Theatre in Coventry built.[1] and her mother was a dancer, who then later went into directing, then went to RADA and Central School of Speech and Drama, which Caroline would later attend.

After studying at the Central School of Speech and Drama, Caroline worked in rep theatre, which she credits, as many actors within these pages do, with her experience in a variety of roles.

She toured extensively with the National Theatre, in particular playing Mary Boyle in the 1966 third West End revival of *Juno and the Paycock*, directed by Laurence Olivier.

In 1970, Caroline John married Geoffrey Beevers, who would later go to play a desiccated incarnation of 'the Master in The Keeper of Traken' (31 January – 21 February 1981).

Caroline John worried that because of her theatre background she might have appeared too highbrow. She forwarded a bikini photograph around to agents and casting department so she didn't seem too 'classical' (*Companions*, HSW p.58) for television. As a result, she received more replies and interviews that when she sent a standard portrait photograph. Director James Cellan Jones forwarded the photograph to Derrick Sherwin, unbeknownst to John, who then invited her to an interview for the part of Liz Shaw.

The character of Liz Shaw was different to many of the female companions. She was a level-headed scientist, sceptical by nature and able to keep up with the Doctor on an intellectual level.

For such a comparatively short time on the show, John's tenure was varied and eventful. In *Doctor Who*, it was often the case that a companion had been 'carried over' from the previous actor playing the Doctor, but John's first story was also Jon Pertwee's first.

'Spearhead from Space' was also the first *Doctor Who* serial to be filmed in colour. Later, the CSO (colour separation overlay, or 'bluescreen') made its debut as a new special effects method. During her time filming *Doctor Who*, John got to work with her husband in 'The Ambassadors of Death'. In her last story, 'Inferno', John portrayed an evil alternate version of her character, the severe and authoritarian Section Leader Elizabeth Shaw. Playing two contrasting characters was something John remembered fondly.

Liz Shaw's intelligence and sophistication was refreshing and foreshadowed Elisabeth Sladen's Sarah Jane Smith in terms of feminism, however it proved difficult for the show because 'she already knew all of the answers'.[2]

This led to the character being written out, although there were other factors at play too. There was a new director who wanted to take things in a different direction. Although John would have turned down more episodes because she was recently pregnant.[3]

Caroline John said she thought she had been written out of *Doctor Who* because she had not impressed Barry Letts,[4] something she had been led to believe because of a lack of positive feedback during the filming.

After *Doctor Who*, Caroline John worked extensively in theatre, radio and television. In 1975, John had a second child and decided on a hiatus while she raised her family.

Caroline John played Liz Shaw for a year and so did not initially have the chance to become attached to the character. However, she briefly returned in 'The Five Doctors' (1983) and the Children in Need *Doctor Who* special 'Dimensions in Time' (1993).

She appeared more extensively in spin-off media, in particular Bill Baggs' 'The Stranger' and 'PROBE' (1995–1996), written by Mark Gatiss, and co-starring Louise Jameson and Linda Lusardi. Due to copyright, no mention of the Doctor himself was permitted.

In 2003, Caroline John was diagnosed with cancer. After surgery and chemotherapy treatment, she continued working, however in 2010, the cancer returned and was this time inoperable.[5] Two years later, Caroline John died. She was 71.

Showrunner Steven Moffat paid tribute to her portrayal of Dr Elizabeth Shaw as being more than just another companion, but one who challenged the Doctor and kept him 'on his toes'.[6]

16

John Levene (John Anthony Woods)

Born	24 December 1941
Companion	Sergeant John Benton
First Appearance	'The Invasion' (2 November – 21 December 1968)
Final Appearance	'The Android Invasion' (22 November – 13 December 1975)

JOHN LEVENE was born on Christmas Eve (in his own words) 'breeched, jaundiced and dead'.[1] His mother, Vera Margaret Blake, married Levene's father Austin Anthony Woods, a gunnery instructor from Newcastle.

Levene grew up in Salisbury which, being a centre for clandestine military industrial operations, was heavily damaged in the Second World War.[2]

Levene's childhood was fraught with illness, contracting a blood disease which lasted for at least eleven months. During this time, Levene had to sleep upright because of the strain on his heart; this led to migraines, from which he would suffer for most of his life.

He was also bullied during his childhood, and his father's response was to teach the young Levene to box. However, Levene lacked the physical strength due his being bedridden for such a long time that his inability and unwillingness to fight only led to further bullying. A sensitive and reflective young man, Levene decided to become a nurse in order to balance out what he calls the 'indentured slave[ry]' of his day job as a mechanic apprentice. During this time, he could practice those innate qualities of kindness and bravery, as he felt that these aspects of his personality had neither been noticed nor encouraged.

Dissatisfied with life in Salisbury, Levene moved to the island of Jersey, where he met Diana Wade, with whom he had his first child, Samantha. After initially leaving Diana and his daughter due to a perceived shame of Samantha's unmarried conception, Levene moved to London and, after pressure from his family, married Diana and settled in Wimbledon.

He got a job working in Hope Brothers menswear on Regent Street, where he met Kojak superstar Telly Savalas. Levene says that this meeting was nothing short of life changing, because Savalas suggested to him that he might be able to replace one of the stuntmen who had been injured, complimenting Levene on his physical appearance and dress sense. Despite a childhood fraught with illness, Levene's strength and physical presence would be something fans of *Doctor Who* would remember him for.

Levene did not end up getting the job, however it had awoken in him a desire to become an actor. His lack of confidence further began to ebb away when he met actor Joe Baker, who enjoyed his jokes. Levene then signed up to the Denton de Grey acting agency and signed up for his equity card. Other actors already shared various permutations of his birth name so he created his stage name to distinguish himself from them.

Ever enthusiastic, Levene threw himself into some of the early roles which came his way. His first acting jobs were walk on roles in *Undermind* (1965) and *The Newcomers* (1966), then playing a Nazi guard on *Adam Adamant Lives!* (1967).

Levene credits his appearances in several episodes of *Z-Cars* in 1967 as a pivotal point in his early career. It was where he first worked with *Doctor Who* director Douglas Camfield, from whom he sought direct, honest advice about how to become a better actor.

Having already appeared as a Cyberman in 'The Moonbase' (1967) and a Yeti in 'The Web of Fear' (1968), Levene was cast as Corporal Benton in 'The Invasion'. Levene's character would go on to appear as a series regular, the 1970s feeling like a personal Golden Era. He enjoyed a close friendship with his co-stars Nicholas Courtney, Roger Delgado, Katy Manning, Richard Franklin and Jon Pertwee, but also maintained precious relationships with Barry Letts and Douglas Camfield.

Levene remembers his time on *Doctor Who* with heartfelt fondness, particularly the feeling of kinship with the UNIT team. His penchant for physical acting was not without its hazards, injuring himself on more than one occasion.[3]

Levene's relationship with Jon Pertwee extended very much to outside filming of the host, visiting his house many times; however, after Jon Pertwee left, Levene found himself somewhat distant from the Fourth Doctor Tom Baker. This was in part owing to the storylines which, having previously been set entirely on Earth due to the Doctor's exile, now took place in the TARDIS and at various off-world locations and times.

Though Levene left the show in 1975, he reprised his role as Benton in the spin-off 'Wartime' (1988) by Reeltime Pictures. In 'Wartime', the backstory of Sergeant Benton was explored and we learned his first name was John. Keith Barnfather talks about 'Wartime' during his interview in this book.

John Levene left the acting world for a while and became, briefly, a private detective. A lifelong love for singing and performing led him to work with Chandra's Fantasy Cruises as an entertainer, his work included being a bingo caller and a stand-up comedian. His latest incarnation was Gentleman Johnny Bingo and it was a period he enjoyed very much.

Levene has returned to voice Benton in some of the audio dramas, notably Big Finish productions' 'Third Doctor Chronicles' and 'UNIT: The New Series'.

In 2023, I was fortunate enough to meet John Levene at a Fantom Publishing Event signing, where I bought his honest and thought-provoking autobiography. He was dressed in an exuberant, colourful jacket. He was tanned and looked youthful, with an open, kind face. He told me to stay unique, to always believe in myself, and he inscribed his book with 'love and peace' in shining silver ink.

17

Richard Franklin (born Richard Kimber Franklin)

Born	15 January 1936
Died	25 December 2023
Companion	Captain Mike Yates
First Appearance	'Terror of the Autons' (2 January – 23 January 1971)
Final Appearance	'Planet of the Spiders' (4 May – 8 June 1974)

RICHARD FRANKLIN was born in Marylebone, London. Growing up during the Second World War, he was evacuated and lived in at least eleven different houses. While living in Checkendon, Oxfordshire, he recalls playing what he considered his first role during his childhood, by acting out the character of a witch.[1]

He had a more substantial brush with acting, this time in front of an audience, at Westminster Underschool, where he appeared in an adaptation of *The Ghost of Jerry Bundler* by Charles Rock and W.W. Jacobs. Partly owning to his father's discouragement of an acting career, Franklin had no idea how to pursue such an ambition. After completing National Service with the Royal Green Jackets, Franklin studied Law at Oxford, then Modern History at Christ Church, Oxford.

It was when his brother became seriously ill that Franklin decided to follow his heart and become an actor, leaving his job in advertising to apply to RADA. This was not without consideration and concern for leaving a relatively certain job to go into the unpredictable world of acting, however he sought advice from his actor friends Susan Hampshire and John Standing, who encouraged and advised him.

Like so many performers of this time, theatre was Franklin's first experience of the world of acting. After graduating from RADA, he toured with the Century Theatre Company, now Britain's oldest surviving travelling theatre company.

They brought arts, music, drama, comedy and dance to communities around Britain who had little access to stage productions. He would go on to spend many years campaigning for support for regional theatre in Britain.

He spent six years in repertory theatre, including Birmingham Rep and the Bristol Old Vic, and also appeared in West End shows. Having already had his first television role in Dixon of Dock Green in 1966, Franklin had appeared in *The Saint*, *Blakes 7* and *The Borgias*.

Franklin was cast by producer Barry Letts as Captain Mike Yates, a character who would become instrumental in the now-Earthbound stories, comprising a vital element of the UNIT team. Franklin enjoyed playing Yates who, for a recurring character, had quite a story arc – though Franklin has said on occasion that this could have been further developed.

Franklin worked with two *Doctor Who* actors – Jon Pertwee and Tom Baker. He cites the unexpected death of Roger Delgado, whose portrayal of recurring villain the Master arguably set the standard for all subsequent incarnations, as precipitating Jon Pertwee's desire to leave the show, though there were other factors involved. Franklin had a good relationship with Pertwee, describing him as a 'decent gentleman' and a professional actor who helped keep the team, or family, together and unified.

Franklin would go on to appear on television several times, most notable in *Emmerdale Farm* in 1988 as Denis Rigg, but he was never far away from his first passion – theatre. He was the director of East Riding Youth Theatre, associate director of the grand Theatre in Swansea and the Renaissance Theatre in Cumbria.[2]

Richard Franklin always had something to say, whether passing on his experience and knowledge by directing students at RADA and Webber Douglas, or appearing in pantomime and writing several plays with a satirical and political commentary.

It feels like Richard Franklin never really left *Doctor Who*. His final regular appearance was in 'Planet of the Spiders', though he would return for a brief appearance in 1983 in' The Five Doctors', then in 1993 in 'Dimensions in Time', as part of the BBC's Children in Need campaign. He also wrote and produced the stage comedy *Recall UNIT: The Great T-Bag Mystery* at the Edinburgh Fringe Festival in 1984. He has voiced Captain Yates in numerous audio productions at Big Finish, as well as narrating some of the *Doctor Who* Target novelisations. Franklin also wrote *The Killing Stone*, a spin-off novel featuring Mike Yates which was released as a BBV audio book.

His documentary appearances are numerous, being involved in many of the specials which accompanied the DVD releases of his *Doctor Who* stories, including *The UNIT Family* and *Life on Earth*.

In addition to the rich tapestry of his acting, writing and directing life, Franklin was also politically active. He stood for parliament as an independent in 1970, then a Liberal Democrat in 1992, before joining the Referendum Party and then the UK Independence Party.

On 25 December 2023, it was announced on Richard Franklin's Twitter page that he had passed away, peacefully in his sleep.[3] He had been ill for some time and had been visited on several occasions by many people, including his long-time friend and *Doctor Who* co-star Katy Manning.

There followed a subsequent outpouring of obituaries, sadness and gratitude, from friends and fans across the world, who described him as a warm and friendly gentleman, who had plenty of time for fans and had lived a full and diverse life.

18

Katy Manning (Catherine Ann Manning)

Born	14 October 1946
Companion	Josephine 'Jo' Grant (later, Jones)
First Appearance	'Terror of the Autons' (2 January – 23 January 1971)
Final Appearance	'The Green Death' (19 May – 23 June 1973)

MANNING was born in Guildford and was raised in London. Her father was James Lionel Manning OBE (10 January 1914 – 18 January 1970), who was a well-known British sports writer for *The Daily Mail*. She originally trained as a dancer, having a successful career at a young age. However, she was in a traumatic car accident, which left her so injured that she was unable to continue.[1]

During her convalescence, she stayed with her sister and was offered a contract with MGM. Instead, she turned it down and Manning trained at the Webber Douglas drama school, before doing repertory theatre.

Her first television role was in police series *Softly Softly: Task Force* in 1970, and then John Braine's *Man at the Top* in 1971.

In 1971, manning joined the cast of *Doctor Who*. The story goes that Terrance Dicks and Barry Letts were looking for somebody very different from Caroline John who previously played Liz Shaw. They auditioned a lot of actresses for the role, but the production team seemed to be taken by the fact that Manning got lost at some point on the way to the audition and went to the wrong room.

In many ways, the character of Jo Grant was the very opposite to her successor, Liz Shaw. This was a deliberate decision by producer Barry Letts and script editor and writer Terrance Dicks.[2] She was younger and less experienced. Her aesthetic was more fashionable, which appealed to younger and older viewers, albeit for different reasons. In the show, the stories Manning appeared were an even mix, more or less, of those set in time and space, and those set on contemporary Earth.

Manning is part of what's often referred to as the UNIT family and she developed strong friendships with Nicholas Courtney, John Levene, Richard Franklin and Roger Delgado, as well as, of course, with Jon Pertwee.

Katy Manning's career has spanned fifty years, stretching from the United Kingdom, the USA and Australia. After leaving *Doctor Who*, director Douglas Camfield (who had worked on the show many times) cast her as Anna in the in *Armchair Theatre* episode 'The Golden Road' (1973). Manning's character begins renting a room at the house of married woman, Cass, a relationship which develops into a groundbreaking exploration of female same-sex attraction, which was mostly unheard of in Britain at the time.

Manning has been heavily involved in the theatre, with her first role being in 1970 in *Union Jack and Bonzo* at the Traverse Theatre, then from 1973 to 1975, she appeared with Derek Nimmo in *Why Not Stay For Breakfast?* by Gene Stone and Ray Cooney.

Between 1972 and 1974, she was married to actor Stewart Bevan (10 March 1948 – 20 February 2022), with whom she appeared in her final episode of *Doctor Who*, leaving, in a case of art imitating life, to get married to his character Professor Clifford Jones. Between 1976 and 1981, Manning was married to actor Dean Harris, with whom she gave birth to twins, Jonathan and Georgina. Manning moved to Australia to take advantage of the climate, as they were both unwell at the time. While in Australia, she continued acting in the theatre, as well as directing, and married actor Barry Crocker.

Manning has appeared extensively in Big Finish Productions audio dramas, both as Iris Wildthyme in *Doctor Who* and in the Iris Wildthyme series. In 2010, Jo Jones (neé grant) returned to the television screen in *The Sarah Jane Adventures* episode 'Death of the Doctor', 2010, alongside Elisabeth Sladen and Matt Smith.

Interlude 3: Katy Manning Interview

SOMETIME IN 2022, I contacted Katy Manning to ask if she would be interviewed for this book but my email got buried. It wasn't until a year later, when I decided to try her again, that I received not only a reply, but apologies for missing my email and a confirmation that she would be delighted to be interviewed. I was delighted too and there was certainly no need for an apology.

When we spoke, Katy leapt straight into telling me about her exuberant and adventurous life. It is rare to meet someone who willingly shares so much of themself and yet retains their personal boundaries of professionalism and courtesy. She is an open, caring woman with an enormous heart and she gave me the time of my life with this interview.

[Katy Manning] So I have no intention of re-living my life to end up in a two-dollar basket in a charity shop three years later and also I feel that so much of someone's life involves so many other people – I never, ever want to talk about somebody else. And I've had some very interesting people in my life!

So you travel between the UK, Australia and United States. I imagine that as soon a you get to one continent there's something or someone to miss on the other?

I grew up in a world where my father was away a lot, my parents were away a lot, everybody was always off somewhere. Sometimes after a big party, my father would say, 'Right, everybody jump in the car.' Off we would go and end up in Italy or somewhere. And you learn, especially having gone through the time with my twins and my mother, the family in America, little children do not like to hold a telephone. So we didn't have all that instant communication, but we still managed to stay together. It's in our family genes. So all that 'missing' becomes very negative and doesn't get you anywhere. So I'd write letters and the children would make tapes. We'd have photos and montages of everyone. So everybody's always with you. Even if they've gone off on their Awfully Big Adventure, they're still with you because they're part of you and part of your life.

So being in the moment seems to come naturally to you. I often find myself being quite retrospective.

Well, when you go forward, you're going into non-reality. You know how people get this huge anxiety about tomorrow? Using time that you could be living now worrying about something which could be completely different from the way you've translated it in your head. Especially if you're having a bad day – everything's going to be terrible! And then if you go back, you're never really in the present, in the moment.

But that doesn't mean you can't have all the stuff behind you. But I think it's a jolly good idea to have it, all in your heart, all in your mind, but get rid of any of it you don't want, unpack the bag at every station you get off at. 'Nah don't want that!' Boom. Off. Because you don't want to carry the weight on your shoulders of things you don't need.

A great approach!
You know there's a wonderful thing, it comes from Peter Pan and it's called living in the O between the N and W. That's your past, that's your future and the O is where we are now.

There's a lot of Buddhist sentiment in that which resonates with me.
When you've grown as old as I am, you've kind of been through everything. I don't just throw something away, I look at everything. Like religion. You should look at every religion before you say you're not buying any of it. And from Buddhism you learn an awful lot about taking responsibly for your life. And when you're growing up and going through the angst of teenage hood – and trust me, I've been a mother of twins so I've had a lot of young people around me. I learned we have a finger called blame. 'I'm this because of that,' but it's actually not that way. Sure, it's a part of what makes you who you are, but you have to take responsibility for every action. I've done some silly things in my life, because you have to if you're going to be exploring!

I was going to ask if you could sum up your approach to life in a few words. I have this question written down, but I feel we've already got there!
Stay in the moment. Remember, every day is basically an adventure. I get up in the morning and my whole life can change in thirty seconds and one email. So consequently, it's very much and adventure which can only happen if you don't know what's going to happen. Otherwise it's not an adventure.

I love that. And you have a lot of time for fans.
I mean with conventions, I've been doing that solidly. But I have this thing about meeting fans and being with them. I have got so many wonderful friendships out of fandom. When people ask me what the greatest thing is for me which came out of *Doctor Who*, I honestly and truly from my heart say it's the fans, it's the people I've met.

I care deeply about people. I love people. I get so excited when I'm in a group of people that I become a little … over the top! People just make me happy. There's something about *Doctor Who* fans. I've been given this wonderful job that's taken me into a world of being able to embrace and understand and in many cases do a lot of support too. This is something that's been given to me and I'm just so grateful. I don't know whether you notice on my Twitter that it's not about self-promotion, but showing that I'm there.

I follow you on Twitter and every time you post, it's like a ray of sunshine. I think I saw one recently where you were on your way to a Fantom event and you were behind a big plant.
Ahh that was the cuttings of forsythia for the two boys who run Fantom. I absolutely adore them. It's little things like that. Giving the fans something else. There's nothing wrong with self-promotion. But I'm not so good at selling myself, because I'll be walking around and just see a flower, or a cat or something weird and I want to put it up there. I want to entertain and give people something to make them smile.

Everybody in the street – I stop, I always carry lots of change and I always give, regardless. I don't judge people and I have so many other people around my area and they know me. I always give something, give them a hug. It's just to put that little smile there.

We need to do that for each other so much more. We're all becoming very insular with social media, feeling like we're being attacked. I mean how can you take any notice of someone who doesn't know you?! If someone's having a go, just ignore them. People say, 'Oh no, I'm losing followers.' But I ask who really wants people like that around you? It's quality, not quantity, that we want in our life. I'd rather have one good friend that a dozen people I'm not sure about.

I've been right through the '60s. I live everything. The '70s, the '80s – my least favourite time – and the '90s, right through to now. Done it all. In my family, we call the friends I've had for forty years, we call them family. I might not see them for three years or speak, because I don't have the need to constantly communicate, but the moment you knock on the door or speak on the phone, boom, they're there. Those are the friendships one should nurture.

I mean if someone ever asks me after a time 'What have you been up to?' I can just feel myself going urgh! [Katy flops down on her sofa, dramatically]. I think, goodness, just in three days, that'd be a tome.

You said the '80s was your least favourite time. Can I ask about that?
Well I can be very flippant and say fashion, right? But it was a time when money became so important. Having money became more important than anything.

Things changed. And I don't think it was the most powerful time for women, either. To me, I was seeing that it was all becoming about money, how much it cost, what you wore. For me, that's not a comfortable place to be. Everywhere I went, everybody was trying to out-dress everyone else.

But, of course, we have to remember that when I make a statement, it's my experience. A lot of people use an opinion as a fact, but it's not.

I wondered if I could ask about your father, because he was a politician and I understand he was very progressive. But I can't find much information about him.

There's nothing up there because it was all in the era. So going back to the late '50s and early '60s, Daddy was campaigning against apartheid and in the sporting world he fought a campaign, which he won, to have a doctor at the ringside in boxing to say when the fight had to be over, because a lot of damage is done to boxers. There's only so many time you can get punched in the head. I like boxing, but it has to be carefully monitored.

He fought to get pensions for journalists' wives and he was also campaigning in the late '50s, or thereabouts, for women to be able to go back to the workforce and to have creches in places where they were working. The press club which had always been a man's thing, he took it over and opened the doors to all the women journalists. He was also very much in support of gay people, and your choice to be who you feel you are, without anybody being unkind or judgemental. That was a very strong sentiment in our family.

I grew up with someone who was always doing the things that a lot of people are trying to do now. With the type of family I grew up in, everybody was important. Nobody thought along the lines of you're a woman or man and therefore you should do this, no. You were a *person*. As long as you were a good, caring, compassionate human being, that was what we needed.

So whatever your religion, whatever your sexuality – it totally must be accepted. That's how I grew up.

And there's a lot of dialogue about that in the media, and in social media, these days. It feels like we're getting somewhere, but on top of that, at the same time, it can be tricky to navigate too.

A lot of what is being dealt with is because of social media. I mean I came through the era when we didn't even have a television! Now people want to be noticed and they shout loudly. There's also all the crime which can be committed online too. You have to be so careful. It's something wonderful, social media, but we have to learn how to use it properly. There's an ability to open our arms and embrace so many people and to help make changes.

So many technological advancements, things being invented so quickly. But emotionally we're still way back there.

If people don't agree with you, we need to learn not to shout. Use your logic. You don't have to be aggressive when you challenge somebody about the way they are. There's so much we have to learn. I could go on for ages about it!

If we're ever going to have peace on Earth – I mean we jolly well *tried* with flower power – it was a nice time. But I think we need to be kinder to each other and not be afraid. I talk to everybody. If I'm in a lift or something, I can't just stand there. I rarely think before I speak!

It sounds to me when you were filming *Doctor Who* that you had a great time.

I was treated, as I've said on every interview, as an absolute equal. I was never treated in any other way. I cant think of anything negative about *Doctor Who*! I love its growth. I love it now. Every single person that's been in it is applaudable.

You know, I read an interview with you where you said you enjoyed filming 'The Daemons' because you were into the occult.

Well if I said it, it was one of those flippant things! Put it this way, I'm not *into* the occult, but back in the '70s, darling, I did the tarot and waved wands and did the stones, because I needed to learn and know. I've read a huge amount and Damaris Hayman and I talked about it. I'm fascinated by it, but only finding out about it.

Thing about me is I don't belong to anything. I don't eat meat, but I'm not a vegetarian. I don't want to be in a group or have a religion.

It feels like you're more like a verb, than a noun, not being stamped or having badges.

Absolutely! I can't bear it. I won't even go to a club and let anybody stamp my wrist, no! That's my rebel I'm afraid. You can't ever say never about anything. I will never ever dismiss anything!

I've taken to asking this question a lot. If there was one thing you could let the people who are reading my book know about you, what would it be?

Well, for me, it's just letting people know they're not alone. Even though I'm just a face on social media, I want people to feel good. I know more and more people suffer from depression and are having a tough time, who haven't had some of the benefits growing up that I did. And I want to be there to say 'I see you, I feel you'.

People often ask me how I can tell people I love them, when I don't know them. My reply is always this: people tell each other that they *hate* each other and they don't know them. And so I just want to turn it right round and I *can* love people I don't know. I love the very fact that they're there. They all have to know that there is only one of them. They are completely and utterly, brilliantly unique.

Our lives and how we live them is so important. I want people to know that they aren't alone. If I can help even a tiny bit, then that's what I want to do. I just want to help people through loneliness, loss, pain, insecurity.

I think we need to start coming together and supporting each other and having the courage to smile at people – even though they may think you're bonkers.

What I was hoping for in this interview, Katy, is an impression of you, and you've given that to me in abundance. Thank you.

19

Elisabeth Sladen (Elisabeth Clara Heath-Sladen)

Born	1 February 1946
Died	19 April 2011
Companion	Sarah Jane Smith
First Appearance	'The Time Warrior' (15 December 1973 – 5 January 1974)
Final Regular Appearance	'The Hand of Fear' (2 – 23 October 1976)

ELISABETH SLADEN'S family originally came from Salcombe, Devon, and once owned the Salcombe Hotel and a ferry boat service. Elisabeth writes in her autobiography[1] that eventually, the only Sladens who retained anything were her father's parents.

Although her family hailed from Devon, when her father was posted to Liverpool for his work with the Cunard Shipping Line, he met her mother whom he eventually married after an adventurous time of travelling with work.

Elisabeth Sladen's love of performance began when she took dance classes at 4 years old. A positive experience at her first performance for a local festival led to acting classes. During one of her earliest theatre performances, playing Alice in *Alice in Wonderland*, Sladen was sick all over her co-star who we would later come to know as prominent Conservative MP Edwina Currie.[2]

After appearing on *Search for a Star*, she enrolled in London's Youth Theatre and got a job as assistant stage manager at Liverpool Playhouse in 1965. It was here that she met Brian Miller. They married on 8 June 1968.

After being asked to act in plays at St Helens' Theatre Royal, Sladen received excellent reviews from the local newspaper. She eventually got her first television role in ITV's *Playhouse* and in 1970 she appeared in six episodes of *Coronation Street*. Sladen explained the lessons she learned about the difference between acting in theatre and acting in television, namely that in theatre an actor can 'be fairly free with movement and the other actors would respond',[3] but that in television, the action and dialogue is scripted.

She made her first foray into science fiction, in *Doomwatch* and police drama series *Z-Cars* in 1971 and 1972. The year after, she had her first meeting with producer Barry Letts. Although Sladen knew this was a casting meeting and script read-though, she was not told that this was for the new companion, Sarah Jane Smith.

Sladen was adamant that her character was not going to be a stereotypical 'weak woman'. In an interview, she said that she could have justified every scream that Sarah made (*Wine and Dine Interview* 1998) and would be a character who would not compromise her ideals.

Sarah Jane Smith was one of the most popular companions in the show's history. Sladen was not given a lot of backstory for the character, so she worked hard to make Sarah Jane believable, saying that 'you had to make it real, because if you don't believe it, nobody watches you'.[4]

When Philip Hinchcliffe took over from Barry Letts as producer, Sladen knew that he would want to make some changes to the show. Wanting Sarah Jane to leave while she was still popular, Sladen decided it was time for her to finish on *Doctor Who*. She told Hinchcliffe 'Don't marry me off, don't kill me off. Can I just go?'.[5]

Elisabeth Sladen's portrayal of Sarah Jane Smith had been so popular that a spin-off series was devised. In 1981, *K-9 and Company: A Girl's Best Friend* was released. It was intended to be the pilot episode for a forthcoming series, however, this did not happen.

Sladen reprised her role on the shows twentieth anniversary special 'The Five Doctors' (1983) and returned almost thirty years later to appear on the revived series, appearing first in 'School Reunion' (2006), and then later 'The Stolen Earth' and 'Journey's End' (2008), and in 2009 returned in 'The End of Time'. In an interview, Sladen remarked how the atmosphere was the same, the amount of takes was the same, but everything was much bigger.[6]

In around 2005, Children's BBC mooted the idea of a spin-off show aimed specifically at a younger audience. To the excitement of fans everywhere, Sladen would return in *The Sarah Jane Adventures*, which ran for five seasons between 2007 and 2011. Providing backstory for her character, the SJA was hailed intelligent, sophisticated and was popular not only with children who were perhaps too young to watch *Doctor Who*, but also their parents, for whom Elisabeth Sladen remained a firm favourite.

Although Sladen acted a little after she left the show during its initial run, in 1985 she and her husband, actor Brian Miller, had a daughter, Sadie. Sladen devoted her time to being a parent.

In 2011, Sladen was diagnosed with cancer and she died two months later, on 19 June 2011.

From show-specific *Doctor Who Magazine* to the mainstream media, from former co-stars to show-runners past and present, the sadness expressed at Elisabeth Sladen's passing was immense – and unsurprising. She had touched the lives of so many people, with her career and her friendship, that anybody who paid tribute to her remarked upon her humour and intelligence, as well as her natural charisma and dedication.

Her daughter Sadie Miller is an actor and writer. She, as nobody else could possibly do, has recreated the character of Sarah Jane Smith in many Big Finish Productions audio dramas. Along with her father Brian Miller, they ensured the posthumous publication of Sladen's autobiography.

20

Ian Marter (Ian Don Marter)

Born	28 October 1944
Died	28 October 1986
Companion	Harry Sullivan
First Appearance	'Robot 28 December' (28 December 1974 – 18 January 1975)
Final Appearance	'Terror of the Zygons' (September (30 August – 20 September 1975)

IAN MARTER was born in Warwickshire and graduated from Oxford University in 1969. He became a stage manager at the Bristol Old Vic theatre. In 1968, he married Rosemary Leyland, with whom he had two children, Toby and Rupert.

In 1970, Marter auditioned for the role of Captain Mike Yates but was unable to commit due to other work. However, Marter made a guest appearance in the 1974 *Doctor Who* story 'Carnival of Monsters', and then later was cast as a regular companion Surgeon-Lieutenant Harry Sullivan. This happened just at the cusp of Jon Pertwee's Third Doctor regenerating into the Fourth, played by Tom Baker.

At the time, the actor for the Doctor had not been decided, so production were looking for somebody who could play the more physical aspects of the show, just in case the Fourth Doctor happened to be played by an older actor.

Marter speaks highly of his time on the show. Those who have watched, for example, 'Genesis of the Daleks' (1974) will have witnessed the tour de force which was Tom Baker, Elisabeth Sladen and Ian Marter at their very best. Marter pays Harry as a dependable, professional man, although with an element of self-awareness with regards to his somewhat antiquated attitudes to women, often calling Sarah-Jane 'old thing', much to her annoyance. This good-natured tension between Marter and Sladen does not come across as if it's played for laughs, although it is humorous. Neither does it appear to be to Sarah-Jane's detriment, but more like a brief commentary on the changing attitudes towards women at the time.

Marter found his co-stars to be generous colleagues and all three of them were reciprocative of the critique and being the scenes character development which they shared with each other.[1]

Tom Baker writes fondly of this time, saying that they would all take their meals together when they were filming on location and that working life had become 'full of fun'.[2]

That Marter's character Harry Sullivan was no longer required to be quite as action-oriented as promised was something Marter found difficult. On an interview with Patrick Stoner in 1984,[3] Marter described Harry as well-meaning and chivalrous, ultimately a bit of a walking disaster, though still likeable.

There were plenty of times Marter's character got into trouble, whether having his head grazed by a bullet or his foot nearly chewed off by a giant mutated clam, however Marter portrayed a degree of heroism not seen for a while on the show. I personally found Marter's performance of Harry Sullivan to be thoroughly good-natured and memorable, a man who, although he was capable of putting his foot in it, had unwavering loyalty to the Doctor and Sarah.

He comes across as very humble about his novelisations of *Doctor Who* and, while talking about the show, he accounts for the popularity of *Doctor Who* being largely down to its ability to self-reference and not take itself too seriously all of the time.

Ian Marter did not decide to leave *Doctor Who*, however his character was written out, sadly with an unsatisfying conclusion. However, Marter retained a passion for the show and novelised several stories, including 'The Invasion', 'The Dominators' and some of the serials in which he appeared like 'The Ark in Space' and 'The Sontaran Experiment'. He also wrote novelisations for several films, including *Splash* (1980), published under the pen name Ian Don.

Having become good friend with Tom Baker, they collaborated to write a script for a film called *Doctor Who Meets Scratchman*, which ultimately came to nothing.[4]

Marter continued to act, appearing in ITV's *Playhouse* (1980), *BBC2 Playhouse* (1981), *Bergerac* (1985) and *The Return of Sherlock Holmes* (1986). By the early 1980s, he was living and working in New Zealand, which meant that when producer John-Nathan Turner asked him to appear in the *Doctor Who* twentieth anniversary story 'The Five Doctors', he was unable to commit.

Ian Marter died on his 42nd birthday, 28 October 1986, of a heart attack related to his long-term diabetes. His final *Doctor Who* book *The Rescue* was released posthumously, as was the novelisation of *Doctor Who Meets Scratchman.*

21

Louise Jameson (Louise Marion Jameson)

Born	20 April 1951
Companion	Leela
First Appearance	'The Face of Evil' (1 – 22 January 1977)
Final Appearance	'The Invasion of Time' (4 February – 11 March 1978)

LOUISE JAMESON was born in Wanstead, Essex and grew up in Woodford Green. When she was 4, she had her first ever acting role as Miss Muffet. Recounting the story of this debut, she tells how in her desire to portray a sufficient level of fear experienced by the titular character, she threw her bowl exuberantly up, which, being made of glass, shattered on the floor, bringing a sudden halt to the performance.

She went to RADA at the unusually young age of 17 and did work for the Royal Shakespeare Company – notable roles include *Romeo and Juliet* and *The Taming of the Shrew*.

One of her first television jobs roles was in *Cider With Rosie* (Dir. Claude Watham 1971), and she would go on to have role in *Z-Cars*, *Disciple of Death* (Dir. Tom Parkinson 1972) and *Emmerdale Farm* in 1973, then later *Emmerdale* in 2022, as a different character.

In the 1970s, Jameson was an official prison visitor, or OPV, run by the National Association of Prison visitors. OPVs are unpaid volunteers appointed by the governor of a local prison to liaise with inmates on an independent basis. The purpose of this being to check on prisoners' welfare and, in some cases, the OPV is the only the visitor they might have.

It was during this time that Jameson met Leslie Grantham, who was serving a life sentence for murder at Leyhill Prison in Gloucestershire. He had been performing in plays during his sentence and Jameson encouraged him to pursue acting. He did so and in 1984, played Kiston in the 1984 story 'Resurrection of the Daleks'.

The characterisation of Leela was originally thought up by Phillip Hinchcliffe, the producer, and Robert Holmes, the editor. They found a character who'd been developed by writer Chris Boucher, which fit perfectly.[1] Auditions for the part were extensive. Over twenty actors were auditioned, including Pamela Salem, Carol Leader (now a successful Jungian psychotherapist) and Gail Harrison.

Leela was a complex character, though ultimately popular. She had a penchant for occasional violence, though was intelligent and well-reasoned. Jameson remarks in an interview that the trade-off between having an intelligent and strong female companion seemed to be the revealing leather outfit.[2]

After leaving *Doctor Who*, Jameson went on to co-star in *The Omega Factor* (1979), playing Department 7 physicist Dr Anne Reynolds. She has been active to this day in audio dramas, reprising both her roles as Leela and Dr Reynolds for Big Finish Productions, as well as the *Sapphire and Steel* audio story 'Wall of Darkness' (2008). Jameson has also appeared din many documentaries, as well as the commentaries on some of the BBC DVD releases of her original *Doctor Who* stories.

Jameson has had numerous roles in some noteworthy theatre productions, as well as writing and directing them. In 2007, Jameson toured the UK in her one-woman show *Face Value*, a commentary on her 'near decision' to have cosmetic surgery.[3]

In 2013, she starred in *Gutted* by Rikki Beadle-Blair, an energetic and challenging play about life in South London. In 2016, she toured in Agatha Christie's *The Mousetrap*.

Louise Jameson is a patron of the Domestic Abuse Volunteer Support Services, based in West Kent. She is also a patron of The Off West End Theatre Awards, nicknamed The Offies, an award dedicated to celebrate independent theatre. In 2023, while presenting an award, she spoke of the importance of fringe theatre and independent venues, highlighting how important it is to have safe spaces to explore challenging, non-mainstream issues.

In a particularly popular recent appearance, Louise Jameson reprised her *Doctor Who* role for the Blu-Ray release of her *Doctor Who* stories. She appears as Leela, a confident, honourable and mature woman in Gallifreyan robes, in the middle of the Time War, confronting the Daleks.

22

John Leeson (John Francis Christopher Ducker)

Born	16 March 1943
Companion	K9 (voice)
First Appearance	'The Invisible Enemy' (1–22 October 1977)
Final Appearance	'Journey's End' (5 July 2008)

LEESON was born in Leicester, into quite a religious family, his father being a clergyman. He worked for some time in a bookshop, then as a hospital porter. He joined the Leicester Dramatic Society and then went on to train at RADA.

Leeson developed an interest is Restoration plays, guided by his teacher Eddie Griffiths. Restoration drama came from a time just after the Puritan Rule of England, which forbade basically anything fun, including theatre. Fortunately, this ended in 1660, and theatre began to flourish, with innovative parody, humour and even rudimentary special effects.

Between 1972 and 1973, John Leeson played the cuddly and troublesome Bungle in Rainbow. The costume was apparently quite hot, especially when it was changed to be far more cuddly than its initial conception, which resulted in Leeson having to take salt tablets due to the constant high temperature.[1]

Leeson married BBC assistant Judy Griffiths in 1969, with whom he had a son, Guy Ducker. Born in 1972, Ducker became a film-maker and script-writer.

K9 was initially conceived to only appear in 'The Invisible Enemy' (1977), but the producers enjoyed the character so much that K9 was kept on. In his autobiography, Tom Baker devotes quite a few paragraphs to describing, in frank – and I think highly amusing – detail, how much he detested the character, calling it 'boring' and 'expressionless'.[2] However, Baker and Leeson got on superbly and Baker is emphatic that he believes Leeson's talent could have been put to better use.

Leeson, thinking he was only going to be in one story, decided to go all in with the character, beginning with rehearsals, where he would famously spend a lot of time on all fours although Baker refutes this.[3] During filming, Leeson was conscious of the technical limitations of the prop, which was radio-controlled, and not very fast.

After he left *Doctor Who* Leeson was concerned that, voicing K9 and being off-screen, he might have difficulty getting work; however, he continued to act and did a lot of voiceover work and presenting, including being the continuity announcer for Channel 4.

Leeson stated that he was aware that acting work was becoming 'slender',[4] so he took it upon himself to diversify.

This author shares one of Leeson's most notable passions: wine. Leeson became accredited at the Wine and Spirit Education Trust and teaches introductory course in London. He is heavily involved in wine cruises in the Seychelles, Bordeaux, Portugal and Spain. He writes extensively for the Trust, lectures in a professional capacity about wine, and is a tutor for The Wine Education Service Ltd. Most of this work is done under his birth name, John Ducker.

Leeson has a versatile, warm voice, which he has given extensively to a thoughtful and very special charity called Calibre Audio,[5] which provides audiobooks to those who find reading difficult, for whatever reason. It has been running since 1974 and access is free to children and young people.

For twenty-five years, Leeson also served as Justice of the Peace, otherwise known as a magistrate, and twice stood as a candidate for the Liberal Democrats in local elections for Ealing.

Leeson has also written *Dog's Dinners: A Collection of Favourite Recipes* (2014, Fantom) and his autobiography *Tweaking the Tail* (2014), and has appeared on numerous occasions at fan conventions as well as signings and 'meet and greet' events.

23

Mary Tamm

Born	22 March 1950
Died	26 July 2012
Companion	Romana (First Incarnation)
First Appearance	'The Ribos Operation' (2–23 September 1978)
Final Appearance	'The Armageddon Factor, (20 January – 24 February 1979)

MARY TAMM was born in Bradford, Yorkshire. Her father was Estonian and her mother, an opera singer, was Russian. Despite not having grown up in Estonia and being English by birth, the country figures largely in Tamm's life.

Tamm's parents had been forced to flee from Estonia, as had so many others. The country had gained independence following the First World War, but the non-aggression treaty between Nazi Germany and the Soviet Union meant the country was soon occupied by Soviet forces once again. Joseph Stalin initiated deportations, nationalist purges and mass 'disappearances'. Consequently, between 1945 and 1952 Estonia's demographic changed dramatically. Some of Tamm's paternal uncles died in Stalin's prisons.

In the Bradford household, Tamm spoke mainly Estonian. Bradford has a long history of being a multicultural city, so it's no surprise that it had an Estonian-language school, which Tamm attended on Saturdays. She did not learn English until primary school.

According to Tamm, growing up in Bradford was very patriarchal, and despite its rich diversity the city could often be insular towards people of non-English ethnicity. Since she was of Estonian descent, she said integrating could be very difficult.[1]

After her mother died, the Tamm finally visited Estonia for the first time and she realised that she wasn't so different, that other people spoke the language still and she felt a connection to the country. Eventually, she decided to find the strength in her differences to make something of herself and her background lent her the drive to do this.

She gained a scholarship to Bradford Girls' Grammar school in 1961 and then joined the Civic Theatre. From 1969 until 1971, she studied at RADA. In 1971, she got her first acting work at Birmingham Repertory Company, including the role of Margaret in *First Impressions* (by Abe Burrows) and Helen in *Action Replay* (by Fay Weldon).

She moved to London a year later and appeared in the Broadway musical *Mother Earth* in 1972, when it played at the Roundhouse in Camden.

Tamm did a screen test with six other actors for the role of Time Lady, Romana. Initially, Tamm wasn't interested in the role, as she had the impression that the Doctor's female companions were mainly there to scream, ask questions and be generally helpless.' There was a bit of snobbery there,' she later admitted. 'In those days it was seen as a children's programme.'[2]

Despite her initial misgivings, Tamm discovered that Romana had been conceived as something of an equal to the Doctor. One of the first things Tamm's Romana did was retort to the Doctor's assumption of her inexperience by criticising his Time Lord Academy graduation score (51 per cent on a second attempt).

The chemistry between Tom Baker and Mary Tamm was evident from the first scene. Baker, Tamm and John Leeson (the voice of K9) would hang out together for drinks after filming, even though Leeson's presence in the studio was not required. The closeness between them, amplified by Tamm and Baker's similar sense of humour, ensured that Tamm had an enjoyable time on the show.

Although Tamm's role did begin as an equal to the Doctor, there developed similarities between Caroline John's experience, in that having two protagonists in the format to which *Doctor Who* existed did not work. It's this author's opinion that opportunities like this were sadly missed and one might wonder what would have happened, had the producers at the time given credence to the idea that a companion could be capable and intelligent.

As Romana's role reverted to more familiar, safe territory (at least for the writers), Tamm decided it was time to leave. There is some confusion over what would have been a scene showing Romana's regeneration into her second incarnation, played by Lalla Ward. According to Tamm, she would have been happy to film it, but was not asked to do so.

Mary Tamm had a varied and full career as an actor. After leaving *Doctor Who*, she appeared in BBC 1 television show The Treachery Game (1980) and the follow up The Assassination Run (1981), starred in The Hello, Goodbye Man in 1984 and played Penny Crosbie in Brookside from 1993 to 1996.

She was in Paradise Heights (2002), Jonathan Creek and the underrated *Crime Traveller* TV series starring Michael French.

Tamm has been a voice actor with Big Finish productions, playing Romana opposite Tom Baker. She recorded seven of these audio dramas, plus appeared in the 2007 DVD box set of 'The Key To Time', as well as recording commentary on the BBC DVDs.

In an interview with fellow actress and friend Jenny Runacre in 2016, Tamm says of acting, that 'one must have the absolute need to do it, as if one cannot possibly do anything else'. Referring to Richard Briers' quote that 'You have to *have* to do it.'[3]

She also opined that the decline of repertory theatre has had a complex impact on actors who are just beginning their careers, that acting is a very expensive and risky undertaking now. She encouraged people to concentrate on their art, but to diversify and think creatively about how they can support themselves at the same time.

Mary Tamm died on 26 July 2012 after an eighteen-month long battle with cancer. She was 62.

The news was a shock to fans and fellow actors alike. Her agent Barry Langford confirmed the news and spoke of her as one of his closest friends. Tom Baker called her 'wonderfully witty and kind'; Colin Baker paid tribute as a caring and down to earth woman.

Her tragic loss was compounded when her husband Marcus Ringrose died suddenly after Tamm's funeral. Tamm's agent went on to say 'He adored her. If you can die of a broken heart, then that's what he died of – his heart just gave out.'[4]

24

Lalla Ward (Sarah Jill Ward)

Born	28 June 1951
Companion	Romana (Second incarnation)
First Appearance	'Destiny of the Daleks' (1 September – 22 September 1979)
Final Appearance	'Warriors' Gate' (3–24 January 1981)

THE HONOURABLE SARAH WARD, known as Lalla Ward, has a thoroughly interesting family history.

She is the daughter of Edward Henry Harold Ward, Viscount Bangor, hence her reverential official title. Viscount Bangor is a title in the Peerage of Ireland and their official seat is Castle Ward, County Down. Castle Ward was originally named Strangford Manor, but it was renamed after its purchase by Bernard Ward in 1570. There it remained in the family, until another Bernard Ward was elevated to the title of Viscount I in 1770. In the 1950s, Edward Ward, Viscount VII Bangor, sold the house, including its library and a rich history of papers and correspondence, to the National Trust in lieu of death duties.[1]

Lalla Ward's father was a war correspondent for the BBC, stationed in Finland doing the Second World War. Her mother, Marjorie Alice Banks, who often collaborated with him was his fourth wife. She died by suicide in 1991.[2]

She has a brother Edward, a half-brother William Maxwell David, who is now the 8th Viscount Bangor.

Lalla Ward's great-grandmother Mary Ward (27 April 1827 – 31 August 1869) was a naturalist, illustrator and science writer. Mary Ward published *Sketches with the Microscope* in 1857, marrying together her extensive knowledge of microscopy with her illustration skills, to produce a collection of fascinating microscopic water organisms.[3]

Mary Ward was tragically killed in 1869 in what is commonly believed to be the first fatal accident involving a motor vehicle, however her published works live on in the Castle Ward library.

Lalla Ward already had many acting credits under her belt by the time she joined the cast of *Doctor Who*. Her first was Dr *Finlay's Casebook* (1969), as well as *Leap in the Dark* (1977) and as Lottie in *The Duchess of Duke Street* (1977).

She first appeared as Princess Astra in the *Doctor Who* story 'The Armageddon Factor' in 1979, but later would be become Romana's second incarnation, replacing Mary Tamm. An on-screen reference was made to Romana's identical appearance in 'Destiny of the Daleks', after Romana was seemingly trying on different bodies (the first example of a Gallifreyan being able to do this).

Writer Graham Williams asked Ward if she would play Romana on the suggestion of Tom Baker, who had enjoyed working with her on 'Armageddon'.[4] Ward considered this story to be a six-episode action and everybody seemed relieved to be able to skip the usual audition process, knowing they already had an actor with whom the Doctor could get along.

Ward had a great deal of say over her character's costume, reclaiming her hatred of having to wear a school uniform when she was younger by coming up with the idea that Romana should wear one. Ward vividly curated what she imagined Romana might wear, acquiring various pieces of lavish and mismatched costumery from various places she might have visited.

Her eventual departure from the series was a mutual arrangement between herself and John Nathan-Turner. By this time Lalla Ward and Tom Baker had got married, though their marriage lasted less than two years.

She speaks fondly of her time on *Doctor Who* and has vivid memories of what was obviously an exciting and dynamic time in her life.

Ward has been on the committee for the Actors' Charitable Trust (TACT) for two decades. It is now called The Actors' Children's Trust (ACT), a membership association which supports the children of actors on a financial, practical and emotional basis.[5]

Ward shares her great-grandmother's love of the natural world. It is easy to see the influence of her ancestor, as she has a remarkable career as a ceramics and textiles artist. She has produced embroidered works documenting rare and endangered animals, referring to her textiles as 'thread drawing'. In 2009, she exhibited her work and raised £24,000 for the Durrell Wildlife Conservation Trust. Her work has appeared at the National Theatre, London, and in 2012 her exhibition named 'Stranded' documented the wildlife of the Galapagos Islands.

Ward has also produced knitting patterns, with extensive instructions and inspirations. Many of her books, though sought after, are still available.

She met evolutionary scientist Richard Dawkins, having been introduced by their mutual friend, the writer Douglas Adams. Adams and Ward knew each other as he had been a writer on *Doctor Who* at the same time she had player Romana. Ward and Dawkins married in 1992, and announced in 2016 that they had amicably split, but remained friends and colleagues.

In 2018, the journal of British horror films *Little Shoppe of Horrors* reported on social media[6] that Ward and her partner, experimental psychologist Nicholas Rawlins, had been caught up in the riots which happened at Rawlins' university in Hong Kong. Fortunately, they both remained safe, but had to temporarily abandon their home. In 2020, Ward and Rawlins married.

Interlude 4: Interview – Keith Barnfather, founder of Reeltime Pictures

AN IMPORTANT part of *Doctor Who* mythology, like many other cult fanbases, is the extended universe – in print, audio and visual media such as spin-offs and documentaries. Over the years, the contribution of many imaginative and dynamic individuals has contributed to the growing story of the show and provided further information both in-universe and behind the scenes.

In terms of visual media, Reeltime Pictures is probably the most well-known production company associated with *Doctor Who*. Since its inception in 1984, Reeltime Pictures have produced an immense catalogue of interviews with cast and crew members, known as the *Myth Makers* series. They have also created several spin-off films which build upon some of the events and character acts in the main television series.

I simply could not let this book continue without involving them somehow. To that aim, I tracked down founder of the company, Keith Barnfather. Fresh from a series of hectic weekends, he was only too happy to tell me the background of Reeltime Pictures and to discuss just how extensive his involvement has been with the *Doctor Who* universe.

Keith, you've just returned from The Capitol Seven Wonders *Doctor Who* convention. How was your weekend?
The Capitol is organised by the Doctor Who Appreciation Society and of course I was one of the founding fathers of DWAS and organised the first two conventions. So whenever I attend a DWAS event, it's like going home. And after, let's see … good God, we started it in 1976, so in two years' time it'll be forty years old.

You must have a celebration.
I think they're planning that at the convention. So for me it's like a fine old wine that I love to revisit.

Should I refer to the company as Reeltime Pictures or Time Travel TV?
Just to clarify, Reeltime Pictures Limited is the production company and all the programmes we make are made by Reeltime, but our outlet, our distribution

arm, is Time Travel TV. When I was setting up our new website so you can buy downloads as well as Blu-Rays, DVDs and VHS, everything is through Time Travel TV. I think that's a much better marketing tool than Reeltime Pictures. That's why we did it. It's been successful, but it does confuse some people, if I'm honest.

So Reeltime Pictures was founded in 1984. Could you tell me about what inspired its inception?

Well, after I left school, I worked for the BBC and then Channel 4 when it began in 1982. I stayed at Channel 4 for a couple of years, worked in engineering and then went up to what they call business development. Most of your readers would understand it as their version of BBC Enterprises.

It was a small department to start with and I was one of the first people they brought in to handle all of their editing and duplication. I had to learn film prints, negatives, positive, intermixes, internegs, as well as VT and duplicating different formats. That was the job I had when I went up to business development. I learned about budgeting, programming and editing.

So I left in 1984 to set up Reeltime. That was a conscious effort because I wanted to move into production completely. So I aimed at essentially doing corporate and business television to start with, but I always intended that I would get into doing *Doctor Who* spin-off and cult television spin-off material. The first year we did our first *Myth Makers* with John Leeson and Michael Wisher on the same day back-to-back.

When *Doctor Who* initially went on hiatus in 1989, did that effect your output or how you worked?

I can't honestly say that it did. Our customer base has remained fairly steady. It's commonly called The Wilderness Years, but I've never thought of it in those terms because I think it was just as prolific as when the programme was on. Fans had to develop their own entertainment because there was no *Doctor Who* being made. You had the explosion of books during that time, *Doctor Who* went from strength to strength.

But we were already producing. We'd already done 'Wartime' in 1987 and we'd carried on. At no time did I think because the show as off-air that we would benefit. I've always said that it would be back. We just carried on.

The thing which affected us most was that the BBC decided we were doing the right thing and started doing behind the scenes programmes to go on the end of their own releases. When we started, we were making behind the scenes with the actors, documentaries, but the BBC were only making *Doctor Who* on VHS with nothing else. What we were doing was completely new.

I do remember the only special feature I think I saw was on the 'Silver Nemesis' VHS, which was the American making-of documentary. It sounds like you were providing something people didn't know they needed – and it was really popular.
Yes, having worked in business development for Channel 4, I learned a lot about marketing and where there was a hole in the market. I knew from the start that we could do something which was original and new. We did two productions in the early days – 'Return to Devil's End' and 'Who On Earth is Tom Baker?' They're pretty legendary now.

You mentioned 'Wartime'. I think it was the first official spin-off.
Over the years there's been a bit of a blurred line between fan productions and professional productions. Some fan productions are incredibly well-made and some professional productions are not so much, so I think my definition would be 'licensed' and 'unlicensed', to a degree. Of fan-made productions, there were many in the late 1970s and early '80s. People like Mark Sinclair doing fan films in Britain.

Some of them are technically brilliant, but they weren't professional films by my definition – and my definition only. All the stuff that Reeltime has ever done is professional by the following definition: that however small the budget, it was budgeted and licensed. We've never featured the Doctor or the TARDIS because those things are quite rightly copyright to the BBC. But everything we did was licensed to us.

And on occasion, like when we made 'Downtime', which was our biggest production, the BBC were happy to license the characters to us, because at the time the show was off-air. They had no specific plans, except the TV movie. But they weren't looking at it as a product which they wanted to keep. So we negotiated with them.

It's challenging navigating all the politics and the licensing – with anything.
That's the nature of television – most businesses, in fact. For me it was very straightforward. When I first mooted any ideas to do elements from *Doctor Who*, I had to circumnavigate around the restrictions, which is why we did 'Wartime'. We got the license, sorted it out and announced that we were doing it.

And what you accomplished with 'Wartime' and 'Downtime' – which is the first one I watched – was enthralling. It had Nicholas Courtney, Deborah Watling, Jack Watling and Elisabeth Sladen all together in what turned out to be quite a prophetic story.

And it's beautifully poignant, because all of those people are no longer with us.

I think 'Downtime' will probably remain unique in terms of its budget for an independent spin-off. It was thanks to Ian Levine and Andrew Beech, who were the co-producers, who basically put the money in. Two thirds of the budget came from them and the remaining third was form Reeltime, so I'll always be grateful to them. It will always be biggest budget production and every penny of it is on screen. For what we spent on it, it looks incredible.

Having Christopher Barry to direct it was wonderful. I was basically a line producer. I just made sure it happened. Line producing or production managing, whatever you want to call it, people who do that are few and far between and it usually costs a lot. We couldn't afford that, but I knew what to do so I was organising the whole shoot, rather than actually sitting and watching it being made. Most of the time, I was running round making sure things were ready for the next bit of filming. Which was absolutely fine. It was a wonderful two-weeks' or ten days' filming. Something I'll never forget.

And in 'Wartime', one of the producers was John Ainsworth, right? He appears in this book for an interview too.

He did say to me at the time that it was a very generous credit! But it was he who found the location, he showed us around during the filming, because we didn't know it. Even now if I watch 'Wartime', it looks great, it's a clear and concise story. Given that it was the first thing many of us had ever done, and given that we had no time to film it, we managed to produce something which I think stands the test of time. And I have such gratitude to John Levene for taking a chance and Michael Wisher for just being so steadfastly brilliant at all times.

Everyone loves Benton. To see more of him, more depth to the character, was so rewarding.

Yes, and I'll blow a trumpet for the novelisation by Stephen James Walker. We liaised closely on that, along with Andy Lane and Helen Stirling, who didn't have time to write it. We all talked about it a lot and Andy and Stephen built the storyline to fit around the drama, and the actual book in narrative terms is about four times longer than what you see on the film, but what it also does is stitch together the Reeltime universe. There are mentions of Captain Cavendish, which then links 'Downtime' and 'Daemos Rising'. So we then had a history of our productions tied together and it fits perfectly.

You've been doing so much with Time Travel TV, but one of the most recent releases was 'The Monster Man', which is about Neil Cole's Museum of Classic Science Fiction.

Yes! I literally just came back from the event last weekend. This weekend just gone was the Capitol, of course. I'm so tired. Neil and I are really close friends and I admire and respect him in so many ways. He runs the museum up in Allendale in Northumbria. My family, going back, come from that area. In Lanercost Priory, there are around fifty Barnfather graves and I can trace my family history right back to the farms. So whenever I go there, I feel at home. I've made good friends in the village so I'm always looking for an excuse to go back.

I met Neil first when we made Lockdown. Sophie Aldred and I went up to Allendale and we filmed all the links for that in his museum. If you're looking for fans who are doing something special in their homes, there's nothing more special than building an entire museum in your basement.

That inspired me to do a series about all the classic *Doctor Who* exhibitions and that kickstarted that series. So 'Doctor On Display' came about and we did the Allendale Classic Sci-Fi museum as our first episode and then we did Longleat, Llangollen, Blackpool, Blackpool 2, and we have a couple more productions coming up. In particular, one on the USA tour next which I'm really looking forward to.

That last one is generating a lot of interest. British fans don't know much about it, but for American fans it's a pivotal part of their fandom. It was the first time they had seen actual *Doctor Who* props. This travelling tour went around America for a few years in the back of a trailer and that's a fascinating documentary we're doing. So when we did the classic sci-fi museum, afterwards, Neil and I were trying to think what I could do as an excuse to go back.

I really wanted to do something to explain exactly what he does with the monsters in the museum. There are very few people in the world who preserve costume and monsters from films. There are great, talented people who make them, but often once they finish, they're not kept in good condition. When they're exhibited or stored, they're in conditions where, especially latex, they will degenerate. So what Neil has done has developed techniques to repair and preserve these items. And he's a genius. So that's what the documentary is about.

That's where the idea about the event came from. We called it The Monster Men and we got together these geniuses who make them. Mike Tucker, Robert Allsopp, Stephen Mansfield – all people I've known for forty years. It's crazy and it was a wonderful weekend. That was a week ago.

I saw the photos from the weekend and all I could think was that it looked wonderful. I'm a big fan of Mike Tucker and I remember seeing photos of Stephen Mansfield, lying on the floor in all sorts of awkward positions, operating Fifi.
That sounds terribly rude, but I know what you mean.

[*One of my most prized possessions is a copy of* Ace! The Inside Story of an End of an Era, *signed by both Mike Tucker and Sophie Aldred. Of the many photographs within is a series from behind the scenes of* The Happiness Patrol *(1988), showing Stephen Mansfield and Sue Moore operating the animatronic puppet of Helen A's beloved, but ferocious, pet.*]

These things are artefacts and how wonderful it is to preserve the past. I have been to some of these museums and I remember seeing these costumes. I see bits and pieces turning up on eBay and I wonder how that happens.
Some people care more about making money than preserving things. There's nothing really wrong with that.

One of the greatest things about Neil's event, though, is that it's so relaxed and open. You pay for your ticket and then you can just hang around and chat with these people for as long as you all like. You can take photos, talk. It's like the old days when it was about the sheer joy of the programme.

There's a constant thread whenever I talk to anybody involved in the show about the magic of it and how important it is. And I'm struck by how much time people give to talking about it, especially when someone like me comes along and asks for interviews. Like yourself, today, being here.
Well, I like to turn that around and say that I'm the lucky one. Reeltime has an incredibly supportive client base. If we didn't have that, regular customers who buy what we make, we wouldn't do what we do. Being semi-retired, I only really do the cult television stuff now, not the corporate work. I do work with my wife on the Greek language programmes, because she's Greek-Cypriot. But apart from that, I only do this and I consider myself to be one of the luckiest people in the world to actually work on something I would have done for free.

And it's all because of the fans out there who have supported us, because it's them who've made it possible. So if they want to talk to me at a convention, if they want me to do anything that I can practically, to say thank you, I will always do it.

That's really nice to hear. Do you think there'll come a time when you're doing *Myth Makers* episodes, of the Nu-Who companions, as time passes?
I'd love to, in time, move on and do the Nu-Who companions. There are lots of them I would love to do. The thing is, I grew up with classic *Who*, meeting the

Deborah Watling in Downtime (1995). (Copyright, Reeltime Pictures 2025)

John Leeson in Downtime (1995). (Copyright, Reeltime Pictures 2025)

Above: Nicholas Courtney and Elisabeth Sladen in Downtime (1995). (Copyright, Reeltime Pictures 2025)

Left: Nicholas Courtney in Downtime (1995). (Copyright, Reeltime Pictures 2025)

Above: Tom Baker, the Fourth Doctor. (Copyright, Reeltime Pictures 2025)

Right: Sophie Aldred in Mindgame (1998). (Copyright, Reeltime Pictures 2025)

Also, Sophie Aldred in Mindgame (1998). (Copyright, Reeltime Pictures 2025)

Carole Ann Ford. (Copyright, Reeltime Pictures 2025)

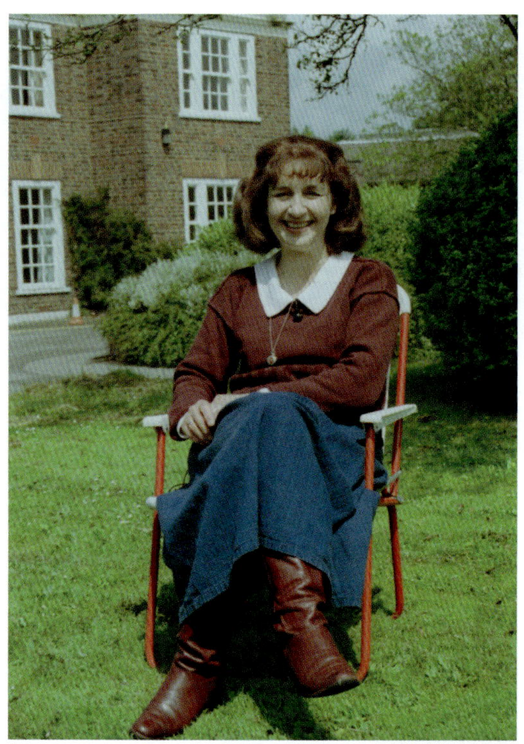

Caroline John. (Copyright, Reeltime Pictures 2025)

Mark Strickson. (Copyright, Reeltime Pictures 2025)

John Levene, Richard Franklin, Jon Pertwee (The Third Doctor) and Nicholas Courtney. (Copyright, Reeltime Pictures 2025)

John Levene. (Copyright, Reeltime Pictures 2025)

The author Dana Fox and Sophie Aldred at a Fantom Events signing. (Copyright, Paul Phipps-Williams, Fantom Events)

The author, Dana Fox and Mark Strickson, at a Fantom Events signing. (Copyright, Paul Phipps-Williams, Fantom Events)

actors, filming and interviewing them. But I haven't had anything to do the new series. It's a generational thing and I feel that maybe it should be left to the next generation to take that on. Reeltime is now so established that we can carry on, even when I can't run it any more.

Perhaps something will come along to change that, but I'm at a point in my career now where I've interviewed virtually everybody from classic *Who* that you could possibly interview.

So you touched upon the 'Lockdown Survival Guide' earlier. It seems to me that *Doctor Who* fans really come together to support each other. During lockdown there was a lot of reaching out and people supporting each other. There was a lot of input from a lot of people for the 'Lockdown Survivors Guide'.

Well, the first thing I'd say is that when you speak to the actors, the one thing people will say is that we're all one big family. Fan and actors can get to know each other, of course. It's a wonderful community and one of the things Sophie Aldred and I were talking about was how much meeting fans and going to conventions meant. When things opened up again, I kept in mind just how much I'd missed it, so that if it ever got a bit too tiring, I remember it's fun and lovely that people want to know what people are doing.

Lockdown itself, well, my wife and I were in Cyprus. I had a lot of programming to edit so I was catching up, but a lot of the time I was looking on social media and watching what people were doing. And my brain works in such a way that I thought it was incredible and this should be a programme! I also turned it around and thought that maybe if people thought what they were doing, what they were creating, could have an end result in a programme for us to show, then it adds meaning.

We had an incredible response when we put the word out. We asked people to send us what they'd made, what they'd be producing and what came through was utterly amazing. I couldn't believe the talent and dedication, the creativity and the madness! I'm very proud of 'Lockdown'.

I think Reeltime have made some documentaries that nobody would ever have made and I think all power to us for that!

Your productions have gone off on some amazing tangents. I'm thinking of stuff like Mark Strickson in America. *Doctor Who* is always there in the background. And with *Myth Makers*, it's actually been an invaluable resource for me writing this book.

I suppose one of the things with *Myth Makers*, which is our core seminal series, was that I didn't want to do interviews about *Doctor Who*. I want to do an interview about an actor's career. I want to learn about them, what got them into acting, why they carried on and how they got their first role. I want to know all that rather than just about *Doctor Who.*

If you remember Parkinson, who's been much imitated, but never equalled. His chat show was the yardstick for interviewing, because it wasn't about Michael Parkinson, it was about the person he was interviewing. That, I think, has been often forgotten, in my opinion. I wanted us to have something like that and we got it. They're not just about *Doctor Who*. You're learning about the actor and their life, rather than just about the part they play.

What would you like readers of this book to know about you, or your ethos or about Reeltime and Time Travel TV?

Right from the start, the one thing I have always done is do something first. Before Reeltime started, I organised the first ever Doctor Who Convention in the world. I was one of the people who set up the DWAS. When I started Reeltime, I did the first interview series with actors that was released on home entertainment and since that time, we've made 180 more. So I want to say that if you believe in something, if you care enough about it, you can achieve it. It's down to you as an individual.

If I can do it, you can do it. And I think that's something that both as a series and as a character, *Doctor Who* would say the same thing.

25

Matthew Waterhouse

Born	19 December 1961
Companion	Adric
First Appearance	'Full Circle' (25 October – 15 November 1980)
Final Appearance	'Earthshock' (8–16 March 1982)

MATTHEW WATERHOUSE was born in Hertford and had two brothers. Tragically, when Matthew was 6, his brother 2-year-old brother died after falling out of his chair. Later, when Matthew was 16, his older brother also died, by suicide.

Matthew got a job at the BBC's Lime Grove, clipping newspaper articles and filing them. Ever resourceful, he sought out BBC casting director Jenny Jenkins and was cast in the 1980 television adaptation of *To Serve Them All My Days*.

Matthew was cast as Adric after audition for John Nathan-Turner. When he received the call confirming he had the part, he 'burst into tears and laughter',[1] which is understandable given his long-term love for *Doctor Who*. He appeared on *Pebble Mill* and *Top of the Pops* upon the public announcement of his joining the show. He was 18 at the time of his casting, the youngest male actor to play a companion on the show.

Waterhouse has cited Tom Baker as personal hero of his, though filming with him could apparently be quite difficult at times, especially during the period of time when Baker and co-star Lalla Ward were going through some personal troubles – although the hostility did not reportedly interfere with filming, there were moments during rehearsals when the tension was evident. In contrast, Waterhouse found Peter Davison to be a serious and even-tempered actor and apparently got on very well with him..

In a shocking ending to the character, Adric was killed. Peter Davison writes that the character's death was unpopular with Matthew Waterhouse and further mentions that although his co-stars took it seriously, it was difficult not to spoil takes with laughter.[2]

However, Waterhouse writes that due to the death of his brother, he felt like he was drawing on something dark and real[3] as an actor, and that he had not told anybody on the show about this. Clearly, there was much more to this scene for Waterhouse than meets the eye.

Matthew Waterhouse had a few television roles afterwards. He has also provided commentaries for the DVD extras on 'Earthshock', 'The Visitation', 'The Keeper of Traken' and many others, while also joining Big Finish Productions after initially declining to reprise his role as Adric.

Waterhouse published *Blue Box Boy: A Memoir of Doctor Who in Four Episodes* (Headmusic 2010), which provides an honest and raw account of his life and his time on the show. Waterhouse chose to write a memoir, rather than a strict autobiography, and he wrote it in third person, which is not an unheard of narrative device for a memoir. As such, *Blue Box Boy* reads with an air of objectivity, with a phenomenological approach, rather than speculative opinion. It's an incredibly valuable volume and often darkly funny.

The elements of black comedy and rich, world-building fantasy which Waterhouse does so well are also evident in his fiction books. He has written *Vanitas* (2013), *Fates*, *Flower* (2013) and *Sugar* (2016), which he describes as 'metaphysical camp'.[4]

26

Janet Fielding (Janet Claire Mahoney)

Born	9 September 1953
Companion	Tegan Jovanka
First Appearance	Logopolis (28 February 1981)
Final Regular Appearance	'Resurrection of the Daleks' (15 February 1984)
Special *Doctor Who* Appearances	'The Power of the Doctor' (23 October 2022)

JANET FIELDING was born in Brisbane, Queensland, Australia. Her father was a parasitologist, who headed up laboratories and contributed to biological research. and her parents moved around a fair bit before settling in Brisbane.[1]

When in high school, Fielding was drawn to either law or journalism, but had various interests and found it initially difficult to decide upon a career path. Eventually, she studied a degree in English and Journalism at the University of Queensland, with the aim of becoming a journalist.

Fielding got into theatre after doing some rehearsed readings in a literary capacity. Her first performance was in *Wrong Side of the Moon*, with the Queensland Theatre Company, where she starred as Rapunzel, opposite Geoffrey Rush.

Fielding got work as a censor with the Australian Broadcasting Control Board and very nearly became a journalist in Melbourne, but decided against it because of the poor pay. Fielding became involved with The Popular Theatre Group, which was first formed in 1974, and whose anti-Apartheid stance and progressive political engagement appealed to her.[2]

She took an opportunity with some of the ex-troupe members to go to England for a three-month run of a show, where she encountered writer and actor Ken Campbell, who invited her to be part of an operatic version of HP Lovecraft's *The Case of Charles Dexter Ward.* After that, she acted in Campbell's 24-hour show *The Warp* at the Institute of Contemporary Arts in 1979. He later encouraged her to get experienced at repertory theatre, which she reluctantly did.

Fielding was in the play *Crown Matrimonial* in 1980,[3] directed by Charles Savage and written by Royce Ryton. It was during this time that she landed the role as Tegan Jovanka.

Fielding won the role as she had been recommended to producer John Nathan-Turner (Howe Stammers Walker *The Eighties*) by the Actors Alliance organisation because she was genuinely a 'bossy Australian'. Initially written only for only three stories, she was kept on and became an enduringly popular character.

Janet Fielding's entrance into the TARDIS in 1981 was reminiscent of the very beginnings of the show. Having mistaken the TARDIS for an actual Police Box (or at least not realising its true nature), she became lost in its vast corridors. Upon the character's eventual first meeting with the Doctor and Adric, after stumbling back into the console room, she demanded to speak to whoever was in charge. From that very first moment, Fielding brought a forthright and principled character vividly to life.

Fielding had a relationship with her co-stars which, it appears, only happens in the show when the blend of actors is just right. Peter Davison[4] speaks highly of her and mentions that she had battled cancer (in 2013) and he was doubly fond of her. In his interview with me, which you can read later on, Mark Strickson describes how they all very much got on. The banter between Fielding and her co-stars is clear on some of the newer DVD commentaries which she has provided and they can often roast each other severely.

In 2022, Fielding reprised her role as Tegan in 'The Power of the Doctor', the Doctor now being played by Jodie Whittaker. She has been involved in several Big Finish Productions audio dramas, appearing as Tegan alongside Peter Davison and Mark Strickson.

In her personal life, Fielding was married in 1982 to *Daily Mirror* foreign editor Nicholas Davies. They divorced in 1991.

After she left *Doctor Who*, Janet Fielding has been anything but quiet. Even a cursory glance at her involvement in a range of admirable projects will tell you that the outspoken demands for fairness and equality which she brought to Tegan are qualities which Fielding genuinely has in abundance.

In 1991, she co-founded the Women in Film & Television International (WIFTI), a global network with over 10,000 members, dedicated to advancing the professional development of women in film television. In 2009, she managed a study of what makes a successful woman in the visual arts and collated evidence supporting the presence of strong female role models, mentorship and highlighted the attitudes and culture within the industry which needed to change in order to support women in their roles.[5]

She had also been the director of Marina Martin Associates, an acting agency whose clientele included Paul McGann, who went on to play the Eighth Doctor. She also was responsible for Sylvester McCoy's screen test for his role as the Seventh Doctor.

Fielding moved to Ramsgate, Kent, in 2008 and declared that she immediately felt in love with the town. She has been vocal in her support of young people in the area and committed herself to the charitable initiative Project Motorhouse, which aimed to convert a vacant motor museum in the area into a building which would provide facilities for local businesses to teach young people successful management skills.

Though the initiative concluded in 2022 without necessarily achieving its aims, Fielding's heading up of the project successfully engaged a number of young people over the years, particularly during the Covid-19 pandemic. One only has to look at the comments sections of the news reports over the years to see the local community's celebratory response, as well as the sadness that the project had to close.[6]

In 2023, Fielding organised an event in Margate called 'Tea With Tegan', in support of a judicial review of the reopening of the local Manston Airport, Kent. Having closed in 2014 due to becoming financially unviable, its owners proposed reopening the airport, a plan which was met with great concern from local residents.

I was delighted to attend Tea With Tegan, as I live minutes from the venue, the historic and resplendent Walpole Bay Hotel, overlooking the ocean. At the event, which was very well attended, Fielding was generous with her time and held a series of raffles, competitions and games, all with the aim of raising money for what is locally agreed to be a worthwhile cause.

Janet Fielding is nothing short of a force of nature. I found her to be open, charming and forthright in equal measures, which is entirely what I expected.

Fielding has acted as Tegan in numerous Big Finish Productions audio dramas and frequently attends *Doctor Who* conventions and has given multiple interviews.

27

Sarah Sutton

Born	12 December 1961
Companion	Nyssa of Traken
First Appearance	'The Keeper of Traken' (31 January – 21 February 1981)
Final Appearance	'Terminus' (15–23 February 1983)

SARAH SUTTON was born in Basingstoke, the daughter of an airline pilot. Sutton studied at Elmhurst Ballet School from age 7, and aged 9 she successfully auditioned for the part of Baby Roo in the *Winnie the Pooh Musical* at the Phoenix Theatre, London. During the first part of the audition, Sutton became upset due to the sudden realisation that she was on a very large London stage; despite this, she did get the role and did three seasons of the run.

Sutton had numerous television roles from 1973 onwards, including the miniseries *Late Call* in 1975 and a starring role in TV series *The Moon Stallion* (1978). Her character in the latter was a blind character named Diana Purwell. Today, it's likely that a visually impaired character would be played by an actor with a similar impairment, however Sutton extensively researched and studied for the role.[1]

Sutton began, but didn't complete, a diploma at Guildhall School of Music & Drama, London. She was saved from studying for the various levels, which she disliked, by landing the role of Nyssa on *Doctor Who*.

Sutton received news about auditions for the character of Nyssa from her agent, just after she returned from a holiday in Barbados. She read for 'Keeper of Traken' director John Black and then John Nathan-Turner. Not too long afterwards, she was offered the role.

Created by screenwriter Johnny Byrne (27 November 1935 – 2 April 2008), Nyssa was initially only going to be in the show for one episode. Production, however, saw that the benefits of having someone closer to Adric's age, who could also bridge the gap between Tom Baker's departure and Peter Davison's arrival, and as a counterbalance to Tegan's hot-headedness (*Companions* HSW).

Sutton enjoyed the role; the freedom of playing a character who was not human allowed her to be unconventional. Nyssa was from aristocracy, and being a scientist she was orderly, precise and somewhat cloistered. Her co-star, Fifth Doctor Peter Davison, thought that her experience as an actor from such a young age meant she was used to the luxury of more production time and she would have benefited from better scriptwriting.[2]

It was an overabundance of TARDIS characters which led to Nyssa being written out of the series. After she left the show, Sutton studied at the Guildhall School of Music and Drama. In 1986, she appeared in *Policy For Murder* by Tony Clayton and had further television roles, such as *Casualty* in 1989 and *Unnatural Pursuits* in 1992. By this time, she had married Michael Bundy and when she gave birth to her daughter Hannah, Sutton stepped away from acting.

Sutton was reunited with her co-star Janet Fielding (for a special which appears on the BBC Studios Blu-ray *Doctor Who*: *The Collection* – Season 20. In this special trailer, Tegan receives a mysterious text message instructing her to meet at the 'Blue Box' in the fairground. After an initially rather tense wait in a spooky abandoned funfair, Nyssa appears and they embrace fondly and reminisce about their time with the Doctor. The short was extremely well-received by fans.

It's a well-known fact that during filming of *Doctor Who*, Sutton and her co-stars, Peter Davison, Mark Strickson and Janet Fielding, got on extremely well. Sutton was sad to have left the show, which was apparently a production decision rather than hers.

Sutton has been involved in several *Doctor Who* documentaries, including 'Putting the Shock in Earthshock' (2entertain DVD, 2003), 'Anti-Matter from Amsterdam' (BBC documentary 2007) and has provided commentary with some of her co-stars for the DVD versions of 'The Keeper of Traken', 'The Visitation' and 'Black Orchid'. She has also played Nyssa in several Big Finish Productions audio dramas.

28

Mark Strickson

Born	6 April 1959
Companion	Vislor Turlough
First Appearance	'Mawdryn Undead' (1–9 February 1983)
Final Regular Appearance	'Planet of Fire' (23 February – 2 March 1984)

MARK STRICKSON was born in Stratford-Upon-Avon and went to King Edward VI Grammar School. He successfully applied to RADA, out of thousands of other applicants, which he thought was extremely lucky and found the training hard work, but extremely important to his acting career.

HIs early roles were small, on shows like *Strangers* (1982) and then *Juliet Bravo* (1982). His next role was as regular character Terry in the BBC television show *Angels*, which was a springboard for many soon-to-be famous British actors, including Lesley Dunlop and Pauline Quirke. It was during his time on *Angels* that he met Gary Downie, production manager, who was also, of course, the producer for *Doctor Who*, and life partner of showrunner John Nathan-Turner. He was subsequently offered a choice: continue on *Angels* in a regular role or join the cast of *Doctor Who*.

Strickson played Turlough, a unique character: an alien exile with a sinister motive. The original reason for even having a companion was to ask questions, and for the audience to relate to them. But immediately, Turlough was different.

Strickson thoroughly enjoyed the role and the character development, which saw a story arc involving Turlough making his choice between the Doctor and the tempting, yet untrustworthy, Black Guardian.

Strickson's career after leaving the show has been particularly enthralling. He became a documentary producer of wildlife and nature films, turning the legendary late Steve Irwin into a virtual household name.

It is difficult to overstate Strickson's contribution to documentary television, nor is there space to list the phenomenal number of audio dramas and documentaries he has been in. Mark Strickson maintains an enthusiastic connection to *Doctor Who* and I was delighted to meet him in person at one of the legendary Fantom Films signing events, where he inscribed the cover of my VHS copy of 'Mawdryn Undead'. As I mentioned in the introduction, this was one of the very first *Doctor Who* cassette tapes I ever bought, so it was a particularly resonant moment for me.

It was not, however, the first time we had spoken. A year prior, I had the pleasure of interviewing him for this book.

Interlude 5: Interview – Mark Strickson

WHEN I WAS lucky enough to interview Mark Strickson for this book, we met online, as he was speaking from New Zealand. I told him how I essentially grew up with Turlough, as much as I did with Sarah Jane Smith, Tegan and Ace. Though I continued by telling him that I found Turlough shifty and intimidating:

[Mark Strickson] Good! He was not only shifty, he was obviously powerful. I went to an ordinary English grammar school and I was prefect. The relationship between Hippo and Turlough was something I had to go back to my school days in order to remember, that somebody would do what you told them because you were more powerful.

Fans often comment that I was too old to portray a schoolboy and I always say yes. That was the whole thing. You should have picked that up from scene one that something was wrong about this guy. You should have been suspicious!

He didn't fit. There was something definitely off about the character.
I think they wrote really well for my character … I very much brought my own personality to Turlough. After filming the scene with the car, John-Nathan Turner asked if he could have a word. I thought 'What have I done?', but he asked me if I could be a bit more posh. I said 'No, John. That's as posh as I get.' And, to his credit, he said 'That's fine, Mark. You stay as you are because you've got to be Turlough for years.'

And you ended being what I would consider to be one of the most recognisable companions.
I won't beat around the bush, it was lovely job. I worked with lovely people and it was a fantastic job to do. We're all still friends.

You're on the convention circuit a lot and that's so nice to see you and the other cast members are still buddies.
We all like each other. It's not hard. It was never hard. I got on really well with John Nathan Turner, the directors and the crew were lovely and the cast were gorgeous. I always say if you go into work and meet nice people, life's a breeze.

There were lovely moments and you remember those. There was one moment when we were filming a story with Rula Lenska ['Resurrection of the

Daleks'] and we had a bit of time off. *Top of the Pops* were recording next door and we went in and had a bit of a dance to Culture Club who were playing.

Now that is pretty cool.
It was *really* cool! Boy George finished and I'd get on my bike and go back to the boat I was living on at the time. It wasn't this glamorous life, it was just a really nice job, if I can describe it like that.

I was thinking about the differences between *Doctor Who* now and then. The show is cool now. I mean, it's really cool.
It is cool now. It wasn't cool when I was doing it.

I was bullied at school for liking it so much. And from what I've read, it was very touch and go with the budget when it was being made.
Well, you can quote me on this: I think you either love science fiction and get it or you don't. There are people who love *Lord of the Rings* and people who find it the most boring thing ever. I get it. It's a different brain. I think when I was in *Doctor Who*, there were people in the upper echelons of the BBC who didn't get it.

But they seem to get it now. The budget is huge.
It was almost cancelled when I was in it. I don't know why it's been so successful over the years!

[When Mark Strickson left *Doctor Who*, he and his wife at the time emigrated to Australia. They both decided they wanted to see what else they could do other than acting, though it appears that the climate was also a factor.]

It was the late 1980s. There had been two terrible summers. When we flew to Australia, we realised we got one thing right: the weather. The sea was blue, the sun was shining, but we did realise we needed to earn a living.

So I did a year on a medical series [Angels] and my wife did lots of radio. But we really did want to do something different, so we enrolled in zoology courses in Armadale which is about half an hour from Sydney. But while we were there, our marriage broke up. We remained friends, we bought two houses on the same block and we remain friends to this day. After that, I decided I wanted to make nature programs. So I moved back to the UK, to a little village outside Bristol.

I made a few programs and sent them off to a various film companies. This is where the funniest coincidence happened. A company called Partridge Films called me and the guy on the phone said: 'I know this is a silly question, but you're not the Mark Strickson who was in *Doctor Who*?' And I said that I was.

He then said, 'I'm the Andrew Buchanan who was the production manager on your last episode!'

So on the basis of that, the first films happened and we got commissions. It was like a dream come true, being back in Australia, living in a land cruiser, travelling on my own and filming crocodiles!

That is quite astounding. I've watched some of your documentaries. I have to ask, how accurate is it that you discovered Steve Irwin *and* that the shooting style you used was pretty much revolutionary for nature programmes?
It's completely accurate. That is totally right. I had no idea that I'd create a revolution in nature TV. I guess that's why I've never stopped working.

The first thing we made with Steve Irwin broke the mould with presenter-led television. It was because the programme was about snakes. There's a golden rule in natural history television that you have to get on the same level as the eye of what you're filming. If you've got a snake, you have to be on the ground. In this case a tripod wasn't going to work. So with my cameraman, Jeff Goodman, we made the decision to get the camera off the tripod.

And we did another thing. It was the first documentary to be made on video, instead of film. With video, you have this amazing thing. You can record the previous twelve seconds before you started filming. If you press the start button, it records the twelve seconds before that.

That's time travel, surely.
Yes! So we got the most amazing natural history moments. We were the first to show a snake popping out of an egg!

So life ended up very exciting, by the sound of it.
Well, the thing is, I really liked acting. I never made a conscious decision to stop acting, but when I made that first Steve Irwin film, it was so successful that I became a world-wide known director. It was amazing and I've never stopped doing it. I've lived in Scotland, the Middle East, Australia, New Zealand. I've kept being a television producer and I'm not unhappy about that. But I would love to go back to acting. I miss my acting friends and the vibe of it. Being a producer is a very lonely life!

I spend much of my time hunched over various keyboards and drawing tablets. I think I know what you mean.
Yes, my editor and I sit in rooms editing and making films. It's not very social and it can sometimes make life difficult for the people you live with. There's

no team that makes these films. It's me! I write my own scripts, I have to time code them and it all has to be sent off on time.

That's intense.
It's very intense! But there are perfect moments. I remember stopping one night in the middle of the Outback, somewhere between Darwin and Brisbane. I was rolled up in the back of the land cruiser trying to sleep and I could hear crocodiles fighting. I remember trying to sleep and just thinking this was amazing. Here you are, doing this! A boy from Stratford-Upon-Avon and here you are doing this.

A sublime moment. How wonderful!
Precious moments. I mean, I've had malaria and almost died. It's very dangerous in these remote places because there's no medical care. I was really sick and almost died on a couple of occasions … but, my God, it's been good!

I was reminded of an interview with you from 1997 – a bit of a while ago now. But you said something which resonated with me. You said that your philosophy was to tread gently on the planet.
It's *really* important to me that I tread gently. It's in my will that there's no service, nothing. Just bury me in the cheapest way. For me, the aim will be to leave no sign that I've ever lived. It's fundamental to me. I don't want any reminder that I was here, which obviously might be fairly impossible.

But it's so important to me. I hardly spend any money on clothes. I wear my son's old shoes. I have enough second-hand clothes to last me until the day I die. In fact, Peter Davison once said to me: 'You've got nice trainers!' And I replied that I'd bought them for my son five years ago.

I always think about flying and that is a huge issue for me too. If I knew then what I know now, I'm not sure I would have lived here at all. Because I do fly back to the UK to see my parents. I fly economy, I would never fly business because you're taking the seat of six economy. So yes I want to tread gently, but we all have to juggle that in our lives.

I think if you look at the scales and the balance in your life, everything you've done to raise awareness of the natural world, plus the way you generally live, I think you're still in credit.
I hope so.

Treading gently is the exact opposite of what we're told to do these days.
I know. I have a son and kids are very consumerist. Kids want the latest thing and I'm okay with that. I remember that. I'm okay with it to a certain point,

but I hope I set a lesson to him with my wife. She and I are absolutely not consumers. So I hope my son might leave home having watched us and will have learned some things.

Kids seem to either absorb their parents' influence or completely reject it. I know which I did.

Yes, and I'm up for that too! Maybe after ten years of rejecting it, he might remember. But for me, I'm never happier that when I'm sitting in the greenhouse watching stuff grow.

29

Gerald Flood

Born	21 April 1927
Died	12 April 1989
Companion	Kamelion
First Appearance	'The King's Demons' (15–16 March 1983)
Final Appearance	'Planet of Fire' (23 February – 2 March 1984)

GERALD FLOOD was born into a Naval family, in Portsmouth and spent most of his life in Farnham, Surrey. During the Second World War, he was a runner with the Royal Air Force. Flood's job was to carry important communications from post to post during air raids, often under heavy fire, armed with only a light weapon.

During his National Service, he performed in amateur theatre in Singapore, before returning after the end of his service to work as a filing clerk. His time in amateur theatre had apparently awakened a desire he'd had from an early age to be an actor, but he found it difficult to find support, as the country was still in a very early post-war economy. So in 1949, he joined the Farnham Repertory Theatre and then in 1951 joined theatre founder Arthur Brough's rep companies in Maidstone and Folkestone, Kent.[1]

It was in Farnham, however, that he met Anne, who he married in 1950.

He went on to have numerous theatre roles, including Rosencratz in *Hamlet*. He maintained dedicated support towards local theatre, eventually becoming a member of management at Farnham Castle Theatre, which would later become Redgrave Theatre.

His first prominent television role was that of Conway in *Pathfinders in Space* (1960), as well as its sequels. Among his many eventual television credits are *Crane* (1963–1965), *The Rat Catchers* (1966–1967), *Harry in Bachelor Father* (1970–1971) and as Ronnie in *Second Time Around* (1974–1975).

Gerald Flood provided the voice for the Fifth Doctor's robotic companion named Kamelion. Flood was offered the role by John Nathan-Turner, who he met while he was acting in *Relatively Speaking* (by Alan Ayckbourn in Brighton, 1982). Coincidentally, Colin Baker, who would go on to play the Sixth Doctor, was also in the play.[2]

In Kamelion's inaugural episode, 'The King's Demons', Flood also played King John, while his pre-recorded lines for Kamelion were played.

For a variety of reasons, the companion Kamelion has passed into *Doctor Who* folklore as one of the most unique and troublesome phenomena to ever appear in the show. The prop was designed by Chris Padmore and Mike Power who together owned a firm called CP Cybernetics. It was not originally built for *Doctor Who*, but John Nathan-Turner went to visit CP Cybernetics in Oxford and was very much taken by the prop. The creators considered it a work in progress at the time and despite warnings from cast and crew, Nathan-Turner went ahead with it.

Although an optimistic idea, it became clear very early on that the Kamelion was not entirely up to the task. Peter Davison would often have to prop up the robot while acting with it and the servo mechanisms in the neck would not often turn the head in the right direction.

Flood had a few more roles after *Doctor Who*, including the 1985 series *Bleak House* and a journalist in *Mornin' Sarge*, three years later. Sadly, his television roles were rare, and Gerald Flood died from a heart attack on 12 April, 1989.

30

Nicola Bryant (Nicola Jane Bryant)

Born	11 October 1960
Companion	Perpugilliam (Peri) Brown
First Appearance	'Planet of Fire' (23 February – 2 March 1984)
Final Appearance	'The Trial of a Time Lord Mindwarp' (4 October – 25 October 1986)

NICOLA BRYANT was born in Guildford, Surrey to Denis and Sheila Bryant. She grew up in the rural Surrey hills with her younger sister Tracy and a dachshund. When she was only 3 years old, Bryant began dance classes and piano lessons, although she could not continue dancing due to her asthma. So instead, she started at the amateur dramatics and did in fact continue learning classical ballet and music. She learned to play the flute, piano and guitar.

Bryant applied to many different drama schools, however because she had been moved on year ahead in school and was only 17, all of the responses to her applications were pretty much the same: go and get more life experience.

What happens next speaks to Bryant's determination and playful sneakiness. Having become familiar with each of the schools' expectations, she returned to each one with a wonderfully clever approach and tailor-made each application to suit the school. For the Webber Douglas Academy of Dramatic Art, she adopted a more classical approach with her audition and convinced them that she had enjoyed a very eventful life, despite her young age.

She got accepted. In an interview with 'The Sirens of Audio',[1] Bryant recounts how one of the panel members for the Central School of Speech and Drama (for which she had also been interviewed), was also on the board for Webber Douglas. Having applied under a different name, she began to worry that he might recognise her, however it soon transpired that her inventive ploy had been an enlivening diversion from an otherwise uneventful day.

Nicola Bryant's first professional television role was as Peri Brown, companion to the Fifth Doctor. The responsibility of introducing Peri in her first story fell to writer Peter Grimwade, though she was developed by script editor Eric Sward and showrunner John Nathan-Turner. Nathan-Turner, having been encouraged by the response to Tegan, decided he wanted another non-British actor to play the next companion – and he decided this time she should be American.

It was Terry Carney who first noticed Nicola Bryant and asked her to action for the part. She had been playing an American in *No, No Nanette*, her latest theatre role and, knowing what the producers were looking for, was encouraged to keep up the accent and pretended to be from the States.

The audition was delayed while Bryant quickly racked up some dancing work at cabaret and clubs in order to get her Equity card, as it was a condition that all *Doctor Who* cast were members of the Guild. In the meantime, the clock was ticking and Bryant became aware that her agent still had not told John Nathan-Turner that she was not, in fact, American. When she landed the role, there would be three months between the good news and the start of filming. During this time there were numerous media appearances during which she had to keep up the accent.

After three years in the role and two Doctors, Bryant decided to leave. On the whole, Bryant has recounted how much fun she had on the show. She had a comparatively brief but pleasant time with Peter Davison. She got on extremely well with Colin Baker, with whom she would co-star together in 'The AirZone Solution' (1993), albeit as different characters. Their on-screen chemistry is always palpable.

At an event ran by *Doctor Who* group Sheffield Watchers in 1997, Bryant recounted some of Colin Baker's pranks, including biting her bottom during filming, only a few days into the show.

Frazer Hines guest starred in 'The Two Doctors' and, as I have noted elsewhere, Hines is notorious for his practical jokes. The pranks he and Colin Baker played on Bryant and Patrick Troughton were uproarious, including soaking Bryant with water and pushing her face into a bowl of muesli in the BBC canteen.[2]

Bryant clearly has an adventurous and unconventional edge to her: she very much enjoyed the gruesome way in which Peri was written out of the show, which involved her mind being overwritten by the villainous Lord Kim (played by Christopher Ryan). This, of course, is later revealed to be possibly apocryphal, and Peri may indeed be quite safe.

When Nicola Bryant left, she was briefly considered for the role of Captain Janeway on *Star Trek: Voyager*.[3]

She has been a prolific theatre actor, with numerous roles including Hermit in *A Midsummer Night's Dream,* Honey in *Who's Afraid of Virginia Woolf?*, *Spring's Awakening* and *Absurd Person Singular* at Vienna's English Theatre. Her television roles have included playing Martine *on The Biz* from 1994 to 1997 and *Star Trek Continue* in 2017.

Bryant also starred opposite Colin Baker in *The Stranger* direct-to-video film series. This science-fiction drama was produced by Bill Baggs and ran from 1991 to 1995. *The Stranger* is sometimes termed a *Doctor Who* spin-off. Although the films feature many actors who starred in *Doctor Who* and the stories have echoes of the show, they are closer to homages and stand very strongly on their own. No mention of the Doctor, or indeed very much else of *Doctor Who*, was allowed due to copyright.

Bryant has rarely been far away from *Doctor Who*. She narrated the *Doctor Who: Short Trips Podcast* series, *Doctor Who: The Monthly Adventures*, and has reprised the role of Peri in several Big Finish Productions audio dramas, opposite both Peter Davison and Colin Baker, as well as directing some of them. She provided commentaries for all her stories when they were released on DVD.

Bryant is passionate about charity work, in particular animals, being a supporter of Dogs on the Streets, an organisation which dedicates itself to supporting dogs belonging to homeless people. Nicola Bryant is also a qualified hypnotherapist. In 2020, she hosted a quantum hypnosis session online, organised by The Royal Vauxhall Tavern and in aid of charities Dogs on the Street and Chimney Farm Rescue.

Bryant's partner is writer Nev Fountain, who has contributed to several Big Finish audio dramas. He is perhaps most famous for his comedy writing, in particular the television and radio show *Dead Ringers*. Having met Fountain, and with her mother having fallen unwell, she did return to live again in rural Surrey.

31

Bonnie Langford (Bonita Melody Lysette Langford)

Born	22 July 1964
Companion	Melanie (Mel) Bush
First Appearance	'The Trial of a Time Lord: Terror of the Vervoids' (1–22 November 1986)
Final Appearance	'Dragonfire' (23 November – 7 December 1987)

BONNIE LANGFORD grew up in Surrey and attended the Arts Educational School, then Saint Catherine's School, a private Catholic school, and then the Italia Conti Academy of Theatre Arts. Langford's mother Babette ran a dance school and, at the age of 93 at least, still did run a school for young, aspiring stage actors.

Langford's family has a history of performance. Her maternal great-aunt was a ballerina, toured with Pavlova and opened a dance school. Her mother joined that and then took over the dance school. Both of her sisters are performers.

Langford appeared on *Opportunity Knocks* when she was just 6 years old, singing Shirley Temple number *On the Good Ship Lollipop* and then became prominent playing Violet-Elizabeth Bott in *Just William* (1977). She became known as a stereotypical precocious child actor, which she found frustrating when it came to transitioning to an adult actor.

She was prolific in stage productions, including *Peter Pan The Musical*, *Cats* and *The Pirates of Penzance*, but experienced the pressures of overwork and celebrity status, feeling as though Bonnie Langford the person was neglected in lieu of Bonnie Langford 'the brand'.[1]

John Nathan-Turner outlined the character of Mel as a 21-year-old computer programmer, with vivid red hair and a strong, even 'irritating' personality.[2] She was cast without an audition because Nathan-Turner had her in mind already. Although, as is sometimes the case, *Doctor Who* mythology provides the alternative story that it was because she shared an agent with Colin Baker.

However, the actual story is that Langford was in Joe Allen's Restaurant in London where she met Nathan-Turner and his partner and *Doctor Who* director. Nathan-Turner was devoted to his role as producer and had an idea of the next companion firmly fixed in his mind, as well as generating ratings for the show. The role went to her particularly easily as she was a very well-known actor and she fit the character profile.

Langford's further involvement in *Doctor Who* took an unexpected turn in 2022 when it was announced that she would be returning to appear in 'The Power of the Doctor' and 'The Giggle'. Her return was well-received by fans and Langford herself, noting that the character had been allowed to develop so that she could finally shed the screaming cliched female role.[3] She returned in a substantial capacity in 2024, appearing in 'The Legend of Ruby Sunday' and 'Empire of Death'.

Langford has been nothing but enthusiastic and positive about *Doctor Who* since its return, hailing its new-found depth and diversity, proposing that at its heart, the show has always been ideologically progressive, with a positive message about inclusion and representation.[4]

After Langford originally left the show, she appeared as a celebrity contestant on *Dancing On Ice* in 2006 and then began playing more theatre role, including *Guys and Dolls* (2006–07) and Chicago (2009–10). She became at home in London's West End theatres.

Langford had a substantial role in *Eastenders* between 2015 and 2018, playing Carmel Kazemi. Her vivid and emotional performance led to her winning the 2016 Best Newcomer in British Soap Award.

She has also reprised her role for an extraordinary amount of *Doctor Who* Big Finish Productions audio dramas, particularly the 'Doctor Who Main Range' and 'The Sixth Doctor Adventures', as well as narration for many of the audiobook versions of her stories.

She married Paul Grunert in 1995 and gave birth to her daughter Biana in 2000, though she and Grunert divorced in 2015.

32

Sophie Aldred

Born	20 August 1962
Companion	Dorothy (Ace) McShane
First Appearance	'Dragonfire' (23 November – 7 December 1987)
Final Regular Appearance	'Survival' (22 November – 6 December 1989)

SOPHIE ALDRED was born in Greenwich, London and grew up in Blackheath nearby. She went to Blackheath High School until 1980 and then went to Manchester University to study drama. Aldred's first performing roles was in children's theatre, notably Polka Theatre which still runs to this day, focusing on community-based theatre for young audiences, as well as Penny Bernand's Theatre of Thelema, which later became Quicksilver Theatre.

Aldred received a call from her agent who said that the producers of *Doctor Who* were looking for somebody for three episodes, which we can assume was the 1987 three-part story 'Dragonfire'. At the time, she was part of the chorus in *Fiddler on the Roof.* Being cast as Ace, Aldred was delighted enough, but the role turned into something much bigger, as Bonnie Langford was considering leaving the show.[1]

Aldred's time on the show, and her character Ace, was nothing short of iconic. In direct contrast to Mel, Ace was streetwise, tough, somewhat troubled and carried a lot of emotional baggage. It's fair to say that a female character who was so forthright had not been seen in this particular way on the show before.

Aldred bonded very quickly with Seventh Doctor Sylvester McCoy, with whom she shared many qualities, not least an irreverent outlook on the Thatcherism of the time, but also a sense of anarchic comedy and a love of theatre, McCoy having toured with the Ken Campbell Roadshow.

Initially, Aldred has said that she had a tough time with showrunner John Nathan-Turner, whose experience with actors was somewhat more

'Joan Collins-sh type glam'[2] as Aldred put it. However, Ace proved to be extremely popular with fans, her rebellious nature immediately something that most young people could identify with, and after a few stories, Nathan-Turner and Aldred found common ground and their relationship bloomed.

Aldred realised very quickly that the character of Ace was pretty unique. She never screamed (although she did shout a few times), her costume was not only era-appropriate, but practical, enabling Aldred to have a more physical role than many female companions had ever had.

Ace was the final companion to appear with the Doctor in the classic series of the show before its cancellation, however Sophie Aldred's involvement in *Doctor Who* was far from over.

Interlude 6: Sophie Aldred Interview

OFTEN, WHEN I have reached out to actors from *Doctor Who*, I worry that I'm being something of a nuisance. I imagine that I might come along, asking all the usual question which they have answered countless times before. Actors are busy people and I fear I might be imposing on their time.

None of this has been true with anybody I have spoken to for this book, least of all Sophie Aldred, who was only too happy accommodate what was a pretty tight deadline for me.

Sophie thanks for joining me. How's your week been?
Well it's been a busy week. I've done some recordings and that's been really good fun. I do a lot of work for a personal growth, training and development organisation. I lead introductions to their basic course. I absolutely love self-development, personal growth and making a difference. I know that one of the places I make a difference is with *Doctor Who*. Since I've done this course, it's actually exploded that as well.

So you teach on the course?
Well I'm an introduction leader. So I lead introductions for anybody who's interested in it and I've created a project from a possibility that I invented for myself – of being loving, joyful and being a contribution to people. And from that came curating my family treasure. So I'm making a film, a documentary, about my mother and then I'll do one about my father.

People of generations to come will be able to hear their stories. I'm collating boxes that my mum's given me of photos from the past. One of my sons is involved – he's into ancestry.com. It's expanding and expanding. I realised that my parents aren't getting any younger and their stories will go unless someone records them.

I've also got my grandmother speaking about her stories. She got struck by lightning on coronation day.

Woah.
I know! She tells the brilliant story about it. She was on a golf course, playing golf, while my grandfather took my mother, who was 15 at the time, to watch the Queen being crowned. And my grandmother was playing hard because she didn't want the other person to win. So she put her golf club up like this [Sophie demonstrates

an exuberant golfing stroke] and the lightening went right through her. She should have died. But luckily she was wearing a silk scarf and that saved her!

So I've got my grandmother telling that story brilliantly, because she was a real character. I've my mother telling her part of the story. I've got my aunt involved too. So I just wanted to get those down so we can have them forever.

That was quite a long answer, wasn't it?!

Well this is why I'm doing these interviews. To get to know those bits of you and for the readers too.
I'm also a trustee for the school that my boys went to, which has since closed down. I'm one of three trustees of the educational trust, looking after land and assets, so that the school can start up again when we've got everything sorted. I've learned *so* much through that about myself and others: planning, sales, land and managing and all that! So that's something else I do.

And I do a lot of voice recording in my airing cupboard.

In your airing cupboard?
Yes, during lockdown I realised I had to get an income. People had said to me when I recorded the occasional thing on my iPhone in my airing cupboard, that my sound quality was really good. So I thought I'd have a go. I bought myself a microphone and sat in the airing cupboard and recorded audio books, Big Finish and all sorts. Because the towels soak up all the sound.

They're like acoustic baffles made of linen.
Exactly! And I used to collect the HelloFresh food boxes from when we'd get the deliveries and inside you get a thick wool mat. I kept them all, sewed them together and put them around the back inside the airing cupboard for soundproofing and it works amazingly.

That's hilarious. So when you do Big Finish, you don't even need to turn up. You can just go in the airing cupboard.
Yes! I do love turning up now that I can, because someone makes me a cup of tea and I see lots of lovely friends. So we do go to the wonderful Roundhouse [Studios] in North Acton and we record there. I do quite a lot of other things there too. But it's great to have the option to record at home. I can do it in the middle of the night or whenever I want to.

I'm not the most technical person but now I can do a bit of sound editing and learn how to export stuff in the right way. So I understand more now and hats off to the sound engineers. What they do is a lot more complex than what I do in the airing cupboard.

Needs must sometimes when we take on these things!
Oh, and actually, I was just thinking also, the wonderful thing about it is being able to record projects in different parts of the world. Last week I was recording a project for someone in the States who was doing a brilliant version of 'The Watcher in the Woods'. It enabled me to talk to him on Zoom, while recording this script. It's amazing what we can do now.

It's weird to think that the pandemic actually ushered us along in terms of technical understanding and adaptation by, perhaps, a decade, I've heard it said. I'd never even touched Zoom before then.
I wish I'd taken out some shares in it. I think the most important think about lockdown was family, actually. I'm lucky enough to have a good husband and two amazing boys. Well, they're young men now. They're my real passion in life.

I don't know whether it was the pandemic, but there's something about not being able to connect with people which made that even more important, to be in communication with friends and family. I made sure I was in communication with people who needed that. People I met through fandom actually, as well, who were on their own and struggling. I think Katy [Manning] did that too. She always does that. She's amazing.

Well, actually Aaron Lowe and I were talking about you in another interview. We spoke about the community Friends of Ace and how that was born from a need to reach out to people.
I think it was a complete no-brainer. What an amazing idea to make a difference to a community that might be struggling. Another person who was doing amazing things back then was Keith Barnfather of Reeltime Pictures. He put the shout out for *Doctor Who* fans who were doing amazing things during lockdown, like making films, learning things, making costumes or doing art work and he got them to film themselves and then he put it all together on a DVD. That was great. People needed some kind of purpose. That was something he needed that too, of course, but for others to be contributing, to be needed was really important.

It was a difficult time. These projects were wonderful.

Would I be able to ask about your early years? You grew up in London and went to Manchester University to study drama. What took you to Manchester?
Well, I had no idea about applying for places. My school, Blackheath High School, was very academic and all my friends were going to Oxford, Cambridge,

getting scholarships. And I thought, well, I'm thick … which really wasn't true! But you know we make these decisions about ourselves?

But more than that, I always wanted to do acting. So I applied to drama school. Now I'm a late August birthday, so at 17 I looked ridiculously young. I went to some auditions for drama school and they all looked at me and told me to go back and get some life experience. I was brought up in very sheltered, middle-class Blackheath, you know. It was brilliant they said that. So I decided to go to university.

My headmistress at school was teaching at Edinburgh and suggested I go there to do English. So I applied there, went up to Edinburgh and it was freezing cold. I stayed in a bed and breakfast, went to the interview. During the night, I was so cold that I had to get up and put all my clothes on and get back into bed. I thought the place was beautiful, but I couldn't be there shivering for four years.

But that's kind of ironic because my son is doing a PhD there now. So I went to Manchester for the interview. I got out at Piccadilly Station, got in a cab. It was drizzling and grey. We drove down Oxford Road to the drama department, which was a concrete block and I just thought 'Yes! This is where I want to be.' I just felt that it was right for me. We had a tour and I spoke to this lovely guy who ended up being my tutor called David Maher. David was American and he looked at my CV and saw I played tennis. As far as I can remember, we spent the whole interview talking about tennis. I got an offer.

But there was that thing that I saw happen with my eldest son when we took him to UEA. He just walked on ahead and I could see he was imagining himself there. He felt at home. I think you know where you're going to belong. It was fantastic for me to go there. I went to gritty, grimy Manchester. When I watched *Life on Mars* I thought 'Yes, that's it!'

I absolutely loved it. I was a bit homesick and lonely at first, but I made some really great friends. The first person I bumped into was this guy called Jed McGuire from Liverpool. I'd never met anyone for Liverpool before. He had Doc Martens up to his knees and he'd been working in Strangeways [Prison] during his gap year. He had little John Lennon glasses on and he asked if I was a Protestant or Catholic. I said I didn't know. Since I'd never been to Mass, he took me off to this Catholic Mass to experience that. For me everything was so new and unbelievable. It was brilliant.

Looking back now, everybody was 18. They were all characters. There was also Simon Hickson in my year who, of course, ended up being half of Trev and Simon. And there was Doon Mackichan, who does a lot with Steve Coogan and she's been in *Good Omens*. She was at my interview. She became a very good friend of mine and we just did production after production.

I also went out with Tim Booth, who was this lovely guy who I met in the cellar bar, dancing madly. I'd never danced like that before. We got together. He wanted to be a pop star and I wanted to be a children's TV presenter. Years later, I got to see him in James when *Sit Down* was number one and I went backstage and we said dreams come true.

You both did it!
Yes! In Manchester, apparently I walked in and I was quite shy, believe it or not. I walked into the drama department, but apparently what I did say was that I'm going to be an actress. And that was absolutely something I always knew that I was going to do.

You had a long time in theatre and then a transition into TV. *Doctor Who* was your first TV role.
It was my first taste of TV!

I remember reading your recollections in your book, *Ace! The Inside Story of the End of an Era*. Suddenly being around all the cameras and on set.
I never went in front of a camera until that first day of shooting 'Dragonfire'. I never even had a screen test. I went to the audition with Chris Clough, talked to him. Bearing in mind, I'm supposed to be playing a 16-year-old. I ended up talking to him about the state of children's theatre in Thatcher's Britain, which I wasn't too happy about, as you can imagine, with all the funding cuts. Then as I walked back to the trailer, I thought 'That wasn't a very 16-year-old conversation…'. I got a recall to talk to John Nathan-Turner and then two weeks later, I got the call. I got the part for three episodes. They were, of course, thinking that if Bonnie [Langford] was going to leave, would I be interested in being the new companion?!

Tough decision, eh?
Let's see, I could continue on Equity minimum, back row of the chorus in *Fiddler on the Roof*… or one of the most sought after iconic parts for a young actor on British TV!

I'm glad you made that choice.

When I heard you were coming back to *Doctor Who*, especially along with Tegan, I thought this was amazing. My next thought was: What's that got to be like for Sophie after thirty years to come back? You have a family, two sons. What was that like?
Well, the thing is, I never left really. Sylvester [McCoy] and I went straight into recording the audio stuff with Bill Baggs and BBV. We just wanted to do anything

because it was so fun. We did stuff with Colin [Baker] and Nicola [Bryant], we did conventions. We were keeping it all going, doing the books, all sorts. And then when Big Finish started up, we did that. So I've never *stopped* playing Ace.

But when I got the call from my agent to say Andy Pryor [*Doctor Who* Casting Director 2005 – present] had been in touch for my availability, well, we all knew what that meant. It was a shock. I was in the conservatory, my husband was reading the paper and there's this call. It was almost like a call I never knew I was longing for all those years. I ended the call and burst into tears. It was just amazing.

The boys are grown up and the thing with filming nowadays is it's all very quick. It didn't mean much of an upheaval at all, because I'm often away for conventions and other jobs. So it's the nomadic life of an actor anyway. It was slightly odd because it was still Covid time, of course.

[*Sophie tells me about filming during lockdown and the pandemic, and how it was actually stranger in many ways than being asked back on the show. The drivers they had would have plastic screens between the front seat and the passenger seats. If you ever went in a taxi during the pandemic, you'll remember this and in some cases it's a habit which has continued to this day. Sophie tells me about the Covid tests which would have to be conducted on the doorstep, prior to production and how there was one person doing the rounds among the actors, one of whom was Janet Fielding. I imagine a collection of Covid tests in a locked box from* Doctor Who *cast members, being driven furtively around the country.*

I did see Janet Fielding at the event which she did at the Walpole Bay Hotel, which was lovely.

Oh yes! The tea event. That looked lovely. It was funny, because although Janet and I know each other from conventions, we didn't really *know* each other. We had lots of time obviously to sit around and get to know each other. All of us share this incredible bond which mirrors that companion scene at the end of 'Power of the Doctor'. Nobody quite can get it what it's like, unless you've lived that experience of being a companion. And we all share that shorthand. We all know what it's like.

That's come up quite often in my research. It's encoded in all of you.

It's funny, because when I first joined, people would say 'welcome to the family'. It's absolutely true. Last year, we did a convention in Pensacola, Florida. There was me, Sylvester, Peter [Davidson] and Janet, Daphne Ashbrook, Paul McGann, Colin and Nicola. And we were all in the same beautiful hotel, which had just been opened. It was a redesigned, renovated church, beautifully decorated, with a restaurant. We just did everything together. It was just like a family holiday. It's just like that and it's so delightful.

Bumping into everybody: Katy, Bonnie, Nicola, Carole Ann Ford, Wendy Padbury. It's just always such a joy and we've always got loads to share.

I think that's wonderful and I've said elsewhere in the book that this seems to be quite unique to the show. I think it fosters something in the fanbase as well, that this happens in real life as well.

And I also think there's something very important that we can offer to the fans. Because so many people come to our tables at conventions and tell the secrets of their hearts to us. It's a real honour to be sitting there, listening to what people say. We all do it in different ways. Katy [Manning] hugs everybody and that's so healing for people. I'm a good hugger too. People feel listened to by us, I think. We have developed this strange skill of therapeutic listening in a way. Realising that when someone comes up to you and says they got really badly bullied at school and all they thought was 'What would Ace do?' To me, that's a privilege to listen to people's stories and to know you've made a difference.

You certainly did with me. You did that work and, I feel weird saying something that you've probably heard a million times, but you made an impact with me.

I never tire of hearing it. It's a rare gift that we've been given, which we didn't even realise at the time. It's also a responsibility in a good way. Not like a burden. It's a responsibility that I feel that I have to people who have loved the character for so long. And there's so many fans which I've known for thirty-five years. It's amazing to see them go through their lives as well.

Of course! Since you said you'd never really stopped playing Ace and have been doing conventions since even before the show first ended, you must have known some of us for a very long time.

I went to my first convention in 1987 not long after 'Dragonfire' and not many people knew who I was. I often bring that up at talks and ask who was there. I'll always get people putting their hands up. I think 'wow', that they will still come and listen to the old stories. It's that comfort and safety of the world of *Doctor Who*.

It's that triumph of good versus evil. Sylvester says there's only about five stories in the universe and one of those is that somebody comes from outside the Earth to save everyone. Many cultures have this, where an otherworldly figure comes to save humanity and the Doctor is one of them.

That folklore trope is something worth considering. *Doctor Who* as the saviour.
And I think in my era, Sylvester and Andrew Cartmel, the script editor, talked about that for a while. You get this idea that he was more than just a Time Lord. 'Who are you?' Is what I ask him at the end of 'Silver Nemesis', and the idea was that he was mystery, you didn't quite know. But there was Omega, Rassilon and him. They were thinking about the Holy Trinity, I think.

That would have been so good, so dark.
Andrew Cartmel been brought up in Canada and his background was graphic novels and comic books, Alan Moore. He was bringing a completely new genre to *Doctor Who*.

[*We speak for a moment about how, if the series had not been cancelled, it could have gone into a very deep, dark and multifaceted direction. Sophie points out that the show needs to do new things all the time because it brings in new fans*.]

I know that when Ncuti was announced, my son, who's a gay drag queen, came running down the stairs and told me he's going to watch *Doctor Who*. He told me loads of his friends who'd never seen the show were texting him and asking what *Doctor Who* actually was. So Ncuti is going to bring, not just a whole new generation, but a new fanbase. That can only be a good thing.

That's an amazing insight. I have no doubt that when a show expands the diversity, its excellent. When Ncuti was announced, my friends and I were so excited.
Already people have said to me, who don't really watch *Doctor Who*, that he shines, this charisma. I asked Jemma Redgrave if he was that beautiful in real life and she said that he was even more so! [Laughs]

So Ace is a gay icon and by default, so are you. A lot of the time in original *Doctor Who*, there was a subtext. We can be more open today, thankfully. The show's always been a bit queer, vastly liberal and forward thinking.
Absolutely. I love it for that. At the time, I didn't have a clue, but when I finally met Rona Monroe who wrote 'Survival' and there was that moment … I had no idea.

You mean you and Lisa Bowerman as Karra. That went over your head, initially?
Yeah! It wasn't in the common dialogue of the time. I would have been delighted, had I known. I absolutely adore the queer and LGBTQ community.

It's always been there. Absolutely the better for it. Andrew Cartmel got away with things during the later years, like 'The Happiness Patrol', with a political undercurrent, whether it was overt or not. But, you know, in 'Remembrance of the Daleks', we had racism. The 'Happiness Patrol' had a story there about Thatcherism. The miners' strike had just finished. There was a huge gap between rich and poor – the Poll Tax, all that. And we were quietly subverting that with quite a few of those stories.

And I think *Doctor Who* fans weren't going to complain, because if you love *Doctor Who*, you are by necessity, I think, an interesting person who is curious about how the world works. You have an interest in something other than right, wrong, good, bad. You have a good moral compass if you're a *Doctor Who* fan.

I think if you look, a lot of the stories have, at their core, love. I think the Doctor is invariably in love with the human race.

People characterise Ace as feisty, rebellious, beating up Daleks with a baseball bat. But she has a massive heart as well and she is totally for fairness. She had that moment in 'Remembrance of the Daleks' where she's at the boarding house, with her hair down, and had obviously fallen for Mike. Then he betrays her and she's furious, not for herself really, but because he's betrayed everything that she and the Doctor stand for. It's more like, 'How could you possibly be that person?' And then there's the sign hanging in the window which reads 'No Coloureds'. She wonders how anybody could be that way.

She's brave and courageous, but she's quite feminine too, a bit of everything. I think that's why she appeals to so many people.

[*It occurs to me that Sophie and I have been talking for over an hour. It also occurs to me that I could listen to her for at least another hour. I decide to ask one final question before we bid goodbye for now.*]

If there's one thing that you'd like the readers of this book to know about you, whether they're a new fan just coming to the show, or have enjoyed it since the beginning, what would it be?
Whoever you are, you are welcome.

33

Daphne Ashbrook (Daphne Lee Ashbrook)

Born	30 January 1963
Companion	Dr Grace Holloway
Appearance	*Doctor Who: The Movie*, also known as *Doctor Who: Enemy Within* (1996)

DAPHNE ASHBROOK was born in Long Beach, California, and grew up in San Diego. She was born into an acting family. Her father, the late Buddy Ashbrook, was a professor of drama at Palomar College, California, and her mother D'Ann Paton has herself acted and Daphne's brother is actor Dana Ashbrook, who played a regular character in all three seasons of *Twin Peaks*.

Of her childhood, Ashbrook has said that being the family business, as it were, it seemed natural that she would become an actress too. Her parents met while in the *Dark of the Moon* by William Berney and Howard Richardson, a controversial stage play which has on occasion been the subject of campaigns to ban its production in some theatres.[1]

Ashbrook's resume is extensive, varied and began at a young age. She had her first role in theatre when she was only 6 years old, playing a Native American in a play directed by her father. and went on to appear in Burlesque … *The Way You Like It* (1982) and *Coming of Stork* (1984).

Her theatre career was interrupted for good reason: she landed her first television role, that of Melinda in *Hardcastle and McCormick* in 1983, then appeared in *Knight Rider* a year later. What followed was a series of relatively small roles, before being cast as Liz McKay in *Our Family Honour*, where she appeared in every episode until its end in 1986.

In 1992, Ashbrook appeared in a very memorable role in 1992 as Lesley in the two-part miniseries *Intruders*, along with a suitably manic Steven Berkoff and the talented Mare Winningham. One of the first films of its kind about the haunting subject of alien abduction, the miniseries was known for its disturbing scenes of otherworldly home invasion and hypnotic regression.

Furthering her range of diverse and sometimes usual roles, Ashbrook appeared in the *Star Trek: Deep Space Nine* episode 'Melora' (1993). Her character, after whom the episode is named, is a member of species who is unable to withstand the gravity of the eponymous space station and so must spend her time there in a levitating support brace of sorts.

Written by Evan Carlos Somers, who is a quadriplegic, Melora's 'condition' can be read as an analogy for disability and it is a role which Ashbrook played with a respectful passion, researching for the role by using a wheelchair while she went to the shopping mall to experience first-hand, not of actually being disabled, but of how members of the public treated her.[2]

Daphne Ashbrook was cast as Doctor Grace Holloway, the first companion to the Doctor since the cancellation the show in 1989. Having no prior knowledge of the television series, Ashbrook was intrigued, and launched herself fully into the role.

Ashbrook's involvement with *Doctor Who* led to a number of 'firsts'. Unlike Nicola Bryant and John Barrowman who, despite his accent, is Scottish, Daphne Ashbrook was a genuine American and the only one to play a companion so far. She was also the first companion to kiss the Doctor, something which predictably caused controversy among fans of the show.

Ashbrook has since become a fan of *Doctor Who* and has fond memories of the production, immediately getting along with Paul McGann, whose eccentric Britishness made him seem even more alien in stark contrast to the American setting.

Although the character of Grace Holloway has not been able to return to the audio dramas, no companion can ever fully escape. As a result, Ashbrook has appeared in Big Finish Productions as Captain Ruth Matheson and has her own *Myth Makers* episode, as well as appearing in *The Doctors – The Paul McGann Years*, both by with Reeltime Pictures.

She has attended numerous conventions, including, most recently in 2024, at the ninth Bedford Who Charity Con, where she reunited with McGann.

Ashbrook has continued to act, proudly considering herself a character actor who enjoys playing people with flaws and unusual qualities. Interestingly, she thinks of her role as Grace Holloway to be 'one of the most normal characters' she had played.[3]

Ashbrook has a daughter, Paton Lee, who continues the family acting tradition, having appeared in several television series, with a recurring role in crime drama *Power Book II: Ghost* (2020–23).

34

Yee Jee Tso

Born	10 March 1975
Companion	Chang Lee
Appearance	*Doctor Who: The Movie*, also known as *Doctor Who: Enemy Within* (1996)

YEE JEE TSO was born in Hong Kong, but his family emigrated to Canada when he was just a baby.

Tso got into acting by, as he put it, sheer luck.[1] One of his earliest roles was in one of a series of short films entitled *Heritage Minutes* (1991), which depicted elected moments in Canadian history. The historical production design and location filming inspired Tso to become and actor and he would soon go on to appear in *Sliders* (1995) and the television series *Highlander* (1995), before being cast in a regular role in *Madison* (1994–95).

Having lived and worked in Vancouver for most of his acting career, Tso answer the open casting call for the *Doctor Who* movie. He went to audition for the part of Chang Lee and, having been invited back for several rounds of interviews as the producers whittled down the applicants, Tso was delighted to have made it to the final one. However, on his way to the audition, a combination of bad traffic and what he described as 'bad time management', led to his being over and hour late.

Being the final round of auditions, many of the high-level producers and executives were present, waiting for him. Understandably, Tso thought he had blown his chances, however with a view to a realistic portrayal of the character, this actually won him the role. Chang Lee was *supposed* to be reckless and errant. Tso got the job.

A long-time fan of the show, Tso describes his time filming the *Doctor Who* movie as some of the most fun he'd ever had.[2] During filming, Tso kept his Nikon camera close by and documented the production behind the scenes, particularly enamoured by some of the beautiful set design. At some point, the photographs were lost, however the negatives were recovered by his wife and, to make the 20th Anniversary of the movie, Tso released *Time and Spaces In 2016*, a full-colour photography book. Now extremely limited and rare, Tso produced an audio-visual version, which he narrated, including interviews with his co-stars.

In 2020, Tso appeared at BritCon Convention in Bellevue, Washington, described as a convention for fans and set up by fans. Though not a *Doctor Who*-specific convention, BritCon was set up to celebrate many different aspects of British cult television.

The complex production of the *Doctor Who* Movie meant that the rights to the character of Chang Lee could not be secured for Tso to reprise him in any audio dramas, but a *Doctor Who* actor never escapes quite so easily and Tso has voiced other characters in some Big Finish Productions, particularly Doctor Goddard in 'Real Time' (2002), Warrant Officer Sato in 'Tales from the Vault' (2011), 'Mastermind' (2013) and 'The Screaming Skull' (2014).

Tso has a remarkable number of acting credits to his name, including the television series *Smallville's Vengeance Chronicles* (2006), *The 100* (2020) and *Snowpiercer* (2020–21).

35

Billie Paul Piper (Leian Paul Piper)

Born	22 September 1982
Companion	Rose Tyler
First Appearance	'Rose' (26 March 2005)
Final Appearance	'The Day of the Doctor' (23 November 2013)

BILLIE PIPER was born in Swindon as Leian Piper, but her parents changed her name a year after. By all accounts, she was a born performer, 'creative from the start',[1] according to her mother.

Piper successfully auditioned for the Tanwood Agency in Swindon and got her job on an advert for an American cereal, then a Cooled advert. It was there she met actor John Pickard, who told her about drama classes, which she dedicated herself to for several years.

When Piper was 13, she joined the Sylvia Young Theatre School, which boasts such notable alumni as Denise van Outen, Alex Pettyfur and Rita Ora. It was here that Piper was first introduced to the diversity of the acting world, in terms of class, sexuality and ethnicity.

It was an infamous *Smash Hits* advert in 1997 which launched Piper's pop career. She became the face of the magazine's re-launch. Innocent Records' founder Hugh Goldsmith thought that Billie Piper was perfect for a solo career. She got a record deal at 15 years old and her debut single *Because We Want To* charted at number one. She was the youngest person (so far) to have a number one hit. To say it was an exciting time is something of an understatement; Billie toured with 5ive, Westlife, Atomic Kitten and Steps.

Piper was interviewed by to Radio DJ and television host Chris Evans, and she began partying and going out with him. According to Piper, they were 'inseparable'.[2] Chris Evans bought her a Ferrari more-or-less out of the blue and there were visits to clubs like Stringfellows and Brown's, as well as holidays and trips.

She and Chris Evans married and moved to Los Angeles. Piper attended acting classes at the Stella Adler Academy. Her first credited film role, except for being an extra in *Evita* (1996), was in *The Calcium Kid* (2004) starring Orlando Bloom. After a few more minor roles in films and television series, Billie Piper got word about the revival of *Doctor Who*.

One imagines that Piper drew on aspects of what had already been an adventurous, and sometimes unpredictable, career. The Doctor has always been someone who takes, accidentally or by design, a normal, everyday human being, and shows them the universe of excitement.

When *Doctor Who* returned to the screen in 2005, that character of Rose Tyler was just that: normal, everyday. Eating chips. She was the first companion to appear on *Doctor Who* since the Doctor Who movie in 1996, and the first regular companion to appear since Ace (Sophie Aldred) in 1989, so Billie Piper was to set the standard for the show's return.

At the audition, Piper impressed producers Russell T. Davies and Julie Gardner. Davies later described her as a 'phenomenon'.[3] The successful appeal of Billie Piper to a new generation of potential *Doctor Who* fans echoed the sudden success from *Smash Hits*. Piper's Rose Tyler was the perfect fit.

The perceptions of women on television and in real life had changed dramatically since the 1960s, '70s – and arguably the '80s, so the roles of women in *Doctor Who* had to change too. The characters of Sarah Jane Smith (Elisabeth Sladen), Tegan Jovanka (Janet Fielding), Ace (Sophie Aldred) and Grace Holloway (Daphne Ashbrook) had made their mark during their respective eras. Billie Piper was adamant that the character of Rose was not going to spend a lot of time screaming or being objectified.

The intense working hours was something which had not changed and during her time on *Doctor Who*, Piper and husband Chris Evans split up. However, Piper is very clear that *Doctor Who* was something that got her through this period.[4]

At the same time as working on *Doctor Who*, Piper starred as Belle in *Secret Diary of a Call Gir*l and, after she left the show, her career has followed an impressive trajectory, joining the cast of *Penny Dreadful* (2014–16) as a series regular, and most recently starring opposite Gillian Anderson in the controversial movie *Scoop* (2024), which told the story of the now infamous Emily Maitlis interview with Prince Andrew.

Her theatre work has been extensive and successful too. She played at the National Theatre in Lucy Pebble's *The Effect* in 2012, but had already debuted in 2007 in the West End, playing Ann in Christopher Hampton's *Treats*. It was during this play that she met Laurence Fox, whom she later married. They divorced in 2016, and have two children. In 2016, she began a relationship with Johnny Lloyd, of indie rock band Tribes, but they separated in 2023.

36

Camille Coduri

Born	18 April 1965
Companion	Jackie Tyler
First Appearance	'Rose' (26 March 2005)
Final Appearance	'The End of Time' (25 December 2009 – 1 January 2010)

CAMILLE CODURI was born in Wandsworth, London. She went to the Holy Trinity Primary School and then Upper Tooting High School. She had a burning desire to become an actor from quite an early age, her first role being at 14 years old in Upper Tooting's adaptation of Wilde's The *Importance of Being Earnest.*

She studied drama at Kingsway Princeton College, King's Cross, and in 1981 she joined the Lyric Youth Theatre, which is now in Hammersmith, but at the time was in the West End. She appeared in the first production they did called *Get Out of That Then*, by Lucy Park, now a teacher at the Young Vic.

Coduri was discovered by agent Mary Selway (14 March 1936 – 21 April 2004), who cast for films such as *Aliens* (1986), *Gorillas in the Mist* (1988) and *Vanity Fair* (2004). After acquiring her Equity Card, Coduri would go on to appear in television series *A Prayer for the Dying* (1987), *Rumpole of the Bailey* (1992) and *Boon* (1987–1991), as well as having roles in well-known films such as *Nuns on the Run* (1990) and *King Ralph* (1991).

Let's face it, Jackie Tyler –Rose's mother – is iconic. Camille Coduri brought a confident, no-bullshit vivaciousness to the character of Jackie Tyler. Coduri has two children with her husband actor Christopher Fulford, and her protectiveness towards Billie Piper's character is real, raw and honest, famously slapping the Doctor after he accidentally kept her away, presumed missing, for a year. Coduri said filming *Doctor Who* was one of the happiest times of her life.[1]

Coduri's presence on the show had a contemporary sincerity which made the events of the first episode of the show's return all the more unusual and threatening, as well as reminding the viewers the Rose had a normal family and a life back on Earth. Coduri wondered, even worried, about her character's popularity, rationalising Jackie's overbearing nature as being what a mother would do out of concern for her daughter and the initial mistrust of the Doctor, regardless of whether it annoyed viewers or not.[2]

Having worked with two different actors who played the Doctor, Christopher Ecclestone and David Tennant, Coduri notes that it was a privilege working with both of them, although they approached the role very differently.

Although Coduri made her final regular appearance in the episode 'Doomsday', she guest starred in the 2008 season finale, 'Journey's End' as well as 'The End of Time'. During filming for the latter, Coduri told Russell T. Davies that she was very emotional about it (RTD *The Writer's Tale.*)

Coduri continued to have links with *Doctor Who* after her final appearance, voicing Jackie Tyler in the Big Finish productions audio dramas and as the narrator for 'Ninth Doctor' audiobooks *The Monsters Inside* (2011), *The Stealers of Dreams* (2011), *Winner Takes All* (2011) and *Rose* (2018).

She has appeared in several television series, including *Ashes to Ashes* (2010) and *Midsomer Murders* (2010), before becoming a regular on *Him and Her* between 2010 and 2013, *King Gary* between 2018 and 2022, *Edge of Heaven* (2014) and as Peggy, Jack's mother, in *Big Boys* (2022).

37

Bruno Langley

Born	21 March 1983
Companion	Adam Mitchell
First Appearance	'Dalek' (30 April 2005)
Final Appearance	'The Long Game' (7 May 2005)

BRUNO LANGLEY was born in Devon, to Australian parents. He subsequently grew up in Derbyshire and attended Harpur Hill Primary School, then Buxton Community School. He is one of eight children, all with a love of music which seemed to run in the family. His father ran a business making ocarina, which is a type of very old, unusual wind instruments made of clay or ceramic.

With his sisters, he had been in junior string orchestras, having learned to play the cello, which he continued until he was 16. His sisters formed the Dirty Pretty Strings, supporting bands such as Muse and The Streets. Langley decided he wanted to become an actor, but continued with his passion for music, forming a band called Wonderland, while training at the North Cheshire Theatre School.

HIs first television role was as Philip Green in television series *Linda Green* from 2001 to 2002, but he is mainly known for playing Todd Grimshaw on *Coronation Street*, a regular main character, between 2000 and 2017.

It was while he was taking a short break from Coronation Street that Langley appeared in the first of the revived *Doctor Who* series to feature the Daleks, appearing in the next episode The Long Game. His character Adam Mitchell had a particularly brief run, owing to his betrayal of the Doctor and his subsequent expulsion from the TARDIS.

After *Doctor Who*, Langley appeared in theatre shows, making his debut on stage *in Romeo and Juliet*, then *Night Sky* at the Old Vic in 2006, coincidentally appearing with Christopher Ecclestone who had played the Ninth Doctor. He then appeared in *Flashdance the Musical*, performing in 2009 at the Cliffs Pavillion in Westcliff-on-Sea.

Bruno Langley is married and has one child and, in 2019, announced he was happy as a photographer and continues to produce music.

38

John Barrowman (John Scot Barrowman)

Born	11 March 1967
Companion	Captain Jack Harkness
First Appearance	'The Empty Child' (21 May 2005)
Final Appearance	'Revolution of the Daleks' (1 January 2021)

JOHN BARROWMAN was born in Glasgow, Scotland. In 1975, he and his family moved to Joliet, Illinois. His father has been working with Caterpillar and was sent to manage one of the factories. During school, he was bullied for his Scottish accent, so he deliberately affected an American accent – he continues to flip between the two to this day.[1]

He studied Musical Theatre at the US International University in San Diego, California. It was during a period of study about Shakespeare that he visited Britain, which was 'interrupted' by his first theatrical role as Billy Crocker in *Anything Goes*, at the Prince Edward Theatre, London. In 2023, he would later return to the show at its revival in Drury Lane.

While appearing in many theatre shows, in cladding *Miss Saigon*, *Matador* and *Phantom of the Opera*, Barrowman became one of the first presenters on BBC 1's new Saturday morning children's television show *Live and Kicking*.

Although Barrowman is perhaps best known for his theatrical stage work, his television and film roles have also been extensive. He appeared as Peter Fairchild in *Central Park West* between 1995 and 1996, Ben in television series *Titans* in 2000, as well as *Desperate Housewives* and *Legends of Tomorrow*.

Barrowman played Captain Jack Harkness in *Doctor Who*, beginning in 2005. Captain Jack would appear as a recurring character, but is also considered a companion to the Doctor. It was the first time that a character in *Doctor Who* had been quite so openly, unashamedly, queer, the character becoming so popular that Russell T Davies developed spin-off series *Torchwood*, which became extremely well-received and ran for four seasons.

Barrowman very much enjoyed playing the character. In fact, he's been nothing but enthusiastic about Captain Jack, once saying that he loved him and that playing him felt like 'slipping back into an old pair of shoes'.[2]

Continuing his enthusiasm for creativity and being a multi-talented artist, Barrowman and his sister Carole E. Barrowman, co-wrote *Hollow Earth*, a fantasy novel partially set in Scotland, which then led to a trilogy and a second series of books. In 2010, the pair also worked with Tommy Lee Edwards for a comic strip, *Captain Jack and the Selkie*. He has also released two memoirs: *Anything* Goes (2008) and *I Am What I Am* (2009), also co-written with his sister.

An openly gay man, Barrowman has been heavily involved in charity work and activism, working tirelessly to confront homophobia and to be open about the struggles remaining for LGBTQ people. He supported Stonewall's Education For All campaign and in 2008 took part in the BBC1 documentary *The Making of Me*, where psychologists and scientists undertook an attempt to explain human sexuality. He married his husband Scott Gill in California in 2013.

His selfless enthusiasm has been deservedly rewarded. For his LGBTQ charity work, he was awarded the Human Rights Campaign Visibility Award and in 2014, he was appointed Member of the Order of the British Empire for services to entertainment and charity. He was also given an Honorary degree from the Royal Conservatoire of Scotland.

At the time of writing, John Barrowman is just about to begin a tour of his show *Laid Bare*, billed as an all-round celebration of his love for music and theatre.

39

Noel Clarke (Noel Anthony Clarke)

Born	6 December 1975
Companion	Mickey Smith
First Appearance	'Rose' (26 March 2005)
Final Appearance	'Journey's End' (2008)

NOEL CLARKE was born in Notting Hill, London. His mother Gemma came to Britain in 1969 and worked as a paediatric nurse, and his father, Alphaeus Baptiste 'Alf' Clarke, is a carpenter. After his parents divorced, he was raised by his mother in Ladbroke Grove in a two-bedroom house on a council estate.

He studied media at the university of North London, but had ambitions to be an actor from an early age. He was asked to audition for *Metrosexuality* between 1999 and 2001, and subsequently began training at the Actor's Centre in London. Further roles included *The Bill* in 2000, *Judge John Deed* and *Waking the Dead*, both in 2001. He then went on to have a recurring role in the reboot of 1980s television series *Auf Wiedersehen, Pet* from 2001 to 2004.

Clarke joined the revived series of *Doctor Who* for its first season in 2005, playing the boyfriend of Rose Tyler. Initially a somewhat puerile and incompetent character, earning the nickname 'Mickey the idiot' from the Ninth Doctor, Clarke's character developed into a more confident person, choosing to remain in an alternate version of Earth to look after his grandmother.

Clarke is well-known for writing the hit 2006 British teen drama *Kidulthood*, in which he also starred. *Kidulthood* attracted attention for its raw, honest and often bleak portrayal of West London teens, garnering praise for showing the events from the perspective of youth, rather than taking a more judgemental approach. A cautionary tale involving drug use, violence and sex, Clarke based the film on his own experiences growing up in Ladbroke Grove. This led some to some critics, who were perhaps far-removed from the real-life setting, to express disbelief that such things actually happen.[1]

The success of Kidulthood led to Clarke being awarded a BAFTA in the *Rising Star* category and his being invited to write and star in its sequel *Adulthood.* Clarke's drive and ambition for the film was that it would encourage people, particularly young people, to reflect on the choices they make in their teens and, while not abnegating a person's autonomy and responsibility, that the choices for young people had become so limited that they had very little to do, particularly in deprived areas.[2]

Clarke continued to write and direct. His work includes *4.3.2.1* (2010), *Fast Girls* (2012) and *Brotherhood* (2016). He also wrote the episode Combat of *Doctor Who* spin-off show *Torchwood.*

In 2018, Clarke co-created, wrote and starred in the Sky One television series *Bulletproof*, which aired for four season between 2018 and 2021.

40

Catherine Tate (Catherine Jane Ford)

Born	5 December 1969
Companion	Donna Noble
First Appearance	'Doomsday' (8 July 2006)
Final Regular Appearance	'Journey's End' (5 July 2008)

CATHERINE TATE was born in Bloomsbury, London, and grew up at the Brunswick Centre, a modernist-style residential and retail centre constructed between 1967 and 1972. Josephine, Tate's mother, was a florist, who, having left her father early on, raised Tate along with her grandmother and godparents.

Tate described herself as shy growing up, using her sense of humour and offbeat personality and dress sense as something of a decoy from scrutiny by her peers.[1]

She initially enrolled at the Sylvia Young Theatre School, but left after a week, eventually applying multiple times to the Central School of Speech and Drama before being accepted. She went on to work at the National Theatre, but had her mind was set on doing comedy. After a successful run at the Edinburgh Festival, as well as some early minor television appearances including *The Bill*, *Men Behaving Badly* and *Surgical Spirit*, pursued stand-up comedy.

Tate describes stand-up comedy as her way of retaining control of her career, not having had much in the way of classical training. She did not initially have much faith in *The Catherine Tate Show*, but when she was approached to put it on television, it became instantly popular.

She thought the character of 'nan' would be being familiar to people, that audiences may either know somebody like her or even be someone like her. Some of the characters' catchphrases have become incredibly well-known, particularly Lauren the schoolgirl. Arguably, we have all either known a Lauren or encountered one.

Tate originally appeared at the end of 'Doomsday', surprising the Doctor directly after the traumatic events of the episode, with the follow-up being the 2006 Christmas Special, 'The Runaway Bride', for which Donna Noble was originally intended to appear as a one-off. However, when Freema Agyeman announced she would be leaving, Tate was asked to return on a more regular basis.

When Tate was announced as the new companion to the Doctor, the reaction was quite mixed, with some articles worrying that casting a well-known comedian in such a prominent role would be a mistake.[2]

Other negative responses were more volatile, perhaps spurred on by the distinct contrast between the character of Rose, who had fallen in love with the Doctor, and Donna Noble who was initially much more abrasive. Catherine Tate was very well-known in the UK at the time. The initially frosty reception to her announcement can be seen as an inverted version of the typecasting which had been so common to actors who had left the show in the past. Only this time, many people were critical of her *joining* the show because of her prominence as a comedian.

Contrary to many of the predictions, Tate's character became extremely popular, her sincerity and unpretentiousness echoing past companions such as Tegan and Ace. Tate would return to the show for the 2023 60th Anniversary Specials.

Tate has made numerous television appearances, notable American series of *The Office*. Working in LA during filming, Tate didn't enjoy the city when she first arrived, describing it as an initially difficult place.[3]

Tate appeared as Miss Sarah Postern in *Big School* (2013–14), *Drunk History: UK* and *Hard Cell* (2022). Tate has voice several characters too, including Lisa in *The Archers*, Magic de Spell in *DuckTales* (2017–22) and has reprised her role in *Doctor Who* audio dramas for BBC New Series Adventures and Big Finish Productions.

Having reigned successfully on television for decades and won many awards for *The Catherine Tate Show*, Tate has also been extensively involved in the theatre. She starred alongside David Tennant in *Much Ado About Nothing* at the Wyndham's Theatre in 2011 and *A Servant To Two Masters* for the Royal Shakespeare Company. She starred as Peggy in *The Enfield Haunting* theatre production, which played at the Ambassadors Theatre, London in 2024.

41

Jemma Redgrave (Jemima Rebecca Redgrave)

Born	14 January 1965
Companion	Dr Katherine Lethbridge-Stewart, known as Kate Stewart
First Appearance	'The Power of Three' (22 September 2012)
Latest Regular Appearance	'Empire of Death' (21 June 2024)

JEMMA REDGRAVE was born in London into a family with a long and rich history of stage and television. Her father was Corin Redgrave (16 July 1939 – 6 April 2010) and her mother was his first wife, Deirdre Hamilton-Hill. Jemma Redgrave is the granddaughter of Sir Michael Redgrave and Rachel Kempson, Vanessa and Lynn Redgrave's niece, and the cousin of Joey Richardson and the late Natasha Richardson.

Redgrave has three brothers, Luke, Harvey and Arden Redgrave, who are a cameraman, a civil servant and a primary school teacher respectively.

The Redgrave Family[1] has been in the acting industry for at least five generations, beginning with George Ellsworthy 'Roy' Redgrave (26 April 1873 – 25 May 1922) who was a silent film star. Among member of this extraordinary family are actresses Lynn Rachel Redgrave (8 March 1943 – 2 May 2010) and Dame Vanessa Redgrave, and Liam Neeson by his marriage to Natasha Richardson. In 2012, the Redgrave Family was honoured by the American Theatre Wing at a special gala held at their annual venue of the Plaza Hotel, New York.

Corin Redgrave, her father, was heavily involved in far-left politics, notably with well-known membership of the Workers' Revolutionary Party and, later, the Marxist party. Of her formative years, Redgrave was not initially aware that her family was any different, however at primary school her teacher would accidentally call her Vanessa.

Jemma Redgrave attended all-girls independent secondary school Godolphin and Latymer in Hammersmith, and then went to London Academy of Music and Dramatic Art (LAMDA) in 1983, when she was 18.

Redgrave went onto play some high-profile roles in theatre, including Lady Teazle in *The School for Scandal* in 1988, at Bristol Old Vic and also appeared playing Irena, alongside Vanessa and Lynn Redgrave in Anton Chekhov's *The Three Sisters* in the West End.

In 2010, Redgrave appeared in *The Great Game: Afghanistan* by Nicolas Kent and Indhu Rubasingham, an unusual production consisting of twelve smaller plays, for a total running time of seven hours every night. Redgrave played five different roles.

Redgrave has appeared in so many television series that it would be utterly beyond the scope of her entry here to attempt to cover even half of them. However, one of her most famous roles was staring as the titular character in *Bramwell* (1995–1998). From 2016 to 2018, Redgrave appeared as Major Bernice Wolfe in *Holby City*.

Jemma Redgrave joined the cast of *Doctor Who* as recurring character Katherine Lethbridge-Stewart, daughter of Brigadier Lethbridge Stewart. Interestingly, the first time the character of Kate had appeared was in 'Downtime' (1996, Reeltime Pictures), played by Beverly Cressman. In 2019, Reeltime Pictures announced that Cressman would also star in a sequel to 'Downtime'. This has not yet been produced, although she did reappear in 'Dæmos Rising' (2004)

Redgrave has appeared as Kate Stewart opposite Matt Smith, Peter Capaldi and Jodie Whittaker, and was also present for the 60th Anniversary Special 'The Giggle'. She returned opposite Ncuti Gatwa's Fifteenth Doctor in 2024.

Redgrave has spoken of the reception from fans to her character, particularly to continuing the Brigadier's legacy, as being very kind.[2] In fact, Redgrave has proven so popular that she has had to fend off many rumours in the media involving a potential spin-off, however there is no news as of yet.

Technically still part of the television series, Redgrave has played Kate Stewart in no fewer than forty-eight episodes of Big Finish Productions' *UNIT – The New Series*.

42

Freema Agyeman (Frema Agyeman)

Born	20 March 1979
Companion	Martha Jones
First Appearance	'Smith and Jones' (31 March 2007)
Final Appearance	'The End of Time' (1 January 2010)

FREEMA AGYEMAN was born in Hackney, London. Her mother Aazar is Iranian-Kurdish, and her father Osei is Ghanaian. They both divorced when Agyeman was young. She has an older sister named Leila and a younger brother, Dominic.

She grew up on Woodberry Down Estate, a practicing Roman Catholic and went to Our Lady's Convent High School, Stamford Hill. Agyeman then went on to the Anna Scher Theatre School and graduated from Middlesex University in 2000, having studied performing arts and drama.

Early on, she changed her first name to make it easier to pronounce. Her first early roles were in *Casualty* in 2004, *Silent Witness* in 2005 and three episodes of *The Bill* from 2004–06, however she appeared regularly in *Crossroads* as Lola Wise in 2003.

Like some of her predecessors, Agyeman first appeared in a one-off role in *Doctor Who*. in the 2006 episode 'Army of Ghosts' as a different character, Adeola Oshodi, who died in the Battle of Canary Wharf. The producers were so impacted by her performance that she was invited to audition for what she thought was a part in *Doctor Who* spin-off series *Torchwood*, however it soon became apparent that it was actually for the role of the new companion.

Agyeman succeeded Billy Piper, and initially she found the size of the role and the importance of the show overwhelming.[1] However, her performance as Martha Jones was complimented in the media and she was popular with fans, going on to be named Best Newcomer at *Glamour*'s Women of the Year Awards 2007.

It is often mentioned that *Dr Who* made Agyeman famous overnight, though she had appeared on television before. Agyeman was the first black companion to regularly travel with the Doctor and, sadly, a prominent reaction from some sectors of the audience was racist abuse.

She spoke in an Ofcom interview during national inclusion week in 2021[2] and she said that although she had a wonderful time on *Doctor Who*, and does agree that she was moved from obscurity to distinction thanks to the show, she did not anticipate the racist responses. With admirable objectivity, she notes that there were criticisms regarding her portrayal of Martha Jones, which are to be expected and even welcomed, but that she 'could not rationalise' the racist sentiments.

Agyeman returned to play Martha Jones in three episodes of spin-off show *Torchwood* in 2008. She praised the character development, noting that Martha had toughened up and matured. While filming, Agyeman was also positive about the writing and script, as well as the pleasant atmosphere of her co-stars, in particular the warm and jovial friendship she shared with John Barrowman, who she revered for his acting experience.[3]

Her rise to prominence can easily be charted through the series of successful and numerous roles she played both during and after her time on *Doctor Who*. She appeared opposite Arthur Darvill in *Little Dorrit* in 2008, playing the character *Tattycoram*; she appeared regularly as Junior Crown Prosecutor Alesha Phillips in *Law & Order: UK* between 2009 and 2011; as well as television series *Old Jack's Boat* and *The Carrie Diaries*.

Diversity and representation is important to Agyeman. She appeared in J. Michael Straczynski's and the Wachowskis' science fiction television series *Sense8* (2015–18), playing Amanita 'Neets' Caplan. According to Agyeman, it has been one of her most important roles to date, highlighting the positive reception to her character's relationship with a trans woman.[4]

In such a short space of time. Agyeman has played a wide variety of roles, though she had said that she'd not yet 'played a role that's true to my upbringing'.[5] In 2023, she appeared as Trish, in the television series *Dreamland*, co-starring with Lily Allen and Frances Barber.

Set in contemporary Margate, the series is based on the creator Sharon Horgan's 2017 Sky Arts short film *Morgana Robinson's Summer*. Agyeman had been living and working in America for so long that she welcomed a role in a more familiar setting and, in fact, very close to her own background and class.[6]

Theatre came later for Freema Agyeman, but her roles have been just as diverse. The stage productions she's appeared in include *God of Carnage* by Yasmina Reza at the Lyric Theatre in Hammersmith, as well as Alexi Kate Campbell's *Apologia* in 2017, directed by Jamie Lloyd. In 2024, Agyeman then appeared in Jamie Lloyd's production of *Romeo and Juliet*, alongside Tom Holland in London's West End.

43

Bernard Cribbins (Bernard Joseph Cribbins)

Companion	Wilfred Mott
Born	29 December 1928
Died	27 July 2022
First Appearance	'Voyage of the Damned' (25 December 2007)
Final Regular Appearance	'Wild Blue Yonder' (2 December 2023)

BERNARD CRIBBINS was born in Oldham. Lancashire. His mother Ethel (1898–1989) was a weaver in a cotton mill; Cribbins was once told that his grandmother had made an investment of sorts by paying half a crown a week to have her trained in the job. Cribbins' father, John Edward Cribbins (1896–1964), was known as 'Jack' who had served in the Royal Army Medical Corps in the First World War but could, according to his son, turn his hand to most things. Cribbins also had a sister named Veronica.

Cribbins' early experience of performing came during the Second World War with a national fundraising campaign called Warships Week in 1942; he volunteered to perform and discovered that he very much enjoyed acting.

Cribbins' had already left school at the age of 13, which was not usual at the time. Having started work as an assistant stage manager, he discovered a passion for acting and performed at Oldham Repertory Theatre, his debut being a play called *Lavender Ladies*.

He had been performing at Oldham Rep until the age of 18, when he was called up for National Service, something which he approached with a sense of adventure and enthusiasm. He returned to Oldham after demobilisation and started again as the assistant stage manager, where he met Gillian McBarnet, whom he married in 1955.

Cribbins' first West End role was in *A Comedy of Errors* in 1956 and appeared in numerous others, including *Not Now Darling* and *Run For Your Wife*. Though he had some smaller roles in the 1950s, the 1960s were very busy for Cribbins. On television, he appeared in *The Best of Enemies* (1961), *Drama 61-67* (1963–14) and *The Troublemakers* (1965).

In 1966, Cribbins was cast in what would turn out to be a prophetic role, playing Tom Campbell in 'Daleks' Invasion Earth 2150 AD', the sequel to 'Dr Who and the Daleks' (1965). He co-starred with Roberta Tovey as Susan and Jill Curzon as Louise. Peter Cushing played the Doctor (who, in these films was also called 'Doctor Who'). The three companion characters were analogous to their television counterparts Susan, Ian and Barbara respectively, but the two Dalek films exist outside of the *Doctor Who* television series.

Bernard Cribbins has been in so many television series and films that it is beyond the scope of this book to list them all. Dedicated to children's television, he had been a storyteller on *Jackanory* between 1966 and 1995. He had become an extremely well-respected actor, even releasing three light-hearted singles through Parlophone, the most famous of which is likely *Right Said Fred* (1962). From 1973 to 1975, he narrated children's television series *The Wombles* and in 1975, he appeared in an unforgettable guest role in the *Fawlty Towers* episode 'The Hotel Inspectors'.

Bernard Cribbins' previous history with *Doctor Who* had not only been to do with the non-canonical movies. In 1974, he auditioned to play the Fourth Doctor. In his autobiography, Cribbins' describes how when Barry Letts asked him what he could bring to the role, he replied that he could fight, which didn't go down very well.[1]

Cribbins would not become the Fourth Doctor, but he did appear in the BBC audio drama 'The Horror of Glam Rock' in 2006. He would then, most famously in the *Doctor Who* universe, be cast as the grandfather of companion Donna Noble, becoming a recurring character and companion to the Doctor.

Cribbins embodied the character of Wilfred Mott memorably, supporting the character of Donna on-screen and developing a joyful and entertaining relationship with Catherine Tate and David Tennant, the latter of which he fond to be one of the most professional actors he had ever worked with.[2] Cribbins spoke in glowing terms of both the cast and the production of the show, citing them as one of the best production units in all his years of acting.[3]

Fans cherished Cribbins in the role, whether brandishing a paintball gun at a Dalek, ensuring its vision was (briefly) impaired, or courteously volunteering to sacrifice himself to save the Doctor.

Bernard Cribbins was rightfully and thoroughly rewarded for his dedication and service. He was awarded the General Service Medal for his service in Palestine during 1948 and in 2009 he was given a Special Award for his services to children's television. In 2011 he was made Officer of the Order of the British Empire for his services to drama, which was parented to him by Princess Anne.

Bernard Cribbins died on 27 July 2022. He was 93.

The tributes which followed his death were as sincere and heartfelt as the man himself. On social media, Elaine Page called him funny, kind and genuine. Catherine Tate said he had left a hole in the world. Russell T Davies and John Simm both individually said Cribbins was a legend. All of those things are, in this author's opinion, most certainly true.

Interlude 7: Interview – John Ainsworth

IF REELTIME Pictures have made their mark with visual media, Big Finish Productions are at the forefront of the audio universe. It is a multi-award-winning company, with hundreds of *Doctor Who* audio dramas, and an extensive catalogue of other cult science-fiction audios, including *Blake's 7*, *The Omega Factor*, *Sapphire and Steel* and *Dark Shadows*.

I first met senior producer John Ainsworth in 2023 at the Tea With Tegan event at the Walpole Bay Hotel, Margate. Of course, I didn't know who he was then. I was sitting at a table, enjoying a splendid afternoon of scones and wine, while Janet Fielding was raising money for a local cause. By this time. I had accumulated a stack of *Doctor Who* books from the stall and was munching on what must have been my fourth cream cake of the afternoon, when we struck up a conversation about another love of mine, the unique television show *Sapphire and Steel*, which ran from 1979 until 1982.

I have been lucky enough to get to know John over the past year and so, when it came to writing this book, I knew I wanted his input, not just from his perspective as a producer, but as a knowledgeable and passionate fan of science fiction.

Thank you for joining me today, John. Big Finish Productions – could you tell me how Big Finish started and what the company does?
Well, the origin was a little fan organisation in the 1980s called Audio Visual which was set up by Bill Baggs. And when the original *Doctor Who* was airing, it was very common for fans to express their enthusiasm for the show by doing fanzines. But Bill decided rather than fanzines, we could do actual drama. And a comparatively cheap way of doing this was audio or radio drama. I got involved fairly early on along with Gary Russell and Nicholas Briggs.

Over a period of years we did about eighteen productions and by the end of it they got quite sophisticated and professional in terms of acting and technical production. We thought it would be brilliant if we could do actual *Doctor Who* dramas, but we never thought it would actually happen. But years later, Jason Haigh-Ellery was able to set up a company, Big Finish, with the idea of doing the audio dramas. The first ones were with Bernice Summerfield, the companion in the *New Adventures* novels and these were adaptations of those.

Those audio productions effectively became the proof that we could do it, which led to getting the license from the BBC with help of Steve Cole, the then editor of the *Doctor Who* novels for the BBC. So he had a relationship with them and he was instrumental in getting the license. In 1999, the first Big Finish *Doctor Who* audio was released and they've carried on since then.

That's so fitting that it germinated from fan enthusiasm. This is one of the things which kept it going through the so-called wilderness years.
Yes, Big Finish came in at the end of the wilderness years, but we were providing new *Doctor Who* at a time when it wasn't on television.

And what's your role in Big Finish?
I'm senior producer, so I look after the day-to-day production, overseeing the production of the different releases. Each release has its individual producer and I have oversight, helping solve any problems, keeping it on track and helping to make sure the productions reach their milestones. The production process of an audio isn't much less than a year long – quite a long process from script to finish and to release. Because of the length, you have to make sure things are on schedule. So that's basically the job and everything that goes with it, really.

It's busy! I've been involved in lots of ways. My first was looking after the website. I wasn't actually around at the very beginnings except for being involved with Audio Visuals. I took over the website. This was the earliest version, quite primitive. But later on, I directed and scripted. I've seen it from all sorts of angles.

So you started when there wasn't *Doctor Who* and then suddenly it's back. The changes which have happened have been extraordinary. I wondered if you had any thoughts about how these changes have been reflected in the companions?
I suppose it's not *always* been the case, but when it's at its best, *Doctor Who* reflects the era and the audience. The companion was always meant to be the one the audience can identify with, but I think there have been instances where that's not been the case. Or when it's been difficult. Such as Leela, who might be harder to identify with. She's great and Louise [Jameson] did a brilliant job of playing her, but the character didn't fulfil that aspect of the role. And then you had Romana who's another Time Lord, and Adric who's not human. I think Tegan was the one who became more identifiable.

But yes, certainly when Russell T. Davies brought it back, Rose was very much of her time and reacting to the same things that you would expect someone from 2005 to react to. And now we have the newer companions, Ruby and Rose.

So I think that's a way of anchoring *Doctor Who* and you do need someone to express a human perspective – and to represent the world at the time.

With change comes criticisms, of course. When people make criticisms of the show, in terms of its diversity for example, it seems to me that it's an inaccurate characterisation of the show, because it's still going strong – *stronger*, even.
The fact it even provokes people to express their views – even if they're objectionable – it's obviously pressing some buttons and that's a good thing.

So how did you first encounter the show?
I couldn't tell you when I first watched it. I was so young. I was born in 1965, and my earliest memories of *Doctor Who* are of Patrick Troughton when I was about 2 years old. My parents watched it and I must have been in my pushchair or on the sofa. I can't imagine it not being there. I literally grew up with it, latched onto it and loved it.

I remember when it transitioned from Troughton to Pertwee. There was a massive change in style. It became very adult, not as comic and light hearted as some of the Troughton era, but I still remember knowing what it was. It was still *Doctor Who* – and I think, how did a 5-year-old know that? But I was gripped, frightened and at no point did I question whether it was *Doctor Who*

It speaks to what's encoded in the show somehow?
Yes! Like when it came back, the whole thing happened again. Russell knew what the elements of it were, how to devise it for modern audiences, because he knew what attracted people to it.

I've been to some of the conventions, many of the Fantom events in London. They're accessible, smaller and very generous with the amount of actors they have. One of the things i've noticed is that the companion actors are also generous with their time, both at conventions and with me personally. I don't recall many shows where that's a thing. Seems quite unique.
Yes I think the whole relationship the actors who played the companions have with the show is interesting. And this is just my observation. It's not uncommon that when the actors leave the show, they initially want to distance themselves from it a bit. Then gradually come back and embrace it and then become really quite part of the family.

In my mind, Sophie Aldred, for example, has always embraced it right from the end of her tenure. And she's always very generous, understanding and very welcoming. But some of the earlier actors, well, typecasting was a thing. I think the happened with Carol Anne Ford, because she became typecast and it stopped her getting roles after. But she has told me just how much she loves it now. She does so many conventions internationally.

So there's a journey quite a lot of them go on. And we have to remember actors are doing their job for the audience and in TV you don't often have an immediate contact with your audience. What's interesting is that some actors have done a huge variety of work but *Doctor Who* is a small part of their career. Yet it's what they became known for and perhaps it leaves them wishing they got as much recognition for other roles in their career.

That evolution you mention, that journey, is very interesting because it's been quite difficult getting interviews with some of the more recent companion actors.
I think all the modern ones, as they have ongoing careers, want to be talking about what they're doing now. I don't think it would harm their career, but I think these days what comes with it is a huge amount of publicity and PR. By the end of it, you've said a lot of the same things and need a break.

That's an interesting observation. It actually tells me volumes about what it must be like to be part of it as an actor. There's always something to understand, even from someone's absence.

I'd like to talk about fandom and how integral it is to *Doctor Who*. It's a vast component of the phenomenon which is *Doctor Who*. What are your thoughts about it?
I think the producers of the show have always listened to the fans, but they do see a difference between a general audience and 'the Fans'. They don't want to alienate the audience. When Russell brought it back, there were no real callbacks to the original series, but after its launch and success, I think they relaxed a bit. I mean, they brought back Sarah-Jane Smith and over the past twenty years its done that more and more. The two eras have meshed, whereas before they were separate entities. Those lines have been blurred and it's great. They've done it without alienating a more casual audience.

It's a fine line to tread. I think they've done it well.
I mean even the episode with Sarah, *School Reunion* … even if you'd never seen Sarah before, you knew who she was. You could also identify with Rose wondering who she was and how the Doctor knew her before. I think producers are conscious of the fact that people who had never watched the show before still needed to understand it and get what was going on.

It's like in soap operas, you have the backstory which is sometimes never seen, but always referred to. It's the grounding. For a time, the original series of *Doctor Who* became the backstory of the new. And you can draw in elements from it, and as long as it's in context, it works.

So, predictable question. What companions resonated with you the most?
Well, I think it's the ones I grew up with, really. Jo Grant was on a poster on my wall. I was always very concerned about her being in danger. And Sarah, who I thought was brilliant. I had the pleasure of working with her in the Sarah-Jane audios.

I interviewed Matt Smith once when he was doing 'Death of the Doctor' and he said that he could tell they'd been companions. He hadn't watched their episodes. He could tell, as actors, that they'd been with the show before. He said the way they reacted to him and made the scenes work.

There's that 'encoding' again, not just in the show, but the actors who've been in it, even if it was a long time ago.

So, science fiction, generally speaking, you're a big fan?
Certainly in terms of film and TV.

In trying to define sci-fi, I referred to Asimov's definition earlier. He said it was about the human reaction to a sudden change in technology or science, or their understanding thereof. Which is probably why I like fiction which shows a destabilisation of established rules. What do you think?
I more or less agree with the definition. I think the key thing is the *human reaction.* Science fiction is about observing humans reacting a realistic way to situations which are currently impossible. If you think back to 'The Three Doctors' where Dr Tyler has been transported through a black hole and he's standing there, trying to work out what's happening. That's science fiction. He's in this impossible situation and he's reacting in a human way.

As for the destabilisation, seeing the change happening – that's the most exciting moment, in a way. I think of *Battlestar Galactica*, where the Cylons initially attack the colonies. For me, that's the most exciting part, the opening.

And I do quite like zombie movies and series. One of the most popular is *The Walking Dead*, but that all takes places afterwards. Then they did the spin off series *Fear the Walking Dead*, where you actually see it happening, seeing the neighbours turn into zombies. And I think this is what I like, the change. Particularly a societal change and it's such a huge one to watch and we begin thinking what would we do. If you've ever seen the original *Survivors* [created by Terry Nation, broadcast originally in 1975] that was the same too.

The classic science fiction thing is 'What if this happens? How will people react?'

That's science fiction.

44

Karen Gillan (Karen Sheila Gillan)

Born	28 November 1987
Companion	Amy Pond
First Appearance	'The Eleventh Hour' (3 April 2010)
Final Appearance	'The Angels Take Manhattan' (29 September 2012)

KAREN GILLAN was born in Inverness to Marie and Raymond John Gillan. Her father is a day care officer, and regularly plays blues and Jazz music on the pub scene in Inverness. Gillan grew up in Scotland, an only child, and spent a lot of her younger years in vintage shops where she discovered a love of Elvis Presley and Nina Simone. In 2013, having grown up listening to her father singing and playing, Karen Gillan encouraged her father to record and release his first album, *Deep Down Inside*.

It was a combination of old music and her father's creative output which initially made Gillan consider a career as a musician herself. She took piano lessons, and later, she would make amateur horror movies with her parents and peers.

Eventually, she developed a passion for acting and by the age of 16 had ambitions to pursue this as a career. Gillan attended Inverness High School and then studied acting and performance at Telford College, Edinburgh, before going on to a place at Italia Conti Academy of Theatre Arts, London. Initially, she supported herself by working in a bar, but was scouted by a modelling agency and would go onto the catwalk at London Fashion Week in 2007.

Gillan did not complete her training at Italia Conti, choosing to take a risk and accept her first role in television series *Rebus*, playing Teri Cotter in 2006. She made appearances on *Harley Street* and *Coming Up* in 2008 and then had a regular role on comedy series *The Kevin Bishop Show*, playing several different characters, between 2008 and 2009.

Karen Gillan (Karen Sheila Gillan)

Karen Gillian first appeared in the *Doctor Who* story 'The Fires of Pompei' in 2008, playing Mira the soothsayer, before landing the role as new companion Amy Pond in 2010.

Gillan described her role on the show as her acting training.[1] She speaks of her time on the show as a period of time where she undertook a steep learning curve, having admitted to knowing comparatively little about the industry before. She credits this, in part, to acting opposite Matt Smith's Doctor, highlighting the transactional relationship between actors and Smith's inventiveness during the role, eliciting a genuine reaction from her during filming.[2]

Gillian's cousin, Caitlin Blackwood, played a young version of Amy Pond in six episodes of *Doctor Who*. Gillan had not met her younger cousin before, Blackwood having grown up in Northern Ireland.

Although Gillian's character Amy Pond left along with Rory, played by Arthur Darvill, she returned in the 2013 Christmas Special 'The Time of the Doctor'.

Since her time on *Doctor Who*, Gillian's career has gone from strength to strength. In 2013, she appeared in *Oculus*, for which she moved to the United States. Later that year, she appeared in one of the plays which were part of *The 24 Hour Plays* on Broadway, which comprised twenty-four actors, six directors and six writers. The series of shows was arranged to benefit the Urban Arts Partnership, a charity which works to promote and advance school students' participation in the arts.

Gillan had shaved her head while appear as the villainous Nebula in *Guardians of the Galaxy* (2014) and so, for the pilot of *Selfie*, for which she was the lead star, in 2014, and throughout filming for the show, she wore a wig.

After several roles in the United States, 2016 saw Gillan write, direct and star in a film, in conjunction with Mt. Hollywood Films, called *The Prey's Just Beginning*. It's working title was *The Tupperware Party*. The film was something of a return to her roots, as it is set in Gillan's home town of Inverness and harks back to her days of making films with a video camera. and explores themes of male suicide.

Of the film's plot, Gillan explained in an interview that although the Scottish Highlands has a reputation of being extremely beautiful and is often voted as one of the nicest places to live in the United Kingdom, there is a side to the town, as with any place, which remains hidden to those who did not grow up there.[3]

Her film was released in 2018 and was nominated for Best Feature Film at the British Academy Scotland Awards. Afterwards, Gillan pledged public support for Mikeysline, the Inverness-based mental health charity, which was set up in response to the suicide rate in Inverness, particularly of two friends, Martin Shaw and Michael Williamson. The charity operates a text-based chat, as well as web chat and a phone line.

In 2024, Karen Gillan participated in Cinema4Gaza, an initiative organised in support of, and speaking up for, the people of Palestine. The group organised silent auctions to raise money, to which Gillan and her former co-star Arthur Darryl donated a one-to-one Zoom chat, plus signed scripts, as a prize.

She has gone on to continue her career, starring in Dual (2022), appearing in *The Call of the Wild* (2020) and has reprised her role as Nebula in further *Guardians of the Galaxy* films. She has also provided her voice for *Doctor Who* BBC Interactive games, appearing once again as Amy Pond.

45

Arthur Darvill (Thomas Arthur Darvill)

Born	17 June 1982
Companion	Rory Williams
First Appearance	'The Eleventh Hour' (3 April 2010)
Final Appearance	'The Angels Take Manhattan' (29 September 2012)

ARTHUR DARVILL was born in Birmingham and between 1993 until 2000 went to Bromsgrove School in Worcestershire. He was born into a creative family.

His mother Ellie Darvill is a well-known actress who has herself recently played characters in Big Finish audio dramas, which is only a small segment of her voice acting career, having numerous credits to her name.[1] During her son's early years, she was a member of the Cannon Hill Theatre, part of the Midlands Art Centre. She toured with the theatre worldwide and was also the voice of the Why Bird in the children's BBC show *PlayDays*.

His father Nigel is a Hammond Organ player whose credit include playing for Ruby Turner, Ska City Rockers and the Fine Young Cannibals. Darvill grew up around music and musicians, so naturally learned music very early and it seemed only normal to him that he would become a performer of some kind.

Not being particularly enthralled by academic subjects, Darvill went to Stage 2 Youth Theatre which is Birmingham's longest running youth theatre. Darvill trained at RADA, where one of his peers was Phoebe Waller-Bridge. His first ambition while training was to be on stage, however he did have a few small television roles. His television roles prophetically saw him appearing as Edward 'Tip' Dorrit in *Little Dorritt* (2008) alongside Freema Agyeman, while earlier in 2007, he had appeared with Matt Smith in the stage adaptation of *Swimming With Sharks*.

Arthur Darvill played the character of Rory Williams in *Doctor Who*. Although Darvill felt like he was somewhat out of his comfort zone of theatre, to suddenly being on a high-profile television show, he enjoyed Rory's character development from 'third wheel' to becoming rather heroic.[2]

Darvill speaks in glowing terms about his time on the show, particularly Rory's departure which he thought was excellent, appreciating how Steven Moffat sought approval from him about how his character would depart the show, praising the writers and producers for their sensitive and inclusive approach.[3]

Although initially he felt that he was finished with *Doctor Who*, Darvill has has played Rory Williams in multiple audio dramas, most notably Big Finish Productions' *The Lone Centurion* series. He cites his love of old radio dramas as a large part of why he was persuaded to return.

After leaving *Doctor Who*, Darvill seemingly did not experience the typecasting which pervaded the careers of so many companions before him, though he and his co-stars Matt Smith and Karen Gillan all expressed interest in reprising their roles, implicitly understanding their shared experience had linked them to the show, likely for the rest of their careers.

Darvill went on to appear in *Doctor Faustus* at the Globe in 2011, playing Mephistopheles, a notable departure from his heroic and selfless Rory Williams in *Doctor Who*. His theatre credits, both before and after the show, are numerous, including Annie Baker's *The Antipodes* at the National Theatre, *Marine Parade* at the Brighton Festival and *Terre Haute* at Edinburgh Fringe. In 2023, he starred in *Oklahoma!* at Wyndham's Theatre, London. On one night, Darvill's drama teacher, with whom he has kept in touch and had been an influential teacher in his life, brought some students to watch the show.

Darvill has always been, and still is, heavily involved in music and composition, having written for theatre productions, including the Bush Theatre, the Young Vic and The Globe, frequently collaborating with Che Walker, with whom he wrote a musical adaptation of Walker's book *Been So Long*.

He is married to actress Ines De Clercq.

46

Alex Kingston (Alexandra Elizabeth Kingston)

Born	11 March 1963
Companion	River Song
First Appearance	'Silence in the Library' (31 May 2008)
Final Appearance	'The Husbands of River Song' (25 December 2015)

ALEX KINGSTON was born and raised in Epsom, Surrey. Her father Anthony, a butcher, was English and her mother, Margarethe, was German. Kingston's maternal uncle is actor Walter Renneisen, who is well known in Germany for his roles in television and theatre. It was while watching one of his plays that Kingston first became interested in acting.

Kingston has two sisters, Nicola (with whom she appeared in *The Fortunes and Misfortunes of Moll Flanders* (1996)) and Susie. Susie is physically and mentally disabled, requiring 24-hour care, due to brain damage during birth. Kingston's mother gave up work to care for Susie, while she spends some of her time at a day centre for adults with disabilities.

In an interview with *Enable Magazine*, Kingston advocated for the need to amplify the voices of carers of people with disabilities, highlighting that each person is unique in their requirements to live a comfortable life and that policy-makers could do much more to take into account the needs of the families.[1]

Kingston went to Rosebery School for Girls, an academy in Epsom, where her English teacher encouraged her to explore her desire to act. She became involved in some of the school theatre productions, before joining the Surrey Youth Theatre. An early *Doctor Who* connection happened when she performed in their production of *Tom Jones* alongside Sean Pertwee, son of the Third Doctor, Jon Pertwee.

She successfully applied to RADA and in 1980 made her television debut in three episodes of long-running children's television series *Grange Hill.* She went on to have a small role in *The Wildcats of St. Trinian's* later that year and then had larger roles in *Henry's Leg* (1986), *A Killing on the Exchange* (1987), before appearing gate film *The Cook the Thief, His Wife and Her Lover* in 1989.

Kingston had a string of roles from the 1980s onwards, until she appeared in her breakthrough role as Elizabeth Corday in the well-known television series *ER*. She stayed on the show from 1997 until 2009. Kingston had neither expected or planned to end up in America with such a prominent role and was initially sceptical of the five-year-long commitment, fearing being typecast and being unable to shake off the association.[2]

Although her departure from the show seemed abrupt to viewers, Kingston maintains that it was a mutual decision, despite some newspapers taking out of context the comments she had made about the disparity in age between herself and her newer co-stars.

Alex Kingston played River Song, joining *Dr Who* in 2008, while Russell T. Davies was still the showrunner, although Steven Moffat wrote her inaugural episodes 'Silence in the Library' and 'Forest of the Dead'. Initially, she was only going to appear in these stories, however when Steven Moffat took over as showrunner for *Doctor Who*, he said he had further plans for the character.

Kingston would return to the show with a backstory hinting at a mysteriously close relationship with the Doctor, which hadn't actually happened to him yet. Her story arc played out in reverse and was a gradual reveal over the course of the series.

The National Space Centre interviewed Kingston.[3] Reflecting on her time in the show, Kingston said she did not consider at the time how her character would become a female role model. The impact she'd had became clear to her when she met fans who told her that River Song's resourceful and irreverent nature inspired them to overcome their own real-life challenges.

In 2015, Big Finish Productions began a multi-series audio play *The Diary of River Song*, featuring Alex Kingston and spanning eight seasons (and counting). Combined with the television series, Kingston has worked with numerous actors who played the Doctor, including David Tennant, Matt Smith, Peter Capaldi, Peter Davison and Colin Baker.

Kingston's career on screen has involved multiple roles, including *Gilmore Girls: A Year in the Life* (2016), television series *The Widow* (2019), before garnering critical and popular acclaim as a major character in *A Discovery of Witches* (2018–22).

In 2023, Kingston returned to the stage after an absence of over twenty years, appearing as Prospero in Shakespeare's *The Tempest.* Forming part of the celebration of 400 years since the playwright published his first folio, her performance was hailed by critics.[4]

Over the years, Kingston has appeared on various shows as herself too, with a particularly memorable episode of *Who Do You Think You Are?* in 2012, where she confirmed her intuitions that she had Jewish ancestry and, incidentally, that her great-great grandmother had run a brothel.

In 2021, Kingston gave her backing and support to the Rainbow Trust's Christmas Appeal – a charity which provides holistic support to entire families with children who have serious illnesses. Kingston highlighted the importance of the ways the support workers provide daily and real-world assistance to families who need it. The appeal raised £63,000 in its first two weeks.

47

Jenna Coleman (Jenna-Louise Coleman)

Born	27 April 1986
Companion	Clara Oswald
First Appearance	'Asylum of the Daleks' (1 September 2012)
Final Appearance	'Hell Bent' (5 December 2015)

JENNA COLEMAN was born in Blackpool to Karen and Keith Coleman. Her father and brother went into business together as joiners, installing fixtures and fittings for bars and retail outlets. In school, Coleman took part in theatre productions. She was in a production of *Summer Holiday* with Darren Day and was reportedly paid in Debenhams vouchers for her part – her first paid role.

After her 'rebellious' teenage years, Coleman became head girl at Arnold School, an independent school in Blackpool. She credits the school and her drama teacher for giving her the confidence to pursue acting, which was fortunate because just before going to York University to study English, she was offered the role of Jasmine Thomas in *Emmerdale*.

In many ways, long-running British television shows might be seen as a replacement to repertory theatre, but only if a budding actor manages to secure a regular role, as Coleman did. *Emmerdale* is filmed on the Harewood House Estate in West Yorkshire, so she moved to Leeds for filming and enjoyed a wealth of acting experience and a regular income.

Eventually, Coleman became dissatisfied with the lack of interesting storylines in the series and decided to leave. After she left *Emmerdale*, she found it very difficult to get further roles, though she did appear in *Waterloo Road* as Lindsay James in 2009. Perhaps this was down to typecasting, having been on a soap opera for so long, but it was certainly not for lack of determination.

Coleman moved to London and worked at a bar, briefly enrolling in an Open University Degree in English literature. She applied to RADA, however did not get in. She moved to Los Angeles and while she enjoyed the audition process, she only landed one role in *Captain America: The First Avenger* (2011). Coleman's career took a turn for the better when she was called back to the UK after landing a role in the *Titanic* miniseries (2012), written by Julian Fellowes. After that, the media began paying attention to her.[1]

Her next role would be as Rosie in *Dancing on the Edge* (2013), by which time she had already been announced as the new companion to the Doctor.

Steven Moffat was the showrunner for *Doctor Who* at this point and during the auditioning process, the production team used an anagram codeword, deliberately chosen to sound like a television show: MEN ON WAVES. Rearranged, the letters spell out 'WOMAN SEVEN', the seventh companion of the revived series.

Moffat has said that the chemistry he witnessed between Coleman and Matt Smith confirmed that they had made the right choice, hoping that the sequence of events would build to a finale just in time for the 50th Anniversary.

Jenna Coleman played Clara Oswald, a character whose history with the Doctor was initially mysterious and convoluted, is uncovered over the course of 'The Impossible Girl' story arc.

Despite being aware of the impact being on *Doctor Who* would have, like many companion actors, Jenna Coleman was unprepared for just how passionate people were about the show. She reportedly felt humbled and grateful while attending conventions and seeing for herself the show's international popularity.

After what might well be called a shaky start to her career, Jenna Coleman secured her place in *Doctor Who* history, which is not to say she did not divide fan response and elicit some lively conversation and speculation among online discussion forums.

She went on to star as Queen Victoria for the full three seasons of ITV's television series *Victoria* (2016–19). In order to rehearse for the role, Coleman read Queen Victoria's journals, which were digitised and made available to the public for Queen Elizabeth II's diamond jubilee, although Coleman restricted herself to only reading up to the point where the series was currently written.

Another noteworthy role, and completely different from Queen Victoria, was as Marie-Andrée Leclerc in television miniseries *The Serpent* (2021), based on the true story of serial killer Charles Sobhraj and his French Canadian lover, played by Coleman. Coleman immersed herself in the role, listening to an imagined playlist of what music she and director Tom Shankland thought Leclerc might have listened to, as well as researching the woman's journals.

Coleman went on to play Johanna Constantine in *The Sandman* (2022), then Liv Taylor in *Wilderness* (2023). Her theatre roles have included Sam Steiner's play *Lemons Lemons Lemons Lemons Lemons*, which ran at the Harold Pinter Theatre in early 2023 and she has narrated the Big Finish Productions audio drama 'The Time Machine' in 2013. Although she has not reprised her role as Clara in any great capacity, she is on record as having played a greater number of named characters in *Doctor Who* than anybody else.

48

Pearl Mackie

Born	29 May 1987
Companion	Bill Potts
First Appearance	'The Pilot' (15 April 2017)
Final Appearance	'The Doctor Falls' (1 July 2017)

PEARL MACKIE grew up in Brixton, South London. Her father is West Indian and her mother is English. When she was 10 years old, she played Nancy in her school production of *Oliver Twist* and, although she always wanted to be an actor, she noticed that there were few strong, black women actors at the time.

Mackie admits to being fascinated by people and spending time imagining what it might be like to be someone different, out of empathy rather than escapism. Of acting, she has delighted in being able to become another person.[1]

Her mother, Suzy Mackie, founded the See Red Women's Workshop in 1974.[2] The arts-based collective was born from a desire to combat negative stereotypes of women in the media, expressing their message through illustration, producing posters for other like-minded groups, calendars, postcards and advertisements.

Mackie's grandfather, Philip Mackie (26 November 1918 – 23 December 1985) was one of the first scriptwriters the BBC employed, along with *Quatermass* and *The Stone Tape* creator Nigel Kneale. Mackie wrote the screenplay for the television adaptation of Quentin Crisp's autobiographical *The Naked Civil Servant* (1975)

She trained at the Bristol Old Vic Theatre School, graduating in 2010. She acted in theatre and her first television role was in the film *Svengali* (2013), directed by John Hardwick. She went on to appear in TV series *Doctors* in 2014 and was in the stage production of *The Curious Incident of the Dog in the Night-Time* at the Gielgud Theatre, London when the news broke about her casting in *Doctor Who*.

Casting for the new companion on *Doctor Who* was, and remains, very secretive. Aside from a few leaks in the past, news about the latest companions has been tightly controlled – and rightly so. During casting for Bill Potts, just like Coleman before her, a production codeword was used: 'MEANTOWN', this time an anagram of 'WOMAN TEN', as in the tenth companion of the revived series. Even Mackie herself had no idea what she was auditioning for, however at the subsequent rounds of interviews, she impressed then showrunner Steven Moffat.

Mackie recalled that she was impressed by the production values on the show, as well as being surprised and delighted by the attention she received, particularly when fans would turn up to the filming locations in Cardiff.[3]

Mackie's character Bill Potts was the first openly gay female, full time companion. Mackie said that there had perhaps been LGBTQ characters on the show before, but that the terminology of the era was different, even just a decade after Captain Jack Harkness' debut, and therefore it was high time for a gay companion. Mackie was positive about the writing, feeling it was realistic and just incidental enough to be genuine, but still important in terms of representation and visibility.

Mackie has been tirelessly and firmly encouraging of diversity, especially within the LGBTQ and black communities. On her Instagram in 2020, she said she was 'Proud to be bisexual. Proud to be Black. Proud of all my LGBTQ+ brothers and sisters and everyone in between.'[4]

In 2022, she publicly announced her engagement to her partner Kam Chhokar.

The period of career-damaging typecasting long since over, Mackie's television career has also grown. After appearing in various films, she was cast in the television series *The Long Call* (2021) as Jen Rafferty, Grafifi in *Best and Bester* (2022) and *Lloyd of the Flies* (2022).

After she left *Doctor Who*, Mackie appeared in Harold Pinter's *The Birthday Party*. Her past theatre credits have included *Only Human* in 2012, Kathy Rucker's *Crystals Springs* in 2014 at Park Theatre, London and *A Mad World My Masters* in 2015 with the English Touring Theatre.

Mackie was cast in *Grenfell: in the words of survivors* by Gillian Slovo. The play tells the stories of the people of Grenfell Tower before, during and after the Grenfell fire in Kensington, 2017. Drawing on interviews from the people of Grenfell conducted by Slovo, the play met with acclaim, most notably for its engaging and emotional impact. It ran at the National Theatre until 26 August 2023.

Mackie played Natasha Elcock, a real person, who is now chair of Grenfell United, a registered family association which represents the survivors the bereaved of the fire.

Mackie became more aware of the details of the Grenfell fire, noting that those responsible still had not been brought to justice. Mackie saw the play as a piece activism and a catalyst for community-building and support.[5]

Pearl Mackie's background and upbringing seems to have been instrumental in her awareness of social inequality, particularly with regards to gender, sexuality and ethnicity. In an interview with *TimeOut,*[6] she praised the existence of smaller, less expensive theatres as being more accessible to young people, as opposed to the West End Shows which are often prohibitively expensive.

49

Matt Lucas (Matthew Richard Lucas)

Born	5 March 1974
Companion	Nardole
First Appearance	'The Husbands of River Song' (25 December 2015)
Final Appearance	'Twice Upon a Time' (25 December 2017)

MATT LUCAS was born in London. His father, John Stanley Lucas (1944–1996) owned and ran a chauffeur business. Lucas' parents both came from Orthodox Jewish families but later joined Edgware and District Reform Synagogue. Subsequently, Lucas was raised in a Reform Jewish household.

Reform Judaism is a particular denomination which encourages and emphasises a versatile and modern-day approach to Jewish faith, believing that in order to be of more use to contemporary followers the religion must evolve with the times. One of the guiding principles of Reform Judaism, much like Quakerism, is that there are many different ways to have faith and to practice Judaism. As such, they openly welcome all people, Jewish or not, of all background, placing particular emphasis on the LGBTQ community, interfaith and intermarried couples, as well as, but not limited to, Black and ethnic minority communities.[1]

Lucas does not consider himself to be a practicing Jewish person, citing his atheism as a reason. In an interview with the *Jewish Chronicle*, he told Rosa Doherty 'I think it would be hypocritical to feign faith […] I just don't believe in God'.[2]

Lucas went to Aylward Primary School and then Haberdashers' Boys' School in Hertfordshire, before studying drama at Bristol University, leaving in 1995 without finishing his degree. He subsequently joined the National Youth Theatre and credits the organisation for being instrumental in supporting his desire to become an actor. Lucas has encouraged other young people with similar aspirations to consider joining.

Matt Lucas has been a long-time collaborator with Vic Reeves and Bob Mortimer, which began in 1992 when he first appeared on their sketch shows *The Smell of Reeves and Mortimer*. In 1995, Lucas appeared with them on their celebrity panel show *Shooting Stars*, which ran between 1993 and 2011. Lucas was predominantly in character as George Dawes, who appeared to be an adult baby, but would sometimes appear as Marjorie Dawes, George's mother. The show was characterised by its distinctive absurdist and surreal humour, often involving elements of slapstick physical comedy and non-sequiturs.

Lucas collaborated with David Wallis to produce sketch show *Little Britain*, which began life as a radio sketch show on BBC Radio 4 before becoming a television series. Lucas and Walliams were long-time fans of *Doctor Who* and there were many on-screen references to the show in *Little Britain*, including characters named Matthew Waterhouse and Sir Michael Craze. The show was also narrated by Fourth Doctor, Tom Baker.

In *Doctor Who*, Matt Lucas played the character Nardole, possibly human, though it was never revealed with any great certainty. Initially, Lucas thought that he would only be doing three episodes, however – as is not uncommon to the show – his role became bigger. The filming experience involved long hours, but at the same time Lucas was writing his autobiography.

Matt Lucas' roles in television, film and theatre have been abundant. He worked once again with David Walliams in the comedy sketch show *Come Fly with Me* (2010–11), a parody of working at a British airport, in which he plays multiple characters. In 2025, he starred in the television series *Pompidou* as the titular character, and narrated *Round Planet* (2016), a satirical comedy series which lampooned nature documentaries. In 2020, Lucas became the host of Channel 4's *Great British Bake-Off*, which he would continue to host for three years.

Lucas took part in a particularly affecting episode of BBC's *Who Do You Think You Are?* Where he learned that many members of his family had been killed in the Holocaust and that his grandmother's cousin, Werner Goldschmidt, had lived with the Anne Frank's family in 1942.

Matt Lucas is an ambassador of TheirWorld, a global children's charity which works to ensure young people who are displaced or whose lives have been disrupted due to conflict, climate crises or emergencies have access to education.

Matt Lucas is openly gay. In 2002, Matt Lucas met Kevin McGee, whom he would marry four years later. They divorced just two years later and McGee died by suicide in 2009. Lucas shared a tribute to his ex-husband, for whom he still had a great deal of affection, saying that he was grateful for the time they had together.

Interlude 8: Aaron Lowe Interview

THE FANTOM signing spectaculars are legendary. If you go to one of their monthly signing events, you can meet some of the wonderful people involved *Doctor Who*, from production and effects, to the very companion actors that this book celebrates. You can get things signed and have your photograph taken with them – and there's a very nice bar just close to the venue, the name of which escapes me.

It was likely due to the proximity of this bar that I had a very bad headache at one such event. Stepping outside for a moment, I made my way through the carpet of Tom Baker scarves and mountains of excited fans with the aim of having a sit down and some fresh air. Chiswick being one of the few areas in London which does not immediately asphyxiate me with pollution (though if it did, it would probably charge you for the privilege), I managed to find both a welcome breeze and a seat.

I also found Aaron Lowe, who upon learning of my headache, proceeded to furnish me with the necessary medication which they so happened to have in their bag. Aaron is a warm and friendly person, with a discerning eye and a charismatic charm.

As the scope of this book increased, I knew I wanted to include the words of a fan and I knew it had to be Aaron. I wanted to get the perspective of someone younger than me, whose first experience with the show came much later than mine. I also knew Aaron had a reputation in the *Doctor Who* fan community as someone who typifies what one aspect of what the show is about: bringing people together.

Aaron was gracious enough to join me for an interview and for the enjoyable conversation which followed, no medication was necessary this time.

Aaron, thank you for joining me today. How's your week been?
It's been okay! It's been a regular working week. I think everyone thinks I have this special interest and that's all life's about, but I've got to pay the rent, and then I get the day off to watch *Doctor Who*.

It's fair to say that you're a big fan of *Doctor Who*. Would you introduce yourself in that context?
Yeah, I don't really have many vivid memories from my childhood, but I still remember that first Saturday night. I know there was me, my mum and my nan

and granddad. They said 'There's this new show coming back on TV. We think you'll like it. We used to watch it years ago.'

I remember nan and grandad's favourite was Jon Pertwee. It's just one of these vivid memories, sitting down and not knowing what was going to happen. That was the first moment that TV became a part of what I wanted to do.

That was the first time I was watching something which blew my mind. I fully believed everything that was going on. I fully believed that they blew up the shop, that the dummies were coming to life. I believed the London Eye was some kind of alien device! It went on from there.

I don't think they thought that twenty years on I'd still be as interested as that night when I was 9 years old. I think they thought it'd be something I'd watch from time to time, and sort of enjoy, but then forget about. That ... didn't happen!

It hooked me in. It opened my eyes. And it was always that thing when I was growing up and times got tough, that the height of when it was getting really bad, no matter how bad it got, there was always this amazing show.

There was a divide in school. Liking *Doctor Who* was 'uncool'. People were saying, 'Oh you don't watch football', or any of the other popular stuff. So I felt like it was my show. So no matter what happened, it was my comfort blanket and it still is.

When things got tough for me, it was during Matt Smith's tenure. I'd gone though Ecclestone, then Tennant. But Smith hit at the right moment, at the right time and the right notes of 'no matter what happens, you're gonna be okay'.

The show has influenced a lot of my decisions too. It was the reason I moved to Cardiff to go to university. At the interview, they asked why I wanted to come to that university, expecting me to mention league tables or student recommendations. I just said '*Doctor Who*'s filmed in Cardiff. It's where I want to be.'

Love it.

And I got a place three hours later via email. It was one of those weird things. I think they appreciated the honesty.

Where are you from originally?

From Derby in the East Midlands. And there was, and still is, a Derby-based *Doctor Who* group. So they used to have a monthly meeting and every few months they'd have a special guest for the evening. It was just in one room, they'd do interviews, autographs. The first one I think they did was Frazer Hines. And that was my first foray into meeting these people.

Initially, if it was an actor from classic *Who*, I didn't know who they were, but I still went because it was the atmosphere and environment I needed. They were all there for the same reason and I didn't have that with my own age. These were people already in their 30s, 40s, 50s, who'd been watching it for years. At 13 I fit in with them and that's the joy of the show. I don't think there's a single one of my friends who I've made through *Doctor Who* who's the same age as me.

Yes, my first convention was Longleat, probably in 1996. I think I was amazed how many adults were there too. There's something extraordinary about the fandom in that way.
It is and I've never liked the debate of whether it's a kids' show or not. Because it's one of those rare shows where it doesn't matter. You can be any age. You can watch it by yourself, in a group, with your family. But there's something in it for everyone, regardless of age. That moment when I was 9, my mum and my grandparents – they all had those memories. We all sat there and enjoyed it. Nobody had grown out of it.

And everybody knows the show. Even if they don't watch it, you can say to someone on the street 'Doctor Who' and they'll know associations like 'Dalek', 'TARDIS, 'sonic screwdriver'.

Yes! I struggle to think of anything on TV which has been embedded in popular culture in such a way.
Exactly. If someone came up to me even and said 'name five footballers', I wouldn't be able to do it. If I did, they'd probably be the people who are retired by now. People don't understand the impact of *Doctor Who*. It's always there in the background.

And even when it wasn't on TV, it was still present. It seemed like a weird decision to cancel it, considering its popularity
I don't understand. There was such a demand. There's no other show on British TV that would carry that torch, like *Doctor Who* fans did.

I'm interested in the diversity that's in the show now. The demographics of the companions has changed a lot. There's so much now. What's it like to see?
It's phenomenal. You go into watching classic *Who*, with an idea of what it's going to be like because you know the state of the world in the '60s and '70s and what it was like. It's always great to see interviews with the older companion actors who say 'that they got paid to scream'. But now it's much more of an equal playing field.

I've always seen myself as a companion, not the Doctor. I identify with them more. I've always wanted to be whisked away by this magical person. And I think for companions, they are the eyes of the viewer.

When it started they were the people who'd stand there and say they didn't understand what the big, technical words meant. Whereas now they take into account that the viewers have more of an understanding of what type of show it is. The companions know more, and so does the audience. And I think that's been pushed forward by the people who play the companions.

People like Pearl Mackie who came on only for one season, but people still talk about Bill Potts seven years on. It shouldn't be a groundbreaking thing to say that this person of colour is a lesbian, but seeing how much that impacted Pearl's life after was phenomenal.

It's not just for the sake of it. Everybody watching is deserving of seeing those adventures through the eyes of someone they can relate to. So people who are LGBTQ, people of colour, viewers who don't necessarily fall into the mainstream, shall we say, they can see themselves represented. And people who've never met such people can see that they exist and that they're just human beings. It's so important.

The types of people that exist, to see them represented on a show that's huge like this is such a weighty decision. It sounds like you think they've done it well.

They have. There's probably still further places they can go. I think they should keep doing what they're doing, keep pushing those boundaries. The more a certain group of people get riled up, the more they should push it. This is a show that been going for sixty-one years and it's always been forward thinking, showing the world how it *could* be, not how it is. What they're showing is that you can still save the universe if you're different, you can still make these friends, have these experiences and it makes a difference. That's what they need to carry on with.

And I think that's why Russell has looked at the world as a whole, brought in people who are at the top of their game. He thinks about what they're bringing from outside – what are they doing for the people who are watching? Because Yasmin Finney outside *Doctor Who* is important too.

I'll explain. Because I do it. I see someone in a film or TV series, then I'll go on IMBD, find them. Find their name and find their Instagram and look at social media, what they do. These people's lives are on a plate. And these kids who are watching the show will do the same thing. They'll have look on social media, look at their other roles, see their activism, see what they represent, what they stand for. And those are the things which will influence them, even if they don't realise it.

Another added layer of responsibility which has come with the digital information age. People who are digital natives – which I'm not actually, technically – the difference is so palpable. It's natural to go and find them online and check them out.
That same responsibility comes with being a fan too. People have the ability to transmit their thoughts and some people don't care what they tweet. They'll say they hate something or someone's role, hit send and not give it a second thought. But then that actor will see it and they will want to react to it and it can fuel the wrong kind of fire.

I created a platform where it was an accepting place for people, in fact where that acceptance and support is fundamental. That's what the show did for me. I want it to do for other people.

So we're talking about the Friends of Ace community, which was what I was looking forward to speaking with you about.
Friends of Ace, yes. It's an LGBTQ+ *Doctor Who* community online. It was something I set up during lockdown. I had my own struggles in the past and I thought, as we were going into lockdown, spending a lot of time with myself was going to be challenging. Weirdly, it was okay for me. But I knew what it would be like for other people. I know what it's like to not be okay, so I spoke to my friend and we clicked and decided this was a really good idea. It went crazy. By the time lockdown lifted, I had about four people who'd sent messages saying that they'd had to spend time quarantining with family, for example, who they weren't out to. But they'd actually come out to their family, they'd spent more time with them and Friends of Ace in some various ways been instrumental to that.

It was almost like having a job through lockdown. I was always scheduling things, making artwork, trying to get the people who we were talking about involved. But none of that mattered when those moments happened and people told me how important it was and how supported they felt. It was all worth it.

That's amazing. What exactly happened in the group when it started? I joined it very much later. You said about scheduling things.
So it was a weekly thing. We would look at the people who'd been in the show and we would celebrate them. If they were an LGBTQ+ character, or actor, or even a fan. And initially, even though *Doctor Who* has an international fanbase now, I wondered what percentage of them were LGBTQ+ … and it didn't actually narrow it down a lot! Because it's always been that place for people who've felt like an outsider for whatever reason.

Every Monday we'd announce who we were going to be looking at. I'd produce a piece of artwork like a digital painting of that person. I think one of the first ones was Luke from *Sarah Jane Adventures*. Then on the Tuesday we'd talk about our favourite moments with them. On Wednesdays it would be fan interactions, sharing photos from conventions where they'd met the person.

It sound like you had a good structure.
Yes, that was important during lockdown, when all the days were blurring together. People would know that if it were Wednesday, it would fan photo day. It gave people a structure. And Fridays was fan art day, so people could produce a piece of artwork and take the four or five days to work on it, to think about that actor or character and what they meant to them.

I wish I hadn't missed all that, myself, as an artist. I imagine it helped a lot of people.
I still get people coming up to me at conventions and asking if I'm the one who does Friends of Ace. That was unexpected. It wasn't a case of me doing it for the glory. I just orchestrated it for other people. I wanted it to get to a point where it was safe for whoever would find it. Since lockdown, there's so many people in my life now because of that group. And people made friends through it and now go to conventions together.

The most joyous thing was Sophie Aldred's involvement. I mean, it was named for her, because it being an LGBTQ+ group, well, you know that in America when being gay was still illegal, people would ask if you were 'a friend of Dorothy's'. That was the code. And Dorothy being Ace's real name … well, it just felt like a perfect name for the group.

And actually one of my closest friends took a year to even get the joke!

So I tweeted Sophie Aldred and asked if it was okay to name it after Ace. I mean if she ever had a problem with something out of her control being named partially after her, I'd have totally understood. But she jumped on board straight away. It was one of those bizarre things which was another moment for a fan to interact with someone they care about. She's been at the forefront of it ever since. She's done more promo for the group around the world than I have!

You go to a lot of conventions and have met a lot of the actors. The actors put a lot of effort into meeting the fans and they're very generous with their time. Isn't that unusual for a show?
I remember being timid and shy at my first ones. The first time I met some of them, I was always asking the default questions, like what was their favourite

episode. But I've got to the stage now where I can't remember the last time I met a *Doctor Who* actor and asked them about *Doctor Who*. Because the response I get when we just engage as human beings is really so important to me. They're a person who has done a job, they have given us a gift and they have that gift of being able to show us these adventures. There's a lot that goes into it, of course, behind the scenes, but at the core of it, they put themselves on screen.

And I've got some good relationships with them. I remember Katy [Manning] was talking to me and she was talking about her father who was in politics in the 1960s. She was saying how he was fighting for equal rights and gay marriage and she told me with Friends of Ace, she saw me as carrying on her dad's work.

How was it to hear that?

I'd never seen myself in that light before. I never had someone that I look up to that much to give me that. It was like a cloudy day and the sun just broke through. I realised I needed to give myself a bit more credit. I think if you do nice things because you're a nice person, you don't think twice. It's not in my nature to automatically think about how it affects people or how much people would hold that.

Giving yourself credit for the effort you put in is important. Life can be a strain.

Which is why we have conventions – and in fact why we have *Doctor Who*. I remember being at a convention and I was having a rough time and someone asked me how it was going, knowing that things were quite bad at the time. But I'd learned from previous experience that if I do that, I end up letting life outside overshadow what should be a good time. A time when you can just close the doors and not let your problems exist within those four walls. That's the one thing I've learned. If you're going to a convention forget everything else. Go to the convention, have those memories, talk to people.

Real life will always be waiting outside. Plenty of time to deal with that. You've been so generous with your time, Aaron. Is there anything else you'd like to say?

The only thing I'd mention is that growing up, *Doctor Who* was always the introduction to those people as actors and they seem to go through the big stigma occasionally of being in the show and then go and do something completely different. In some cases, it led to them giving up acting or even, at least for a time, resenting being on the show, because it typecast them.

This comes up again and again, yes.

But now it's like a springboard. You can see what amazing stuff Freema is doing. You can see how Karen Gillan went off to Hollywood. They use this as platform to show their skills. Back in the day they needed to scream and ask questions. But now they get the technical jargon. The action sequences – they get to showcase their whole range. I'm so glad they're given these opportunities.

I think that's why some of the older actors have come back and will be coming back in the future, because there's so much more to these people. Big Finish has always done that too. It's bridged the gaps and brought more out of them.

It's a show that looks forward but should also celebrate its past and it's doing that very well.

50

Bradley Walsh (Bradley John Walsh)

Born	4 June 1960
Companion	Graham O'Brien
First Appearance	'The Woman Who Fell to Earth' (7 October 2018)
Final Appearance	'The Power of the Doctor' (23 October 2022)

BRADLEY WALSH was born in Watford, Hertfordshire. He attended Francis Combe School in Horseshoe Lane, Garston, Hertfordshire. Not an academic student, when he left school he became a jet engineer for Rolls-Royce.

He began a career as a footballer when he was 18, going professional for Brentford reserves. His football career ended after fracturing both of his ankles. Though unable to play professionally, Walsh still plays for Soccer Aid, a charity organisation which supports UNICEF in its bid to provide humanitarian aid to children worldwide.

While he was in Majorca on holiday, he won a talent competition, which inspired him to apply to be a Pontins bluecoat. From then, he began performing stand-up comedy, which in turn led to his being invited to support Leo Sayer in 1985.

Walsh's career began its long, consistent and sometimes surprising trajectory when he began hosting television show *Midas Touch* from 1995 until 1997, when he later replaced Nicky Campbell of the extremely popular primetime game show *Wheel of Fortune*.

To say that Walsh is a versatile talent is an understatement. He began acting, becoming a regular on *Night and Day* as Woody Dexter (2002–3) before adding to his credentials as a household name in a two-year run on *Coronation Street* as Danny Baldwin in 2004 until 2006, when he left under a mutual agreement after his contract ended.

During a meeting with showrunner Chris Chibnall, he was offered the role of Graham O'Brien and, as has often been the case, Chibnall was tight-lipped about the details, only telling him later that it was a role on *Doctor Who* and that he should probably prepare himself for an extraordinary time.[1]

Chibnall wasn't kidding. When the series returned after Peter Capaldi's exit, the Doctor had regenerated into a woman, an announcement which, as you might expect, seemed to polarise the entire nation and excite the fanbase beyond any previous measure since its return in 2005.

Walsh gave high praise to his co-stars and the production team, saying that filming in Wales had made the place feel like 'a second home' to him.[2]

The phenomenal impact of having a female Doctor and, in general, the show's iconic status, was not lost on Walsh. He acknowledged the punishing filming schedule and extremely challenging work as being not only rewarding and exhilarating, but also partly why he decided to leave.[3]

On the show, viewers last saw Walsh's character Graham delivering a monologue about how amazing, but also how isolating, traveling with the Doctor had been. Eventually, we see that he is in a room full of former companions, including Jo Grant, Ian Chesterton, Ace, Tegan and Mel. The scene has since become infamous and it underscored Walsh's down-to-earth, sensitive performance.

The British audience knows Bradley Walsh. He has been a household name for decades and continues to surprise and delight audiences. He has appeared on panel shows such as *Play to the Whistle* (2015–17) and, furthering his authentic image as a relatable man, appeared with his son Barney Walsh in five seasons (soon to be six) of *Bradley Walsh & Son: Breaking Dad*. In the show, they travel to various countries and engage in various adventurous activities, including G-force training at a space centre, rodeo riding and paragliding.

Since 2009, Walsh has hosted ITV's gameshow *The Chase* and, along with his son, once again, hosted the reboot of *Gladiators*. Bradley Walsh is married to Donna Derby and has one other child from a previous relationship.

51

Tosin Cole

Born	23 July 1992
Companion	Ryan Sinclair
First Appearance	'The Woman Who Fell to Earth' (2018)
Final Appearance	'Revolution of the Daleks' (1 January 2021)

TOSIN COLE was born in Florida, USA, and lived in New York until he was 8. His parents are Nigerian and after they separated, he moved with his father and uncle to London. He went to Abbey Wood Secondary School in Greenwich and came to appreciate Shakespeare because a teacher skilfully made the playwright's work feel relatable.

When he was 16, Cole began going to Intermission Youth Theatre,[1] a project which was set up in 2008 and whose purpose is to work with disadvantaged young people at risk from anti-social behaviour and social and economic deprivation.

It was while at Intermission that Cole began to further relate to the world of acting, being taken to see the play *Sucker Punch* by Roy Williams, and starring Daniel Kaluuya and Anthony Welsh. Cole came to respect and admire the two lead actors who, like him, were Black. 'I saw people who look like me, who sound like me',[2] said Cole. He became further inspired to become an actor himself.

He continued at school, but soon left when he was scouted by an agent. He landed his first role in *Eastenders* spin-off series *E20*, appearing as Sol Levi. He landed on primetime television a year later, appearing in no less than eighty episodes of *Hollyoaks* as Neil Cooper (2011–12), a character who would later meet a dramatic and explosive end.

After leaving *Hollyoaks*, Cole appeared in a range of television series, such as *The Secrets* (2014), *Versailles* (2015) and *Star Wars: Episode VII – The Force Awakens* (2015), as Lieutenant Bastian.

Tosin Cole joined the cast of *Doctor Who* as Ryan Sinclair in the first episode of the eleventh series. When he learned that he was in with a chance of becoming the Doctor's new companion, he was sworn to secrecy – though later stated that he did in fact tell a few people. Having never seen the show before, he was blissfully unaware of the controversy and excitement surrounding Jodie Whittaker's casting as the first female Doctor. Cole, characteristically open and relaxed, seemed unbothered, believing it to be perfectly reasonable that an extraterrestrial who could regenerate could certainly be female.

Being in a show like *Doctor Who* was something Cole had never done before, but he approached his performance and the ensuing media attention with a relaxed attitude, praising the cast, the crew and the diversity of his co-stars. Recalling perhaps what encouraged him to first pursue performing, Cole hoped that if young fans of the show see someone who is familiar to them, then they may in turn become inspired.[3]

Cole played a sensitive and relatable character in *Doctor Who*, and he also made an impact on people through his portrayal of Ryan Sinclair's dyspraxia, a physical disorder which affects a person's movement and coordination. Journalist Tom Gerken, a *Doctor Who* fan who is also dyspraxic, wrote that he found another level of appreciation for the show in seeing his disability portrayed on television so accurately.[4]

Tosin Cole when on to appear in a diverse range of roles after he left the show. He played Moses Johnson in series one of *61st Street* (2022), a legal drama depicting criminal justice corruption in Chicago, and in 2023 starred in the remake of 1990s teen comedy *House Party* (2023).

Cole also appeared in *Till* (2022), directed by Chinonye Chukwu and written by Michael Reilly. The true story of Emmett Till, a 14-year-old black boy who was murdered in Mississippi in 1955. Cole portrayed civil rights activist Medgar Wiley Evers, who was later also murdered by a member of the Ku Klux Klan.

Cole prepared for the role by researching the history of the events, including what he describes as extensive conversations and interviews done with Myrlie Evers, the real-life widow of his character, getting the chance to speak with her directly.

On the versatility as an actor, Cole has stated that he has made a conscious decision to be known not just for one role, and continues to work towards being recognised by reputation, rather than a typecast character actor.

In 2024, Cole starred opposite Heather Agyepong in the world premiere of Benedict Lombe's play *Shifters* at the Bush Theatre, with Cole's performance as Dre winning him solid reviews as an adept and entrancing presence on stage.

52

Mandip Gill (Mandip Kaur Gill)

Born	5 January 1988
Companion	Yasmin Khan
First Appearance	'The Woman Who Fell to Earth' (7 October 2018)
Final Appearance	'The Power of the Doctor' (23 October 2022)

GILL was born in Leeds, Yorkshire. Of Punjabi heritage, Gill is a practicing Sikh. Her parents owned and ran a newsagents in Middleton and she went to Cockburn School in the Beeston area of Leeds.

Gill played Phoebe McQueen in *Hollyoaks* from 2012 until 2015. Having auditioned for roles before *Hollyoaks*, Gill did not consider her audition for Phoebe's character as anything particularly new or noteworthy, however she auditioned for the role partly because it was listed as non-race-specific. When she landed the part, she enjoyed playing somebody whose role was not centred around their ethnicity.[1]

Although Gill's character was involved in storylines central to the show, she decided to leave after three years and branch out, rather than staying within her comfort zone. It was a bold, but ultimately worthwhile decision, as Gill then appeared as Shazia Amin in *Doctors* (2016), The *Good Karma Hospital* (2017) and BBC television series *Love, Lies and Records* (2017).

Gill has been selective in her roles over the years, a factor in her decisions being whether or not the role excites her, whether there is an important motivation or story behind the performance, and her faith as a Sikh woman also has an influence.

When Gill auditioned for the part of Yasmin Khan, she wasn't told much about it, but she suspected that it might have been for *Doctor Who*. As usual, the casting process was secretive and highly classified.

Mandip Gill played a vital role in one of the most diverse casts of the series' history. The storylines were often divisive among viewers and politically resonant. The story 'Rosa' (2018), written by Malorie Blackman and guest starring Vinette Robinson as Rosa Parks, revisited *Doctor Who*'s historical roots and taught that the show could also be educational as well as entertaining. Similarly, 'Demons of the Punjab' (2018) by Vinay Patel provided a compelling look into the time of the partition of India. Gill cites this as her favourite episode, the history of the partition being something which was highly important to her and a personal joy to have been part of.[2]

Both episodes were critically acclaimed and Gill acknowledged how important it was to tell these stories, stating in an interview with the *Guardian* that criticisms of the show's overtly 'politically correct' tone was a misnomer, stating: 'its just *correct'*.[3]

Her character's unrequited love for the Doctor was another important aspect of the production for Gill, who developed a close and enjoyable friendship with Jodie Whittaker while filming. Whittaker expressed her delight that 'the fam' was more than just an on-screen dynamic, celebrating their friendship in glowing terms.

Gill has acknowledged that the acting industry, casting in particular, has progressed in recent years, opening up more roles for ethnically diverse actors who are not playing the clichéd roles which were normally associate with them.[4]

In March 2022, Gill made her West End debut in *2:22 A Ghost Story*, appearing with Tom Felton, Beatriz Romilly and Sam Sainsbury. In 2024, it was announced that she would be starring in the forthcoming drama *Curfew*, a dystopian drama, heralded as part of an important exploration of violence against women.

53

John Bishop

Born	30 November 1966
Companion	Dan Lewis
First Appearance	'Flux' (28 November 2021)
Final Appearance	'The Power of the Doctor' (23 October 2022)

JOHN BISHOP was born in Everton, Liverpool. His mother Kathleen was a housewife and his father a labourer. Bishop grew up in a council house with very little money and he recalls leaving sixth form on his first day because he only had jeans and was unable to buy trousers suitable to the dress code.

He would later return and finish his 'A' levels, before obtaining a grant to go to university. He studied English for one term at Newcastle Polytechnic, which later became Northumbria University in 1992.

He's a passionate supporter of Liverpool Football Club and played semi-professionally for Southport and Hyde United. His brother Edward Bishop (28 November 1961) is a former professional footballer, who played for Tranmere Rovers, Chester City and Crewe Alexandria.

When he left university, he began working for a pharmaceutical company, but by this time he had already begun pursuing his idea of becoming a stand-up comedian. In 2006, he left his job to focus fully on his career as a comic. After a shaky start, Bishop felt that he may have made the wrong choice and that he would have to return to a day job of some description.[1] However, Bishop's career as a comedian began to take root.

He performed in Manchester, before going onto enter competitions designed to platform new and up-coming comedians. He made it through to the finals before winning the North West Comedy Award for best stand-up. In 2009, he was nominated for an Edinburgh Comedy Award for his Edinburgh Fringe Show entitled 'Elvis Has Left the Building'. The reviews were overwhelmingly positive,[2] praising his self-deprecating humour and relaxed attitude, appealing to women as much as men.

The awards he's won over the years are almost as numerous as the number of gigs, panel shows and stand-up performances he has given. Bishop has been a welcome and popular guest on several top British panel shows, including *Mock the Week*, *8 Out of 10 Cats* and *Have I Got News For You*. He has also toured relentlessly, beginning in 2007 with *The Going to Work Tour*, continuing with the wonderfully named *Stick Your Job UP Your Arse Tour* in 2008 and, after period continuous work, is most recently due to begin his 2024/2025 tour *Back At It*.

The character of Dan Lewis was written with John Bishop in mind. In an interview with *Entertainment Weekly*, Bishop said showrunner Chris Chibnall had initially approached him to play the part, but he was busy touring and unavailable. However, when the Covid pandemic began and lockdown occurred his tour, like most other things in the country, was suspended. Filming could take place under strict conditions with minimal cast and crew, and he was able to accept the role.[3]

Having been announced as the new companion, John Bishop appears on *The Graham Norton Show*[4] where he revealed information to a group of drama students regarding his role on the show – before the producers had given him permission. This information was that the character was from Liverpool, which Bishop explained with uproariously irreverent comic delivery, would have been obvious to anybody who had ever heard him speak.

In a BBC press release, Bishop described his character as a humble man who has not really left Liverpool much and doesn't have the desire to. With an innately caring nature and sense of righteousness, Dan Lewis appealed to fans of many different demographics, becoming a celebrated, yet accidental hero of what Whittaker's Doctor, often termed 'the fam'.

After he left the show, Bishop went pretty much straight on tour, so didn't have chance to miss his time on *Doctor Who* until later. John Bishop has become one of the most successful British comedians of our time. In 2024 he appeared as a guest on Irish comedian's eponymous television series *The Tommy Tiernan Show*. He spoke about how he plans to travel on his latest tour by motorbike, citing the new wheels as the result of a mid-life crisis. His wife allegedly nicknamed the risky purchase 'Dignitas on wheels'.[5]

Having lived at Whatcroft Hall, a country house in Cheshire dating back to 1780, Bishop sold the house to the controversial high speed rail scheme HS2, as its proposed proximity would have made the house unsaleable. Bishop had been vocal in his criticism of the project, citing its spiralling financial costs and the environmental impacts.[6]

He married his wife Melanie in 1993, and they have three children.

54

Yasmin Finney

Born	30 August 2003
Companion	Rose Noble
First Appearance	'The Star Beast' (25 November 2023)
Final Appearance	'The Empire of Death' 22 June 2024

YASMIN FINNEY was born in Manchester. Her mother is Jamaican and her father, while English, has Irish and Italian heritage. Her parents separated and Finney was raised by her mother, along with her half-sister.

Finney's first role was in *Mars* (2022), a short film directed by Abel Rubinstein and written by Chris Bush. She then went on to appear in the Netflix comedy drama series *Heartstopper*, where she played Elle Argent. Finney was complimentary of how her character in the show was written, highlighting the importance of having a positive representation of relatable trans characters, though fraught with all the usual challenges and upheavals which permeate everybody's lives.[1]

Finney experienced bullying when she was younger and found herself questioning whether she could even be an actor at all because she couldn't see anybody who was a person of colour and trans on screen.[2]

After she began transitioning, she described feeling even more isolated from her peers. Finney began documenting her life as a trans person in Manchester on TikTok back in 2019. It was there that she found an encouraging community of people who welcomed and supported her. She describes the response to her honest and open journey, presented in short-form video, as incredible. Her content is extremely popular and she currently has over 1.9 million followers.

Finney plays the character Rose Noble, the daughter of former companion Donna Noble and Shaun Temple. Rose Noble is a trans character, non-binary and female-presenting.

Finney's debut episode 'The Star Beast' (2023) was the first story of Russel T. Davies return as *Doctor Who* showrunner and was an adaptation of the comic strip *Doctor Who and the Star Beast*, written by Pat Mills and John Wagner in 1980.

While filming, Finney found some of the scenes reminded her of growing up, particularly when Rose Noble is harassed by some passing boys from the neighbourhood, who call her by her birth name, a process known as 'deadnaming' someone. Rose Noble was, on the whole, greatly received by fans, who were particularly delighted to see a continuation of Donna Noble's character development, now being a mother.

The BBC received over 100 hundred complaints about the inclusion of a trans, non-binary person of colour on *Doctor Who*, which they promptly rejected. Showrunner Russel T Davies, whose previous work includes the groundbreaking *Queer as Folk* (2000) and *It's a Sin* (2021) spoke about Finney's casting and derided the negativity, calling it venomous and destructive.[3]

Although it has not been confirmed at the time of writing, it is very possible the Yasmin Finney will return to *Doctor Who* as Rose Noble.

55

Millie Gibson (Amelia Eve Gibson)

Born	19 June 2004
Companion	Ruby Sunday
First Appearance	'The Church on Ruby Road' (25 December 2023)
Final Appearance	'Joy to the World' 25 December 2024

MILLIE GIBSON was born in Tameside, Greater Manchester and went to the Blue Coat School, a Church of England academy school. She took drama classes at the Oldham Theatre and Music Workshop, which was founded in 1968. It was during her time here that she was scouted by Manchester-based agency Scream Management.[1]

Gibson has been on television since 2017, with her first role as recurring character Indira in *Jamie Johnson* (2017–18), before going on to appear as Mia in *Love, Lies and Records*.

She became a prominent character in ITV soap *Coronation Street*, joining the show in 2019 and leaving in 2022. During her tenure on Coronation Street, her character Kelly Neelan was central to some hard-hitting and explosive storylines, mainly revolving around her character being framed for murder, before leaving to begin a new life.

In 2022, Millie Gibson was announced as the new companion to the newly regenerated Doctor played by Ncuti Gatwa. She told the *Radio Times* that she was still finding it difficult to believe the news and acknowledged the companions who had gone before her, understanding that she had a responsibility to satisfy the fans' expectations.

In a testament to the supportive and nurturing nature of the *Doctor Who* cast and crew, both presently and in the past, Gibson contacted Karen Gillan and asked her about her time on the show. That Gibson felt able to reach out speaks volumes and that Gillan provided advice and support says even more.

While times may have changed, in that the new Doctor is incidentally a black, gay actor, the media furore which erupts whenever a new companion is announced has certainly remained constant. Various newspapers made insubstantial claims that Millie Gibson would only be in a handful of episodes, being swiftly replaced by newcomer Varada Sethu, speculation apparently based upon location filming involving Gatwa and Sethu, with Gibson being absent.

As the rumour mill went into overdrive, Gibson was able to confirm that she would in fact be appearing in the show alongside both Ncuti Gatwa and Varada Sethu. Gibson and Gatwa were on *ABC News* in April 2024 for an interview with Linsey Davis. In the comparatively brief appearance, they were both resplendent in complementary outfits and were unconditionally supportive of each other, with Gibson acknowledging the multifaceted nature of the show and the bond between the two characters.

She said it was her dream and an honour to be the new companion. At the time of writing, we have been introduced to the character Ruby Sunday in one episode only, 'The Church on Ruby Road', and already an in-universe mystery has formed around the character. Perhaps in further editions of this book, I will be able to continue her story and celebrate what is likely to be Millie Gibson's successful acting career.

56

Varada Sethu (Varada Sethumadhavan)

Born	12 May 1992
Companion	Belinda Chandra
First Appearance	Boom (17 May 2024 – 18 May 2024)

SETHU was born in Kerala, south west India, along with her twin sister Abhaya. Her family is of Malayali heritage, of which a substantial diaspora exists in the world. They moved to Benton, Tyne-and-Wear near Newcastle, where Sethu attended the National Youth Theatre. Both Sethu's parents are doctors and alongside her acting training she also studied veterinary medicine at Bristol University, before studying at the Identity School of Acting, London.

One of Sethu's earliest roles was in English: *An Autumn in London* (2013), where she played Megan Scariah. It was the first Malayalam-language film she had played and although she cannot read Malayalam, and feels that the spoken language is no longer her first, she felt at home and welcomed on a film set where everybody was speaking a familiar tongue.[1]

Sethu appears on television in the television series *New Blood* in 2016, then (pre-) apocalyptic science fiction drama *Hard Sun* in 2018 as DS Mishal Ali, before going on to appear in Manisha Chetri in *Strike Back* in (2019) and then in *Andor* in 2022 as Cinta Kaz.

It is arguably in the Disney+ series *Andor* that Sethu became so well-know. Her character Cinta Kaz is portrayed as quiet but with presence, capable of surprisingly action-oriented physicality. Kaz is also in a relationship with a woman, the incidental nature of which was something Sethu praised, saying that it should not be a big deal.[2]

In 2022, she spoke on 'Filme Shilmy' podcast about representation of Indian actors in Britain, where she acknowledged the awareness and effort casting agents, writers and producers were putting into roles for people of Indian heritage, particularly noting that if a character's ethnicity was not intrinsic to the plot, then there should be no reason why a minority ethnicity actor could not play them. The 'default settings' of white, Western faces as the standard is something which is slowly changing.

Sethu discussed the casting of Indian actors on podcast 'The Noel Zone',[3] where she gave her opinion on what the host termed 'box ticking', which has been criticised by voices from the Black, indigenous and people of colour communities as a form of tokenism[4] and merely a way to improve diversity quotients on paper, rather than addressing deeper problems.

Sethu said she hoped she would be chosen for her acting abilities rather than as a box to be ticked, and that she would hardly be aware of any tokenism, as it's not usually discussed openly. That said, she also made a point that in any case, she would use her roles to, as she put it, to do the best job possible.

After much speculation, including rumours that she would be replacing Millie Gibson, Varada Sethu was officially announced as the new companion to the Doctor, but that she would be appearing alongside Gibson, rather than replacing her. Shortly after the announcement, former *Doctor Who* companion Mandip Gill, who is of Punjabi descent, was reported to have contacted Sethu and told her to enjoy her time on the show.

Interlude 9: Non-Binary Voices

WHATEVER ONE hears to the contrary, *Doctor Who* has always been progressive. When the show began in 1963, the producer Verity Lambert was a female at a time when the industry was dominated by men, and the director of the first episode, Waris Hussein, was a gay British Indian man; homosexuality was not decriminalised in the UK until 1967, and certainly was not visible in the popular media.

The show did not always get it right every time, of course, but who *does*? Many of the progressive themes and subtexts depicted in the classic era might seem tame compared to more contemporary episodes, but we should remember that for its time, the show certainly leaned in a progressive direction.

Fans will remember the anti-racist themes explored in Ace's storyline, the anti-nuclear proliferation subtext of 'Battlefield' (1989) and will recognise the Daleks as analogous to the Nazis. Going back further, episodes such as 'Inferno' (1970) and 'The Green Death' (1973) both provided commentaries on environmentalism.

Society has progressed and voices which dissent from the mainstream have only become fiercer and more eloquent in their demand for change and representation. Upon its revival, *Doctor Who* has met these expectations with stories like 'The Zygon Invasion' and 'The Zygon Inversion' (2015), and exceeded them with its casting decisions.

In many important ways, the character of Rose Noble continues the show's tradition as a disruptive positive force, but the reality that someone can be a non-binary and female-presenting might not be immediately understood. As the author of this book, I could have chosen to tell what appears to be only the beginning of this exciting new aspect of the show, hoping that might be sufficient.

However, whenever possible I have chosen to use people's own words. On the occasions I have had a chance to speak with people first hand, it has been invaluable in telling the story of the show from perspectives which are not mine. In keeping with that, I reached out to some fans of the show who, like the character of Rose Noble, are female-presenting and non-binary and I asked them for their thoughts.

Lizzi VonDooLittle Interview

[Lizzi] Jumping right in, I never knew growing up that non binary was a thing. I only found out about it as a term because of drag race a couple of years ago and I'm 50 next month. Suddenly it all made sense.

I'd grown up being allowed to wear what I wanted, unconventional stuff like jumpsuits and dungarees in the '70s and then as soon as I discovered *Doctor Who* and other TV programmes and things in history that excited me, I was permanently dressing as a Native American, a Roman soldier, Tom Baker from *Doctor Who*, the Master, Robin of Sherwood, Michael Jackson in *Smooth Criminal*, Dave Lister from *Red Dwarf*. My mother took me out looking like a boy most of the time and nobody minded.

When I turned 16 I went Goth and veered between dressing like Carl McCoy or Patricia Morrison, depending on mood. You may notice my clothes choices were mostly male and I felt equally comfortable in being either gender or neither. I couldn't say that I ever felt 100 per cent female or 100 per cent male, just happily gender fluid and in-between.

Becoming a mother at 34 and carrying a baby was the closest I have ever felt to identifying as female, because of the hormones and obviously I had no say on that, but I can't say it was a fulfilling experience the whole pregnancy and childbirth thing, although the parenting side is very pleasing and satisfying.

At nearly 50, and a mum to a teenager now, I identify more as a mother, as happy job description than as a physical female, if that makes sense. But then also I am now menopausal and feeling less like any particular gender than ever before. I am vaguely female presenting, inasmuch as leggings and tops and no bra since 2019 can be. I can't be bothered with makeup on a daily basis either. So as long as I don't have to present myself in polite company I am just plain me. Either or neither or both. Does that make sense?

It makes sense to me. Can I ask you for your thoughts on representation in *Doctor Who*, particularly with regards to Yasmin Finney's character?
Personally, as a performer, I have always seen representation in theatre as I've spent the majority of my acting roles playing the male. I played pantomime baddies opposite the dame in community theatre work and Verrier in Clive Barker's *History of the Devil*, at the Liverpool Playhouse, 1996, I think. My character, Miss Von Trapp, was more dark cabaret clown, closer to drag than anything.

I think in theatre, gender has always been happily and acceptably blurred, right back to Greek comedies and commedia dell'arte. I think television has a lot of catching up to do, however. I remember the furore over *Brookside*'s first lesbian kiss. So it has been getting better.

Non-binary hasn't had a huge amount of recognition, though. As I said, I didn't even know it was a thing until Ginny Lemon brought it up.

In terms of *Doctor Who*, though, it's always been either ahead of the curve or at least wholly up to date with society and attitudes. For me, I was always wanting to be the Doctor. Female companions were fierce enough and had attitude. Ace was a good example of the acceptable tomboy and that probably helped with representation for females who were more like me.

In general, I think it's important that we continue to mirror and represent all aspects of society and educate viewers that it's not just a pink and blue binary world. *Doctor Who* is continuing to do just that.

Maria Kinsella Interview

Maria, thank you for agreeing to talk with me. Can I ask about your experience of being a non-binary femme? What does it mean for you?
For me being a non-binary femme has meant accepting myself and who I am, asking questions of myself over time, and cherry-picking from different strata: themes, fashion, idols and music. Applying these to myself, and trying so many things out before settling into a group of signifiers that felt right and comfortable for me personally.

My first experience of femme was to reject it. At first, it was pushed onto me by family as a way I needed to present, a way I needed to behave. By subverting the expectations that others had of me, I came out of it with an identity that feels right for me right now. That could all change with more understanding of myself, and how I feel within myself, how I relate to that selfhood.

My presentation right now is more relaxed than it has been in the past, but that doesn't mean that the desire to be loudly femme has gone away. Sometimes it's dormant, or sleeping, and on those days I'm floating between spaces feeling liminal and not really like anything. I still know my femme-ness is there; it's something I can amplify when I feel I need to. It's more than feminine, it's a roar and it's a shout, it's subverting those signposts and blurring the lines. It's not just the clothes on my back; femme (for me) means so much. Yes, it's the battle against, and eventual acceptance of, pink. But it's also looking at music scenes and honing in on the women that made them great (punk).

When I started, the act of questioning gender was already a rebellion. If you presented as femme, you were 'someone's' femme – as in, you were going out with a butch, and the conversation ended there. There was a lot of femme invisibility, so presenting in this way and playing these high femme 'games' was controversial. I wasn't brave enough yet to always present like this, so

I dressed tougher and played pool and didn't step out of (what was then) my comfort zone until a lot later.

Being taken under the wings of wild gay men and being brought up in the ways of drag and performance gave me an outlet. I was given a playground to explore in a safe environment. I have to mention my drag mother at this point: the fabulous DJ Joe Pop. Every week when I walked into a club night, he would exclaim, 'Oooh you are giving me the Banshees/the New York Dolls/Jordan.' I would go home and look these people up, do research, and dive deeper, discovering what elements inspired me. This led me to create performance pieces of my own, exploring the facets of femme that have made me over time and strengthened my using femme signifiers in my life.

How did you feel seeing Yasmin Finny playing Rose Noble and what did it mean to you in terms of representation and visibility?

I think in the past five to ten years we as a community have started to see more and more excellent queer representation. Surprisingly, most of this has come from animated media shows and movies (*SheRa*, *Kipo*, *The Owl House*, *Nimona*, and many others) which have shown wide expressions of gender that don't align with what society has always prescribed. Things like realistic body shapes and emotional range – for all characters, rather than the traditional top-heavy muscular bodies full of anger for the 'boys', and skinny-legged waifish bodies that regularly burst into tears for the 'girls'. Modern characters are allowed to experience the full range of emotional responses, which leads to great personal development, and better storytelling.

The appearance of Yasmin Finny playing Rose Noble in *Doctor Who* has been part of improved LGBTQ+ representation within the show's new incarnation since Eccleston. It's not that it doesn't mean anything to me and it's not special or important, but we've had a lot of really good representation around for quite a long time.

I can imagine that for a lot of the young non-binary femme trans folks, the little babies who are watching *Doctor Who* while they're starting adulthood, she was answering a question that they hadn't even realised was forming within them. They've got this fantastic character, whether they're watching it for the first time or as a long-term fan, who is going through a similar journey that they might be. The younger teenagers who are gathering those important examples, bits of information about identity and emotion, role models, figuring out where they're coming from, and how they're feeling inside, can see a trans woman playing a trans character.

And so it's important that her trans-ness is incidental, rather than written as her whole personality?

If they are a bit older, then they realise that her entire character is not about being trans. She isn't the comedy foil that you might expect if you grew up in the 1990s. She is strong and independent and interesting and has her own stuff going on. That one aspect of her personality isn't used to drive the story, it just exists. Very much like I was talking about with the cartoons, Rose Noble is a person first and character second. She's not the butt of anybody's joke, she is strong, she is independent, she's got her own hobbies and interests, she's cherished by a family.

That's a really big thing because so many of us in the LGBTQ+ community have experienced being rejected by family. The fact that Donna loves her daughter so much, bringing a 'mama bear' strength if anyone upsets her baby, is wonderful. We don't experience that as often. The love that the Doctor has for his niece, seeing how accepting he is with her, as my family is with my nephews and nieces. It felt completely natural that she was accepted by her family.

The fact that we've got to this point is fantastic. Took a long time, but the fact that we've got here at all is great. I want to see more gender representation, I want to see trans masculine and non-binary masculine, and why not have everybody in this brilliant show? It's about a thousand-year-old, time-traveling, two-hearted, gender-flipping, queer entity – isn't that brilliant? I want it to go on for another 100 years, and where will we be in 100 years? Who knows? That would be fantastic to think about.

Closing Remarks

IT'S CUSTOMARY to draw some conclusions at the end of a piece of work, or at least make some closing remarks. But what can I possibly tell you which has not already been demonstrated by the gestalt legend that is *Doctor Who*? Even now, the story continues. I don't feel equipped to make any conclusions about something so vast and long-lived. The very idea feels out of reach. Perhaps this space is just for me and my little book. Yes, that feels about right.

Having the audacity to even write this book in the first place is something which, if I think about it for too long, fills me with a vague sense of unease. I am under no illusions that this book will be scrutinised and judged (I hope, favourably), which contributes to the feeling I have, which is reminiscent of one of those turning-up-to-work-in-your-underpants dreams.

Unease, because I know the book may not please or interest all of you. I must also allow for the possibility, however tiny, that someone mentioned in this book may not be entirely thrilled to be 'biographied' in such a fleeting way by somebody they have not met. I hope that this book is received in the spirit in which it is given.

In the course of my research, I have been selective about what I present. I have made every effort to substantiate the information and I have restricted myself, on the whole, to facts which are readily available, or words spoken (or written) by the actors themselves. The limitations of space mean that there will be information which is absent. There is a bibliography and a list of resources of which I encourage you to avail yourself. The biographies, autobiographies and guidebooks contain more information than I could ever hope to provide and they have been very valuable to me.

If at any point I have erred, I offer my apologies and if necessary, corrections will be made in future editions of this book.

I also acknowledge that as soon as this book is published, it will be out of date. New companions, of whose existence we are currently unaware, may have been announced. They may even have already appeared. Things seem to move very quickly these days.

All that said, as I write these final words, I must admit a feeling of contentment.

My desire for this book is that you enjoy at least a part of it. That's all, really. It's very simple. I hope that whoever you are, you will be able to find something meaningful here.

Perhaps you will find yourself reflected here somewhere. I know I certainly do. If that is the case, then it is very little to do with me and everything to do with the actors. It is their hard work and talent, their dedication, flair and flamboyance, which makes the show what it is.

It also has a lot to do with *us*, the fans. We must own our share of the responsibility, because we tell the story as well. As we go forward into what is a tumultuous and sometimes frightening world, we should keep the spirit of the show close to our hearts. If we do this, we can live our lives in way that would make the Doctor proud.

In many ways, we are the companions too.

References

Introduction

1. Ingersoll, Earl G., A Conversation with Isaac Asimov Earl G. Ingersoll, Isaac Asimov, Gregory Fitz Gerald, Jack Wolf, Joshua Duberman and Robert Philmus, Science Fiction Studies Vol. 14, No. 1 (March 1987) pp 68-77
2. Sutin, Lawrence (ed), The shifting realities of Philip K. Dick : selected literary and philosophical writings. (Vintage Books, New York 1995)

1. Carole Ann Ford (Carole Ann Lillian Higgins)

1. Howe, David J., Stammers, Mark. Walker, Stephen James, *Doctor Who: the Sixties* (Doctor Who Books, 1992, London) p.4
2. https://www.telegraph.co.uk/culture/tvandradio/doctor-who/9975948/Doctor-Who-It-destroyed-my-acting-career.html
3. Doctor Who: An Adventure in Space and Time, plus Special Guests (Riverside Studios, London. 11 March 2023)

2. Jacqueline Hill (Grace Jacqueline Hill)

1. Bremner, Louise, *A Future in Five Minutes – A Biography of Jacqueline Hill* (Fantom Publishing, 2020, Croydon) p.6
2. ibid. p.19.
3. Howe, David J., Stammers, Mark. Walker, Stephen James, *Doctor Who: the Sixties* (Doctor Who Books, 1992, London) p.10
4. Howe, David J. Stammers, Mark. Walker, Stephen James, *Doctor Who Companions* (Doctor Who Books, 1995, London) p.22
5. Bremner, Louise, *A Future in Five Minutes – A Biography of Jacqueline Hill* (Fantom Publishing, 2020) p.149

3. William Russell (William Russell Enoch)

1. Howe, David J. Stammers, Mark. Walker, Stephen James, *Doctor Who: the Sixties* (Doctor Who Books, 1992, London) p.7
2. https://www.radiotimes.com/tv/sci-fi/interview-doctor-whos-william-russell/

4. Maureen O'Brien

1. https://drwhointerviews.wordpress.com/category/maureen-obrien/
2. ibid.

5. Peter Purves

1. Purves, Peter, *Peter Purves The Autobiography: Here's One I Wrote Earlier* (Green Umbrella Publishing, 2009, London) p.3
2. ibid
3. www.peterpurves.net/wp2/blue-peter/

6. Adrienne Hill

1. Howe, David J. Stammers, Mark. Walker, Stephen James, *Doctor Who: the Sixties* (Doctor Who Books, 1992, London) p.119

7. Jean Marsh (Jean Lyndsey Torren Marsh)

1. *Wine and Dine Interview* 1998
2. Pirani, Adam, Jean Marsh –' Belle of the Bad' (*STARLOG Magazine* #135 October1988)
3. https://www.telegraph.co.uk/culture/tvandradio/9079869/Jean-Marsh-co-creator-of-Upstairs-Downstairs-urges-Cameron-to-make-everything-better.html

8. Jackie Lane (Jacqueline Joyce Lane)

1. p.7 Howe, David J. Stammers, Mark. Walker, Stephen James, *Doctor Who: the Sixties* (Doctor Who Books, 1992, London)
2. Russell, Gary, TV Zone 19 – 'Dodo's travels with The Doctor' (June 1991)

9. Anneke Wills (Anna Katarina Willys)

1. Wills, Anne, *Anneke Wills: Self Portrait* (Hirst Books Ltd, 2007) p.221
2. www.radiotimes.com/tv/sci-fi/doctor-who-companion-anneke-wills-on-achieving-cultural-immortality/
3. *Doctor Who: Tales from the TARDIS* (Midnight Oil Productions, 2013)

10. Michael Craze (Michael Francis Craze)

1. *TARDIS magazine* Vol 7 (Andrew Johnson, September 1982)
2. ibid.
3. ibid.
4. Wills, Anneke, *The Stage* (The Stage Media Company Limited, 24 December 1998)

11. Frazer Hines (Frazer Simpson Frederick Hines)

1. Hines, Frazer, *Hines Sight* originally published as *Films, Farms and Fillies* (Boxtree Ltd, 1997) p.10
2. Hines, Frazer, *Hines Sight* originally published as *Films,Farms and Fillies* (Boxtree Ltd, 1997) p. 35

12. Deborah Watling (Deborah Patricia Watling)

1. Watling, Deborah, Ballard, Paul W.T., *Daddy's Girl: The Autobiography* (Fantom Publishing 2010) p.10.
2. Deborah Watling – *Myth Makers* #10 (TimeTravelTV, 2010. Originally released 1986)
3. Watling, Deborah, Ballard, Paul W.T., *Daddy's Girl: The Autobiography* (Fantom Publishing 2010) p.60.

13. Nicholas Courtney (William Nicholas Stone Courtney)

1. Courteney, Nicholas. McManus, Michael Still Getting Away with it: The Life and Times of Nicholas Courtney (2005) p.21
2. ibid. p.76
3. https://www.theguardian.com/tv-and-radio/tvandradioblog/2011/feb/23/doctor-who-nicholas-courtney-brigadier
4. https://www.tombakerofficial.com/nick-courtney/

14. Wendy Padbury

1. Lock, Alistair. Stevens, Alan. TV Zone Special 03 'The Sixties' (November 1991) p.50
2. ibid. p.51

15. Caroline John (born Caroline Frances John)

1. Caroline John *Wine and Dine Interview*, 1999
2. Letts, Barry, *Who And Me: The Memoir of Barry Letts* (Fantom Publishing, 2009) p.49
3. Beevers, Geoffrey, *One Man in his Time... The Life of a Working Actor* (Fantom Publishing, 2022) p.117
4. Caroline John *Wine and Dine Interview*, 1999
5. Beevers, Geoffrey *One Man in his Time... The Life of a Working Actor* (Fantom Publishing, 2022) p.176
6. https://www.doctorwhotv.co.uk/r-i-p-caroline-john-1940-2012-35147.htm

16. John Levene (born John Anthony Woods)

1. Levene, John, *Run the Shadows, Walk the Sun: A Life* (Fantom Publishing, 2019)
2. https://www.secretspitfiresmemorial.org.uk/
3. *Doctor Who Magazine* #82 (November 1983) p.19.

17. Richard Franklin (born Richard Kimber Franklin)

1. Richard Franklin – Myth Makers #16, (Reeltime Pictures, 1989)
2. Richard Franklin Obituary https://www.theguardian.com/tv-and-radio/2024/jan/01/richard-franklin-obituary
3. https://twitter.com/PlanetFranklin/status/1739348573702213778?lang=en

18. Katy Manning (Born Catherine Ann Manning)

1. https://katymanning.com/biography/
2. Howe, David J. Stammers, Mark. Walker, Stephen James, *Doctor Who Companions* (Doctor Who Books, 1995, London) p.60

19. Elisabeth Sladen (born Elisabeth Clara Heath-Sladen)

1. Sladen, Elisabeth. *Elisabeth Sladen the Autobiography* (Aurum Press Limited, London 2011)
2. ibid. p.19
3. ibid. p58
4. Howe, David J. Stammers, Mark. Walker, Stephen James, *Doctor Who Companions* (Doctor Who Books, 1995, London) p.70
5. *Wine and Dine Interview* 1998
6. *Doctor Who Confidential* Series 2 Episode 3: 'Friends Reunited' (BBC Three, 29 April 2006)

20. Ian Marter (Ian Don Marter)

1. Interview with Richard Marson, *Doctor Who Magazine* #93 (October 1984) p.36
2. Baker, Tom, *Who on Earth is Tom Baker? An Autobiography* (Harper Collins Publishers, London 1997) p.204
3. Ian Marter interview with Patrick Stoner, WHYY Spotlight USA (June 1984)
4. Pixley, Andrew, Hickman, Clayton (ed.), 'Up to Scratch', *Doctor Who Magazine*, #379 (February 2006).

21. Louise Jameson (Louise Marion Jameson)

1. Howe, David J. Stammers, Mark. Walker, *Stephen James, Doctor Who: the Seventies* (Doctor Who Books, 1994, London) p.104
2. https://www.denofgeek.com/tv/the-den-of-geek-interview-louise-jameson/.
3. https://louisejameson.com/face-value-2007/

22. John Leeson (John Francis Christian Ducker)

1. Interview with TV_Film Podcast UK, Rainbow Interview with John Leeson (October 2023)
2. Baker, Tom, *Who on Earth is Tom Baker? An Autobiography* (Harper Collins Publishers, London 1997) p.211

3. ibid p.211
4. Kaldor City, Interview with John Leeson, (www.kaldorcity.com/people/leesoninterview.html, originally published in *Celestial Toyroom Magazine* #324.
5. https://www.calibreaudio.org.uk/

23. Mary Tamm

1. Wireless Theatre Ltd Audio Drama, Mary Tamm – Interview, recorded on 18 August, 2016 (www.wirelesstheatrecompany.co.uk/podcast/mary-tamm-interview)
2. Article: *The Telegraph*, Mary Tamm Obituary, (26 July 2012) www.telegraph.co.uk/news/obituaries/culture-obituaries/tv-radio-obituaries/9430375/Mary-Tamm.html
3. Wireless Theatre Ltd Audio Drama, Mary Tamm – Interview, recorded on 18 August, 2016 (www.wirelesstheatrecompany.co.uk/podcast/mary-tamm-interview)
4. Article: *The Telegraph*, Mary Tamm's widower 'died of a broken heart', (24 October 2012) https://www.telegraph.co.uk/news/9632534/Mary-Tamms-widower-died-of-a-broken-heart.html

24. Lalla Ward (Sarah Jill Ward)

1. Sheila Markham in conversation, William Ward interview (Interviewed for *The Book Collector* Spring 2014) https://www.sheila-markham.com/interviews/william-ward.html
2. Best, Brian, *Reporting the Second World War* (Pen and Sword, 2015)
3. Linda Hall Library, Scientist of the Day – Mary Ward (31 August, 2021) https://www.lindahall.org/about/news/scientist-of-the-day/mary-ward/
4. Howe, David J. Stammers, Mark. Walker, Stephen James, *Doctor Who Companions* (Doctor Who Books, 1995, London) p.86
5. Register of Charities Commission, England and Wales, https://register-of-charities.charitycommission.gov.uk/
6. Little Shoppe of Horrors Facebook page, 'The Journal of Classic British Horror Films' by Richard Klemensen, www.facebook.com/LittleShopOfHorrorsMag/

25. Matthew Waterhouse

1. Waterhouse, Matthew, *Blue Box Boy: A Memoir of Doctor Who in Four Episodes* (Hirst Publishing, London 2010) p.82
2. Davison, Peter, *Is There Life Outside the Box? An Actor Despairs* (John Blake Publishing Ltd, London 2016) p.177
3. Waterhouse, Matthew, *Blue Box Boy: A Memoir of Doctor Who in Four Episodes* (Hirst Publishing, London 2010) p.232
4. Matthew Waterhouse *Doctor W*ho interview, (Cultbox, 2013) https://cultbox.co.uk/interviews/exclusives/matthew-waterhouse-doctor-who-interview per cent5D

26. Janet Fielding (born Janet Claire Mahoney)

1. Interview with Janet Fielding, State Library of Queensland, 2016, https://www.slq.qld.gov.au/blog/interview-janet-fielding-tegan-doctor-who
2. Roberta Bonnin Papers, Playscripts, posters, articles, research notes, transcripts and publications from 1974–99, University of Queensland, https://manuscripts.library.uq.edu.au/downloads/uqfl529.pdf
3. Cast list, *The Crown*, 1980 http://www.chaseside.org.uk/theatre_casts/1980/crown.html
4. Davison, Peter, *Is There Life Outside the Box? An Actor Despairs* (John Blake Publishing Ltd, London 2016) p.172
5. Overview of Women in Film & Television International, https://web.archive.org/web/20161031114052/http://wifti.net/overview.aspx
6. Article, *Isle of Thanet News*, Kathy Bailes, 28 October 2022 https://theisleofthanetnews.com/2022/10/28/end-of-a-13-year-journey-as-ramsgate-youth-charity-project-motorhouse-shuts-down/

27. Sarah Sutton

1. SciFiAndTvTalk Interview, 'Doctor Who's Sarah Sutton – A Touch Of Nobility', 2010 https://scifiandtvtalk.typepad.com/scifiandtvtalk/2010/12/doctor-whos-sarah-sutton-a-touch-of-nobility.html
2. Davison, Peter, *Is There Life Outside the Box? An Actor Despairs* (John Blake Publishing Ltd, London 2016) p.173

29. Gerald Flood

1. Interview With Gerald Flood, Eye of Horus Website, http://www.eyeofhorus.org.uk/content/editorial/interviews/flood.html#watchingwho
2. Cast list, *Relatively Speaking* https://theatricalia.com/play/4n2/relatively-speaking/production/ssk

30. Nicola Bryant (Nicola Jane Bryant)

1. Guest Nicola Bryant on Playing Peri in Doctor Who on TV and Audio & Directing David Tennant, Sirens of Audio YouTube Interview, 2023 (https://www.youtube.com/watch?v=0XW4SZIKy5M)
2. Transcript, *An Afternoon With Nicola Bryant*, (March 1997) https://cavern-of-nicola-bryant.tripod.com/afternoon.htm
3. Article, '10 Star Trek captains who never were, from Peter Capaldi to Chris Pratt', *Digital Spy* (22 September 2017) https://www.digitalspy.com/tv/ustv/a838769/star-trek-captains-auditions-kirk-picard-janeway/

31. Bonnie Langford (Bonita Melody Lysette Langford)

1. Bonnie Langford interview: 'I lost sight of myself as a person', *The Telegraph* (25 January 2019) https://www.telegraph.co.uk/tv/2019/01/25/bonnie-langford-interviewi-lost-sight-person/

2. Howe, David J. Stammers, Mark. Walker, Stephen James, *Doctor Who Companions* (Doctor Who Books, 1995, London) p.108
3. Doctor Who star Bonnie Langford on Mel's return and how the show has evolved since the '80s, *Entertainment Weekly* article, by Devan Coggan (23 April, 2024), https://ew.com/doctor-who-bonnie-langford-on-mel-return
4. Article, Bonnie Langford interview: 'Doctor Who in the 1980s was all terribly serious – I was awful in it', (*The Telegraph*, 18 November 2023) https://www.telegraph.co.uk/tv/2023/11/18/bonnie-langford-interview-doctor-who-sondheim-old-friends/

32. Sophie Aldred

1. Aldred, Sophie. Tucker, Mike, *Ace! The Inside Story of the End of an Era* (Doctor Who Books, Virgin Publishing Ltd, London, 1996) p.2
2. Sophie Aldred Interview, The Den of Geek interview: Sophie Aldred (14 February, 2008) https://www.denofgeek.com/tv/the-den-of-geek-interview-sophie-aldred-2/

33. Daphne Ashbrook (Daphne Lee Ashbrook)

1. Interview: Daphne Ashbrook, Indie Mac User (23 January 2015)https://indiemacuser.com/2015/01/23/interview-daphne-ashbrook/
2. Melora entry at Star Trek Memory Alpha wiki, https://memory-alpha.fandom.com/wiki/Melora_(episode)#Background_information
3. Interview with Daphne Ashbrook, Doctor Freedom YouTube Channel, https://www.youtube.com/watch?v=vCpbawkZDv4

34. Yee Jee Tso

1. https://indiemacuser.com/2015/08/08/3030/
2. https://indiemacuser.com/2015/08/08/3030/

35. Billie Paul Piper (Leian Paul Piper)

1. Piper, Billie, *Growing Pains* (Hodder and Stoughton, London 2006) p.216
2. Piper, Billie, *Growing Pains* (Hodder and Stoughton, London 2006) p.76
3. Davies, Russell T., Cook, Benjamin, *Doctor Who: The Writer's Tale, The Final Chapter* (BBC Books, Ebury Publishing, 2010) p.189
4. Piper, Billie, *Growing Pains* (Hodder and Stoughton, London 2006) p.340

36. Camille Coduri

1. Interview, Flirty at 40 as Camille has the Time of her life (People.co.uk, 2006) https://web.archive.org/web/20060619183635/http://www.people.co.uk/news/tm_objectid=17143641&method=full&siteid=93463&headline=dr-woo---name_page.html
2. *The Signal* – Interview with 'Doctor Who' star Camille Coduri at L.I. Who, https://soundcloud.com/radiofreesignal/the-signal-interview-with-doctor-who-star-camille-coduri-at-li-who

38. John Barrowman (John Scot Barrowman)

1. Interview, 'The house that Captain Jack built', *The Independent* (12 April 2009) https://www.independent.co.uk/news/people/profiles/the-house-that-captain-jack-built-1667535.html
2. Interview: John Barrowman, *The Examiner*, 14 January 2008, https://www.examinerlive.co.uk/whats-on/music/interview-john-barrowman-5043521

39. Noel Clarke. (Noel Anthony Clarke)

1. *Kidulthood* review, The film that speaks to Britain's youth in words they understand, *The Guardian*, 26 February 2006, https://www.theguardian.com/film/2006/feb/26/features.mirandasawyer
2. Noel Clarke Interview, *Female First*, 9 June 2008, https://www.femalefirst.co.uk/celebrity_interviews/Noel+Clarke-52527-page2.html

40. Catherine Tate (Catherine Jane Ford)

1. Catherine Tate Interview, 'Catherine the Great', *The Observer*, 15 October 2005, https://www.theguardian.com/stage/2006/oct/15/comedy1
2. Article, 'Catherine Tate in Doctor Who? I'm worried,' *The Guardian*, 4 July 2007, https://www.theguardian.com/culture/tvandradioblog/2007/jul/04/catherinetateindoctorwhoi
3. Catherine Tate on *The Jonathan Ross Show* (23 January 2016)

41. Jemma Redgrave (Jemima Rebecca (Jemma' Redgrave)

1. The Redgrave family Tree https://redgrave.com/redgraves.htm
2. Interview, 'We weren't brainwashed': Jemma Redgrave on Doctor Who, family tragedy and growing up in a radical acting clan, *The Independent*, 17 November 2013, https://www.independent.co.uk/news/people/profiles/we-weren-t-brainwashed-jemma-redgrave-on-doctor-who-family-tragedy-and-growing-up-in-a-radical-acting-clan-8942604.html

42. Freema Agyeman (Born Frema Agyeman)

1. Interview article, *Question Time*, 29 March 2007, https://www.theguardian.com/media/2007/mar/29/broadcasting.g21
2. Interview, 'All in: New Amsterdam' – Freema Agyeman and David Schulner's reflections on making the diverse US drama, https://vimeo.com/619881248
3. Interview, 'The Millennium Effect', from the *Official Torchwood Magazine* Issue 2, https://millenniumeffect.co.uk/index.php/freema-agyeman-interview/
4. Interview, Freema Agyeman: 'LGBT relationships on TV – I can feel a momentum shift', *The Big Issue*, 14 June 2015, https://www.bigissue.com/news/freema-agyeman-lgbt-relationships-tv-i-can-feel-momentum-shift/
5. Ibid
6. Article, *Fabric Magazine*, https://fabricmagazine.co.uk/people/exclusive-interview-freema-agyeman/

43. Bernard Cribbins (born Bernard Joseph Cribbins)

1. Cribbins Bernard, *Bernard Who? 75 Years of Doing Just About Everything*, (Constable, London, 2018) p.281
2. Ibid p.283
2. Interview, Bernard Cribbins on 'Doctor Who': 'Daleks are dustbins with attitude', *Digital Spy*, 27 May 2013, https://www.digitalspy.com/tv/cult/a483392/bernard-cribbins-on-doctor-who-daleks-are-dustbins-with-attitude/

44. Karen Gillan (Karen Sheila Gillan)

1. Karen Gillan, Interview Magazine, 29 July 2014, https://www.interviewmagazine.com/film/karen-gillan
2. Interview, The Mary Sue Interviews Karen Gillan of Doctor Who, 30 August 2012 https://www.themarysue.com/karen-gillan-interview/
3. https://www.scotsman.com/arts-and-culture/karen-gillan-film-starts-conversation-about-highland-suicides-1431620

45. Arthur Darvill (Thomas Arthur Darvill)

1. Ellie Darvill, professional profile, https://www.mandy.com/uk/v/elliedarvill
2. Interview with Rob Bryon, Arthur Darvill Reveals the REAL Reason Behind His Dr Who Departure, Rob Bryon YouTube channel, https://www.youtube.com/watch?v=SuRY1N4AGcQ
3. Interview, 'Doctor Who's Arthur Darvill on Amy and Rory's "perfect ending"', *Radio Times*, 11 October 2023 https://www.radiotimes.com/tv/sci-fi/doctor-who-arthur-darvill-amy-pond-rory-exclusive-newsupdate/

46. Alex Kingston (Alexandra Elizabeth Kingston)

1. Interview, *Enable Magazine*, Alex Kingston: 'I'd like carers to be heard and respected', December 2014, https://enablemagazine.co.uk/alex-kingston-id-like-carers-to-be-heard-and-respected/
2. Article, 'Why Alex Kingston Left ER In Season 11', Screenrant, 14 Feb 2023, https://screenrant.com/why-alex-kingston-left-er-season-11/
3. Interview, 'In Conversation with Alex Kingston', National Space Centre, 2022. https://www.youtube.com/watch?v=bbkJCeSRTxM
4. Review, *The Tempest* – Alex Kingston is a magnificent Prospero, *The Guardian*, 3 February 2023, https://www.theguardian.com/stage/2023/feb/03/the-tempest-review-alex-kingston-prospero-royal-shakespeare-stratford

47. Jenna Coleman (Jenna-Louise Coleman)

1. Article, 'Why we're watching: Jenna-Louise Coleman, actor', *The Guardian*, 11 March 2012, https://www.theguardian.com/culture/2012/mar/11/jenna-louise-coleman-actor-titanic

48. Pearl Mackie

1. Interview, 'Pearls of Wisdom', *Fabric Magazine*, https://fabricmagazine.co.uk/people/exclusive-interview-with-pearl-mackie/
2. See Red Women's Workshop Wbstie, https://seeredwomensworkshop.wordpress.com/about-see-red/
3. Televised Interview, *This Morning*, 18 May 2017, https://www.youtube.com/watch?v=3Ee5pwP7sac
4. Instagram post, Pearl Mackie, https://www.instagram.com/therealpearlmackie/p/CB-bfqZAX6y/
5. Interview, *Wonderland Magazine*, 18 July 2023, https://www.wonderlandmagazine.com/2023/07/18/pearl-mackie/
6. Interview, Pearl Mackie: 'If you believe in equality, you are a feminist', *Time Out*, 15 January 2018, https://www.timeout.com/london/theatre/pearl-mackie-interview-if-you-believe-in-equality-you-are-a-feminist

49. Matt Lucas (Matthew Richard Lucas)

1. Article, 'What is Reform Judaism?', https://reformjudaism.org/what-is-reform-judaism
2. Interview, Matt Lucas: 'J is for Jewish', *The Jewish Chronicle*, 10 October 2017, www.thejc.com/life-and-culture/matt-lucas-j-is-for-jewish-kigwwqlv

50. Bradley Walsh (Bradley John Walsh)

1. Article, 'Doctor Who star Bradley Walsh reveals Ray Winstone persuaded him to act again', *The Mirror*, 15 September 2018, https://www.mirror.co.uk/tv/tv-news/doctor-who-star-bradley-walsh-13248114
2. Interview, Doctor Who TV online, 30 November 2020, www.doctorwho.tv/news-and-features/bradley-walsh-and-tosin-cole-talk-about-revolution-of-the-daleks-and-leaving
3. Article, 'Bradley Walsh responds to Doctor Who replacement after departure from show', *Hello Magazine*, 12 January 2021, www.hellomagazine.com/film/20210112104338/bradley-walsh-reacts-doctor-who-replacement/

51. Tosin Cole

1. Intermission Youth Theatre, Our Story, https://www.intermissionyouththeatre.co.uk/our-story
2. Interview, 'Doctor Who's Tosin Cole: "Seeing people who look like me on stage made me think I could do that"', *Evening Standard*, 23 October 2018, https://www.standard.co.uk/culture/theatre/doctor-who-tosin-cole-interview-a3968901.html]
3. Interview, 'Doctor Who's new companion Tosin Cole talks TV diversity and sci-fi secrecy ahead of series 11', R*adio Times*, 22 July 2018, https://www.radiotimes.com/tv/sci-fi/doctor-who-series-11-new-companion-tosin-cole-exclusive-interview/
4. Article, 'Doctor Who: How the dyspraxic assistant became my hero', BBC News, 8 October 2018, https://www.bbc.co.uk/news/uk-45784822

52. Mandip Gill (Mandip Kaur Gill)

1. Interview, 'Exclusive Interview with Hollyoaks Phoebe McQueen – Mandip Gill', Punjab200, http://punjab2000.com/exclusive-interview-with-hollyoaks-phoebe-mcqueen-mandip-gill/
2. Interview, 'Doctor Who: Jodie Whittaker & Mandip Gill On Companions, Chemistry & Saying Goodbye To Who', Empire Online, 5 January 2022, https://www.empireonline.com/tv/features/doctor-who-jodie-whittaker-and-mandip-gill-on-companions-chemistry-and-saying-goodbye-to-who/
3. Interview, Mandip Gill: 'Me and Jodie Whittaker are so touchy-feely', *The Guardian*, 5 May 2022, https://www.theguardian.com/stage/2022/may/05/mandip-gill-doctor-who-ghost-story-interview
4. Interview, 'Doctor Who's Mandip Gill recalls the moment she was asked to lose her Northern accent', *Stylist Magazine*, https://www.stylist.co.uk/people/doctor-who-mandip-gill-sheffield-sikhism-accent-northern-regional-companion-yaz-spoilers-character-bio-tv-news-celebrity-interview/232517

53. John Bishop

1. Interview, 'John Bishop: Where did it all go right?', *The Guardian*, 17 November 2010, https://www.theguardian.com/tv-and-radio/2010/nov/17/john-bishop-comedian-interview
2. Article, 'Edinburgh Festival 2009: John Bishop – Elvis Has Left the Building', review, 10 August 2009, https://www.telegraph.co.uk/culture/theatre/edinburgh-festival/6005657/Edinburgh-Festival-2009-John-Bishop-Elvis-Has-Left-the-Building-review.html
3. Interview, 'Doctor Who newcomer John Bishop can't wait to start telling jokes about time travel show', *Entertainment Weekly*, 27 October 2021, https://ew.com/tv/doctor-who-john-bishop-interview/
4. *The Graham Norton Show*, BBC 1 original transmission date 25 November 2022.
5. Article, 'Viewers laud "charming and engaging" interview with John Bishop on Tommy Tiernan Show', *Irish Mirror*, 9 March 2024, https://www.irishmirror.ie/showbiz/viewers-laud-charming-engaging-interview-32315791
6. Article, 'John Bishop sells Cheshire mansion for £6.8m to make way for HS2', *Liverpool Echo*, 7 April 2019, https://www.liverpoolecho.co.uk/news/liverpool-news/john-bishop-sells-cheshire-mansion-16091587

54. Yasmin Finney

1. Article, 'Heartstopper star Yasmin Finney feels "blessed" to be telling a "positive" trans story', *Pink News*, 21 April 2022, https://www.thepinknews.com/2022/04/21/heartstopper-yasmin-finney-trans/
2. Interview, 'Doctor Who's Yasmin Finney: "As a trans teenage girl, I never saw myself represented anywhere on TV", *The Independent*, 9 December 2023 https://www.independent.co.uk/arts-entertainment/tv/features/yasmin-finney-doctor-who-interview-rose-trans-b2460152.html

3. Article, 'If you hate that Doctor Who includes trans people, good luck to your lonely life', *The Metro*, 10 November 2023, https://metro.co.uk/2023/11/10/if-you-hate-trans-people-in-doctor-who-good-luck-to-your-lonely-life-19800335/

55. Millie Gibson (Amelia Eve Gibson)

1. Article, 'Broadbottom's Millie Gibson shines on Coronation Street debut', Quest Media, 11 July 2019, https://www.questmedianetwork.co.uk/news/tameside-reporter/broadbottoms-millie-gibson-shines-on-coronation-street-debut/

56. Varada Sethu (Varada Sethumadhavan)

1. Interview, 'Kerala-born British actor Varada Sethu on playing a rebel in "Star Wars" show "Andor",' *The Hindu*, 22 November 2022, https://www.thehindu.com/entertainment/movies/interview-with-kerala-born-british-indian-star-wars-actor-varada-sethu/article66139458.ece
2. Article, 'Who is Varada Sethu, the rumoured new Doctor Who companion?', *The Standard*, 22 January, 2024, https://www.standard.co.uk/culture/tvfilm/doctor-who-companion-now-varada-sethu-who-is-she-b1133920.html
3. Online interview podcast, 'Varada Sethu On Box Ticking New Doctor Who Actress', The Noel Zone, 2024
4. Article, 'Black tokenism: how to stop box ticking when it comes to diversity', Women's Agenda, 1 June 2021, https://womensagenda.com.au/latest/black-tokenism-how-to-stop-box-ticking-when-it-comes-to-diversity/

Bibliography

Books

Aldred, Sophie, Tucker, Mike, *Ace! The Inside Story of the End of an Era* (Doctor Who Books, Virgin Publishing Ltd, London, 1996)

Baker, Tom, *Who on Earth is Tom Baker? An Autobiography* (Harper Collins Publishers, London 1997)

Beevers, Geoffrey, *One Man in his Time ... The Life of a Working Actor* (Fantom Publishing, 2022)

Best, Brian, *Reporting the Second World War* (Pen and Sword, 2015)

Bremner, Louise, *A Future in Five Minutes – A Biography of Jacqueline Hill* (Fantom Publishing, 2020, Croydon)

Courteney, Nicholas. McManus, *Michael Still Getting Away with it: The Life and Times of Nicholas Courtney* (2005)

Cribbins Bernard, *Bernard Who? 75 Years of Doing Just About Everything*, (Constable, London, 2018)

Davison, Peter, *Is There Life Outside the Box? An Actor Despairs* (John Blake Publishing Ltd, London 2016)

Hines, Frazer, *Hines Sight* [*originally published as Films, Farms and Fillies*] (Boxtree Ltd, 1997)

Howe, David J., Stammers, Mark, Walker, Stephen James, *Doctor Who Companions* (Doctor Who Books, 1995, London)

Howe, David J., Stammers, Mark, Walker, Stephen James, *Doctor Who: the Sixties* (Doctor Who Books, 1992, London)

Howe, David J. Stammers, Mark, Walker, Stephen James, *Doctor Who: the Seventies* (Doctor Who Books, 1994, London)

Letts, Barry, *Who And Me: The Memoir of Barry Letts* (Fantom Publishing, 2009)

Levene, John, *Run the Shadows, Walk the Sun: A Life* (Fantom Publishing, 2019)

Newman, Sydney, Burke, Graeme, *Head of Drama: The Memoir of Sydney Newman* (ECW Press, Toronto, 2017)

Piper, Billie, *Growing Pains* (Hodder and Stoughton, London 2006)

Purves, Peter, *Peter Purves The Autobiography: Here's One I Wrote Earlier* (Green Umbrella Publishing, 2009, London)

Sladen, Elisabeth. *Elisabeth Sladen the Autobiography* (Aurum Press Limited, London 2011)

Waterhouse, Matthew, *Blue Box Boy: A Memoir of Doctor Who in Four Episodes* (Hirst Publishing, London 2010)

Watling, Deborah, Ballard, Paul W.T., *Daddy's Girl: The Autobiography* (Fantom Publishing 2010)
Wills, Anne, *Anneke Wills: Self Portrait* (Hirst Books Ltd, 2007)

Magazines

TARDIS Magazine
Doctor Who Magazine (Panini, London)
TV Zone (Visual Imagine, London)
STARLOG Magazine (Starlog Group Inc, USA)
The Stage (The Stage Media Co., London)

Television Programmes

Doctor Who Confidential (BBC)
Jonathan Ross Show (ITV)
The Myth Makers (Reeltime Pictures)
WHYY Spotlight (PBS)
Wine and Dine interviews (fan-made)

Digital Resources

www.bbc.co.uk
www.bigissue.com
www.calibreaudio.org.uk/
www.cavern-of-nicola-bryant.tripod.com
www.chaseside.org.uk
www.cultbox.co.uk
www.denofgeek.com/
www.digitalspy.com/
www.doctorwho.tv
www.doctorwhotv.co.uk
www.empireonline.com
www.enablemagazine.co.uk
www.ew.com
www.examinerlive.co.uk
www.eyeofhorus.org.uk
www.fabricmagazine.co.uk
www.facebook.com
www.femalefirst.co.uk
www.hellomagazine.com
www.independent.co.uk
www.indiemacuser.com
www.instagram.com

www.intermissionyouththeatre.co.uk
www.irishmirror.ie
www.kaldorcity.com
www.katymanning.com
www.lindahall.org
www.liverpoolecho.co.uk
www.louisejameson.com
www.mandy.com
www.manuscripts.library.uq.edu.au
www.memory-alpha.fandom.com
www.metro.co.uk
www.mirror.co.uk
www.peterpurves.net
www.punjab2000.com
www.radiotimes.com/
www.redgrave.com
www.reformjudaism.org
www.register-of-charities.charitycommission.gov.uk
www.scifiandtvtalk.typepad.com
www.scotsman.com
www.screenrant.com
www.secretspitfiresmemorial.org.uk
www.seeredwomensworkshop.wordpress.com
www.sheila-markham.com
www.slq.qld.gov.au
www.soundcloud.com
www.standard.co.uk
www.stylist.co.uk
www.telegraph.co.uk
www.theguardian.com
www.thehindu.com
www.theisleofthanetnews.com
www.themarysue.com
www.thepinknews.com
www.timeout.com
www.tombakerofficial.com
www.twitter.com/
www.vimeo.com
www.web.archive.org
www.wirelesstheatrecompany.co.uk
www.womensagenda.com.au
www.www.thejc.com
www.youtube.com